# Microsoft Word for Windows 2 Made Easy

*Paul Hoffman*

Osborne **McGraw-Hill**

Berkeley  New York  St. Louis  San Francisco
Auckland  Bogotá  Hamburg  London  Madrid
Mexico City  Milan  Montreal  New Delhi  Panama City
Paris  São Paulo  Singapore  Sydney
Tokyo  Toronto

Osborne **McGraw-Hill**
2600 Tenth Street
Berkeley, California 94710
U.S.A.

For information on translations or book distributors outside of the U.S.A., please write to Osborne **McGraw-Hill** at the above address.

**Microsoft Word for Windows 2 Made Easy**

Copyright © 1992 by McGraw-Hill, Inc. All rights reserved. Printed in the United States of America. Except as permitted under the Copyright Act of 1976, no part of this publication may be reproduced or distributed in any form or by any means, or stored in a database or retrieval system, without the prior written permission of the publisher, with the exception that the program listings may be entered, stored, and executed in a computer system, but they may not be reproduced for publication.

67890 DOC 99876543

ISBN 0-07-881770-6

Information has been obtained by Osborne **McGraw-Hill** from sources believed to be reliable. However, because of the possibility of human or mechanical error by our sources, Osborne **McGraw-Hill**, or others, Osborne **McGraw-Hill** does not guarantee the accuracy, adequacy, or completeness of any information and is not responsible for any errors or omissions or the results obtained from use of such information.

**Publisher**

Kenna S. Wood

**Acquisitions Editor**

Elizabeth Fisher

**Associate Editor**

Scott Rogers

**Project Editor**

Judith Brown

**Technical Editor**

Bob Kermish

**Copy Editor**

Dusty Bernard

**Proofreading Coordinator**

Kelly Barr

**Proofreaders**

Audrey Johnson
Wendy Goss
Nancy Pechonis

**Indexer**

Paul Hoffman

**Director of Electronic Publishing**

Deborah Wilson

**Production Supervisor**

Barry Michael Bergin

**Production Assistant**

George Anderson

**Computer Designer**

Stefany Otis

**Typesetters**

Jani Beckwith
Helena Charm
Erick Christgau
Lynda Higham
Peter Hancik
Marcela Hancik
Susie C. Kim
Fred Lass
Robert Myren
Lance Ravella
Michelle Salinaro

**Cover Design**

Mason Fong
Bay Graphics Design, Inc.

# Contents

|  | *Introduction* | xiii |
|---|---|---|
| I | **Word Basics** | 1 |
| 1 | **Getting Started** | 3 |
|  | Word Processing Terms | 3 |
|  | Preparing for Word | 4 |
|  | Starting the Word Program | 5 |
|  | Entering Text | 8 |
|  | Selecting and Inserting Text | 8 |
|  |     Selecting Text with the Mouse | 10 |
|  |     Inserting Text with the Mouse | 11 |
|  |     Selecting and Inserting Text with the Keyboard | 12 |
|  | Using Word Commands | 13 |
|  | Making Paragraphs in Word | 15 |
|  | Getting Help | 16 |
|  | Leaving Word | 17 |
|  | Review | 18 |
| 2 | **Basic Editing with Word** | 19 |
|  | Lesson 1: Typing Your First File | 19 |
|  | Lesson 2: Saving Your Text in a File | 20 |

|   |   |   |
|---|---|---|
| | Lesson 3: Opening a File | 22 |
| | Lesson 4: Scrolling Around in Your Document | 22 |
| |     Scrolling with the Mouse | 23 |
| |     Scrolling with the Keyboard | 24 |
| | Lesson 5: Changing Text | 24 |
| | Lesson 6: More Ways to Select Text | 25 |
| |     Selecting Text with the Mouse | 25 |
| |     Selecting Text with the Keyboard | 27 |
| | Lesson 7: The Undo Command | 27 |
| | Lesson 8: Making Choices in Dialog Boxes | 29 |
| |     Making Dialog Choices with the Mouse | 30 |
| |     Making Dialog Choices with the Keyboard | 31 |
| | Lesson 9: Inserting Special Characters in Your Text | 32 |
| |     Line Breaks Within Paragraphs | 32 |
| |     Nonbreaking Spaces | 32 |
| |     Inserting Other Characters | 33 |
| | Lesson 10: Printing Your Document | 34 |
| | Review | 35 |
| **3** | **Using Word's Windows** | **37** |
| | Lesson 11: Splitting a Window in One File | 38 |
| | Lesson 12: Moving and Sizing Windows | 41 |
| | Lesson 13: Using Two Windows for Two Files | 42 |
| | Review | 45 |
| **4** | **Moving and Copying Text** | **47** |
| | Lesson 14: Using the Clipboard | 48 |
| | Lesson 15: Moving and Copying Text Within a Document | 49 |
| | Lesson 16: Using the Clipboard with Two Files | 52 |
| | Lesson 17: Moving and Copying Without the Clipboard | 54 |
| | Review | 56 |
| **5** | **Searching and Replacing** | **57** |
| | Lesson 18: Searching for Text | 58 |
| | Lesson 19: Replacing Text | 61 |

|    |                                                                                                 |     |
|----|-------------------------------------------------------------------------------------------------|-----|
|    | Lesson 20: Using Special Characters in Find and Replace                                         | 63  |
|    | Review                                                                                          | 66  |
| 6  | **Using Glossaries**                                                                            | **67** |
|    | Lesson 21: Introduction to Glossaries                                                           | 67  |
|    | Lesson 22: Creating a Glossary                                                                  | 68  |
|    | Lesson 23: Storing, Opening, and Printing Glossaries                                            | 71  |
|    | Lesson 24: Finding Other Uses for Glossaries                                                    | 71  |
|    | Review                                                                                          | 72  |
| 7  | **Pictures in Your Documents**                                                                  | **73** |
|    | Lesson 25: Using Art in Your Text                                                               | 73  |
|    | Lesson 26: Creating Graphics in Word                                                            | 75  |
|    | Lesson 27: Resizing and Cropping Graphics                                                       | 79  |
|    | Lesson 28: Opening Graphics Files                                                               | 81  |
|    | Review                                                                                          | 81  |
| 8  | **Printing Your Documents**                                                                     | **83** |
|    | Lesson 29: Using the Print Setup Command                                                        | 84  |
|    | Lesson 30: Giving the Print Command                                                             | 85  |
|    | Review                                                                                          | 88  |
| II | **Using Word to Format**                                                                        | **89** |
| 9  | **Basic Formatting with Word**                                                                  | **91** |
|    | Lesson 31: Introducing Formatting                                                               | 91  |
|    | Lesson 32: Giving Formatting Commands                                                           | 93  |
|    | Lesson 33: Searching for and Replacing Formatting                                               | 94  |
|    | Review                                                                                          | 96  |
| 10 | **Formatting Characters**                                                                       | **97** |
|    | Lesson 34: Common Character Formatting                                                          | 97  |
|    | Lesson 35: Other Character Formats                                                              | 100 |

|    |                                                                  |     |
|----|------------------------------------------------------------------|-----|
|    | Lesson 36: Introduction to Fonts ....................            | 101 |
|    | Lesson 37: Changing Fonts .......................                | 104 |
|    | Lesson 38: Selecting Character Formatting with the CTRL Key ..................................... | 105 |
|    | Lesson 39: Copying Character Formats ..............              | 105 |
|    | Review ...............................................          | 107 |
| **11** | **Formatting Paragraphs** ........................           | **109** |
|    | Lesson 40: Basic Formatting for Paragraphs .........             | 110 |
|    | Lesson 41: Indenting Paragraphs ...................              | 112 |
|    | Lesson 42: Line Spacing for Paragraphs .............             | 116 |
|    | Lesson 43: Aligning Paragraphs and Using Keeps ......            | 118 |
|    | Lesson 44: Selecting Paragraph Formatting with the CTRL Key ..................................... | 121 |
|    | Lesson 45: Using Tabs ..........................                 | 122 |
|    | Lesson 46: Setting Tabs .........................                | 124 |
|    | Lesson 47: Using Leader Characters ................              | 126 |
|    | Lesson 48: Working with Columns of Tabs ..........               | 126 |
|    | Lesson 49: Copying Paragraph Formats .............               | 128 |
|    | Lesson 50: Highlighting Paragraphs with Borders .....            | 128 |
|    | Review ...............................................          | 131 |
| **12** | **Formatting Sections** ..........................           | **133** |
|    | Lesson 51: Using Word's View Modes ..............                | 133 |
|    |     Page Layout Mode ...........................     | 134 |
|    |     Print Preview Mode .........................     | 135 |
|    |     Zooming in Normal and Page Layout Modes .....    | 137 |
|    | Lesson 52: Introduction to Sections ................             | 138 |
|    | Lesson 53: Using Headers and Footers ..............              | 140 |
|    | Lesson 54: Page Numbering .....................                  | 146 |
|    | Lesson 55: Creating Text with Newspaper Columns ....             | 147 |
|    | Lesson 56: Numbering Lines in Your Document .......              | 149 |
|    | Lesson 57: Positioning with Frames ................              | 150 |
|    | Lesson 58: Setting Margins and Paper Size ..........             | 154 |
|    | Lesson 59: Repaginating and Page Breaks ...........              | 156 |
|    | Review ...............................................          | 158 |

| | | | |
|---|---|---|---|
| 13 | **Using Styles to Simplify Formatting** | | **159** |
| | Lesson 60: Creating a Style Sheet | | 161 |
| | Lesson 61: Using Styles in Your Documents | | 164 |
| | Lesson 62: Working with Style Sheets | | 166 |
| |     Styles in Templates | | 166 |
| |     Basing Styles on Other Styles | | 167 |
| | Lesson 63: Getting the Most from Style Sheets | | 168 |
| | Lesson 64: Using Document Templates | | 169 |
| | Review | | 171 |
| **III** | **Other Word Features** | | **173** |
| 14 | **Creating Form Letters** | | **175** |
| | Lesson 65: Creating the Main Document and Data File | | 176 |
| | Lesson 66: Finishing the Main Document and Data File | | 180 |
| | Lesson 67: Printing Form Letters | | 184 |
| | Lesson 68: Using Merge Instructions | | 187 |
| | Review | | 190 |
| 15 | **Working with Tables and Footnotes** | | **191** |
| | Lesson 69: Introduction to Tables | | 191 |
| | Lesson 70: Creating Tables | | 193 |
| | Lesson 71: Advanced Table Handling | | 198 |
| | Lesson 72: Borders for Cells | | 200 |
| | Lesson 73: Using Footnotes | | 201 |
| | Review | | 204 |
| 16 | **Customizing Word** | | **207** |
| | Lesson 74: Setting the Options | | 207 |
| |     View Settings | | 208 |
| |     General Settings | | 210 |
| |     Print Settings | | 211 |
| |     Save Settings | | 212 |

|   |   |   |
|---|---|---|
| | Spelling Settings | 213 |
| | Grammar Settings | 213 |
| | User Info | 213 |
| | Win.ini | 214 |
| | Lesson 75: Customizing Menus in Word | 214 |
| | Lesson 76: Changing Keyboard Equivalents | 216 |
| | Lesson 77: Changing the Toolbar | 217 |
| | Lesson 78: Storing Your Settings | 218 |
| | Review | 218 |
| **17** | **Outlining** | **219** |
| | Lesson 79: Creating an Outline | 221 |
| | Lesson 80: Collapsing and Expanding | 224 |
| | Lesson 81: Rearranging Your Outline | 225 |
| | Lesson 82: Numbering Your Outline | 226 |
| | Review | 229 |
| **18** | **Tables of Contents and Indexes** | **231** |
| | Lesson 83: Planning a Table of Contents | 232 |
| | Lesson 84: Indicating Table of Contents Entries | 232 |
| | Lesson 85: Creating the Table of Contents | 234 |
| | Lesson 86: Advanced Use of Tables of Contents | 235 |
| | Lesson 87: Marking Index Entries | 237 |
| | Lesson 88: Creating an Index | 239 |
| | Review | 240 |
| **19** | **Proofing Your Documents** | **241** |
| | Lesson 89: Introduction to Spelling Checking | 242 |
| | Lesson 90: Using the Spelling Checker | 244 |
| | Lesson 91: Using the Thesaurus | 247 |
| | Lesson 92: Grammar Checking | 248 |
| | Lesson 93: Hyphenation | 251 |
| | Review | 254 |
| **20** | **Sorting** | **255** |
| | Lesson 94: Sorting Text | 257 |

|     | Lesson 95: Sorting Numbers | 258 |
|---|---|---|
|     | Lesson 96: Sorting in Tables | 259 |
|     | Review | 260 |

| 21 | **Retrieving Documents** | **261** |
|---|---|---|
|     | Lesson 97: Filling In Summary Sheets | 262 |
|     | Lesson 98: Searching for Documents | 264 |
|     | Review | 268 |

| 22 | **Fields, Annotations, Bookmarks, and Cross-References** | **269** |
|---|---|---|
|     | Lesson 99: Introduction to Fields | 270 |
|     | Lesson 100: Creating Annotations | 272 |
|     | Lesson 101: Using Bookmarks | 274 |
|     | Lesson 102: Using Cross-References | 275 |
|     | Review | 276 |

| 23 | **Revision Marks** | **277** |
|---|---|---|
|     | Lesson 103: Using Redlining for Revisions | 277 |
|     | Lesson 104: Saving Revised Documents | 279 |
|     | Review | 280 |

| 24 | **Using Word with Other Programs** | **281** |
|---|---|---|
|     | Lesson 105: Opening Non-Word Files | 282 |
|     | Lesson 106: Saving Files in Non-Word Formats | 284 |
|     | Lesson 107: Linking to Other Programs | 284 |
|     | Review | 285 |

| IV | Reference | 287 |
|---|---|---|
| A | Keyboard Reference | 289 |
| B | Word Commands | 293 |
|     | **Index** | **297** |

# Introduction

*Microsoft Word for Windows 2 Made Easy* will help you master Microsoft Word for Windows version 2. It discusses both the essential and unique features of the program and provides practical suggestions for putting Word for Windows to work for you. This book supplements the documentation, the Word for Windows *User's Guide,* by showing you, in step-by-step fashion, how to use Word. (Throughout this book, Word for Windows will be referred to simply as Word.)

Even though a few of Word's features appear complex, they are relatively easy to master once you understand the concepts behind them. This book is arranged to teach you these concepts in a logical order, and it reinforces the concepts with many practical examples. The examples demonstrate the numerous word processing functions performed in a typical business office, although they are just as useful in any situation that requires word processing capabilities.

Each chapter is divided into lessons that are fully illustrated with pictures of the Windows screen so you will know what to expect as you use the program. There are also review exercises at the end of each chapter.

For those of you who have never used a word processing program before, this book explains basic concepts when they first appear in the text. Even if you have used other word processing programs, you will find that some of Word's features are unique. (For example, Word can display several parts of a file simultaneously). These features, too, are explained in full to help you completely understand the power of Word. You need to know only the basics of using Windows to use this book; you do not need to be familiar with any other word processing program.

If you already have Microsoft Word for Windows or are thinking of buying it, this book is for you. As a beginning user, you will find that the lessons are easy to follow, and succeeding lessons build on concepts learned earlier in the book. If you are an intermediate user, you will find that topics mentioned only briefly in different parts of the documentation are described fully in one location in this book. All users will find that the real-world examples in this book are more helpful than the terse step-lists in the Word manual.

## What Is Microsoft Word?

A word processing program is a computer program that lets you type and save any text (such as memos, letters, reports, and books). Word processing programs such as Microsoft Word let you easily enter text for a document, revise the text once it has been entered (called editing), and print the text out on your printer in a professional form (called formatting).

There is a wide variety of word processing software available for many different computers. Some software gives you the bare minimum of capabilities, while other programs, such as Word, give you many more useful features that make word processing easier.

Word is useful for all types of word processing, such as writing memos, business letters, financial statements, articles, books, and long reports. It is generally easy to use and has many advanced features that you can use or ignore, depending on the type of document you are writing. For example, many people use Word to create attractive brochures and advertisements. The more you use Word, the less you need to worry about what your text will look like; this lets you spend more time concentrating on what you want to say.

## Advantages of Using Word

If you have compared Word to word processing packages that do not run under Windows, you know that it has many features that others do not. Of course, having a plethora of features does not make a word processor good—you have to be able to use these features easily. Three outstanding features of Word are mentioned briefly here and described fully in this book.

### Undo Feature

Since it is common to make mistakes when you edit text, Word has an Undo feature that lets you take out your last change. This means that if you do something you didn't intend to do, you can tell Word to undo it. This feature can save you a great deal of typing and frustration.

### Help Feature

If you are ever unsure of what you are doing in Word, the program can always offer help. This feature prevents you from having to look up information in the reference manual (or in this book) when you just want to know a small bit of information. The help that Word gives you is often more useful than the help you get from other programs. It first gives you help on what you are currently doing and then makes it easy to ask for more information if you need it.

### Windows

One problem with many word processing programs is that you can see only a small portion of your document at a time. With Word, you can see many parts of the text at the same time in different windows. You can also see two parts of a document in one window. This feature is very useful when you are writing a long document; you can look at what you wrote earlier while you write new text. You can even use Word to look at different files on the screen at the same time and to move text between files.

## New Features in Version 2

If you are using Microsoft Word for Windows version 1, you should upgrade your copy. Like every program, Word had some bugs in its earlier versions, and most of these have been fixed in version 2. Contact Microsoft to determine how you can upgrade to version 2.

Version 2 also has many significant new features and improvements to the user interface, which make Word easier to use and allow you to prepare business documents in a more natural way. This book has been completely revised to incorporate these new features (as well as dozens of minor ones).

- The toolbar, a set of buttons near the top of your screen, lets you give commands with a single mouse click. The buttons are labeled with pictures of the actions you can perform. You can even change the buttons on the toolbar to perform different actions.
- You can now move words and sentences without giving any commands. You simply drag the words to the desired new position.
- Word now has its own drawing program so you can create simple graphics without having to run another program.
- The mail merge feature has been greatly simplified yet still retains its power.
- It is now easier to make up your own keyboard equivalents and change the menus.

# I

# Word Basics

# 1
# Getting Started

This chapter explains the few steps you need to follow before you can begin to use Word for Windows and shows you how to start up the program. After following the installation instructions, you can start to edit and format documents immediately; in fact, you will start using Word in Chapter 2 to enter a business letter that is used throughout the next six chapters and in many other sections of the book as well.

If you have no word processing experience, the following section gives you a quick overview of many of the terms you will find in this book. If you are familiar with another word processor, you can probably skim the section.

## Word Processing Terms

Word processing programs give you two major capabilities: editing and formatting of text. *Editing* is the ability to enter text into the program, make corrections, save the text on disk, and later change the text. *Formatting* is the ability to specify how the text will look when you print it out—for example, in boldface or italic in a specific type size and style. Formatting also allows you to add special features to the printout, such as page numbers on each page, and to specify the width of the left and right margins.

In order to make a word processing program work, you give it *commands*, which are instructions that tell the program what you want to do. In Word, you can give commands by using the mouse or by pressing the `CTRL` key or the `ALT` key in combination with one or more other keys.

When you write a document, you *insert* text into a file. This is done by typing the text as you would on a typewriter. Once you have typed the text, you can use editing commands to correct mistakes or to rearrange the text. While you are editing, you can move around in the text so you can edit different parts. When you want to see text that is not on the screen, the word processing program *scrolls*, or moves, the screen to the desired location. When you are done with a file, you can *save* it on disk, and when you want to use the file later, you can tell the word processing program to *open* it from disk.

## Preparing for Word

Word for Windows comes on disks containing the programs and special files needed to run it. Since Word is such a large program, it takes up several disks. Follow the directions in the installation guide that comes with Word to copy the files from the Word distribution disks to your hard disk. The installation program guides you through the choices you need to make when installing Word (such as deciding which directory it should go in).

When you install Word, the SETUP program asks if you want to use WordPerfect keyboard settings. Reply "No" to this prompt since Word's keyboard settings are easier to follow. If you have already installed Word and had answered "Yes" to this, see Chapter 16 for more information on how to change this setting.

After you have installed Word, it is a good idea to store the distribution floppies in a safe place, preferably away from your computer. (Many people even keep their distribution floppies in a different room.) If the copy of Word that you have made on your hard disk or other floppies later becomes damaged or lost, you can reinstall the program from the original floppies.

## Starting the Word Program

You start Word in much the same way you start other Windows applications. Start Windows as you normally do. This leads you to the Windows Program Manager. To start Word, double-click the Word icon, which is shown here:

Microsoft Word

This is the method you will normally use for starting Word.

Another method for starting Word and editing an existing file is to double-click the Program Manager icon for that file. When you double-click a Word document, Windows starts Word and opens that file automatically.

When you install Word, you are asked to personalize your copy. This puts your name and company name into the program; these names are shown each time you start the program. If you work for a company, they may have already personalized your copy for you.

When you start Word without opening a document, you see Word's main window, shown in Figure 1-1. (The items labeled on the figure are discussed throughout this and the following chapters.) The file is named Document1 until you save it to disk with a name of your choice. The next new file that you open during this session will be named Document2, and so on.

It is important to note the difference between Word's program window and its document windows. Word's *program window* is the outside window, the one with the menu bar. When Word starts for the first time, the program window is *maximized*, that is, it is the full size of the screen. The maximized program window has a *restore box* with two triangles in the upper-right corner of the screen:

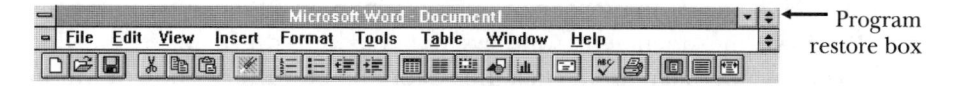

⟵ Program restore box

Each document has its own *document window* that resides inside the Word program window. When a document window is maximized, it takes up the

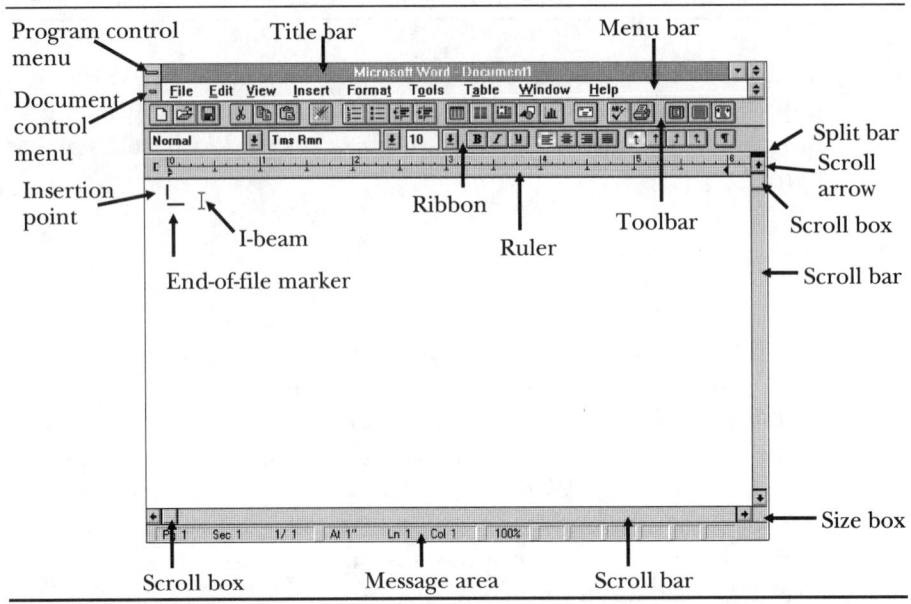

***Figure 1-1.*** *Features of Word's main window*

entire program window. When Word starts for the first time, the document window and the program window are both maximized. The maximized document window has a restore box that appears at the right side of the menu bar:

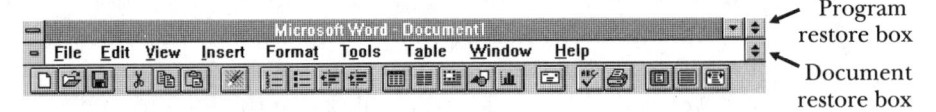

Note that the document's restore box is different from the program's restore box.

If you work on more than one document at a time, it is more convenient to have the document windows not maximized. To make the document window not maximized, click the restore box for the document window. The result is shown in Figure 1-2.

As you can see, many of the features of the Word window are the same as in other Windows programs, but some are unique to Word. Those features seen only in Word are described throughout this book.

**Chapter 1:** *Getting Started* 7

*Figure 1-2.* Word window with document window not maximized

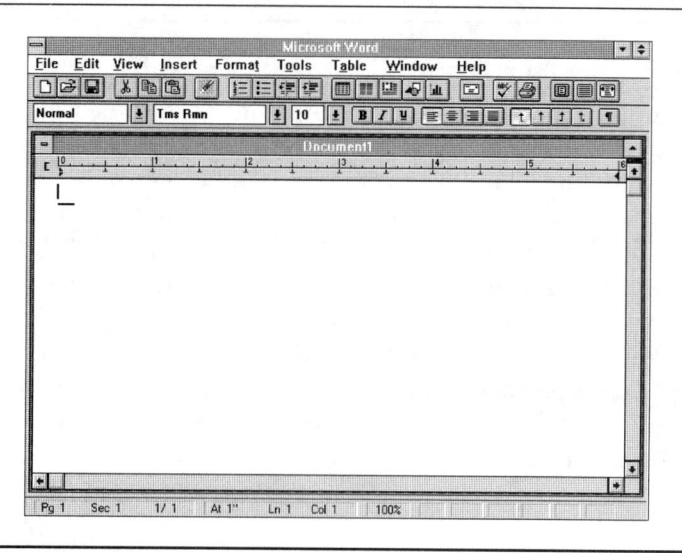

As you can see, many of the features of the Word window are the same as in other Windows programs, but some are unique to Word. Those features seen only in Word are described throughout this book.

One mark on the window that may interest you now is the horizontal line near the top of the document window. This is called the *end-of-file marker* because it shows you where the end of your document is. All text in your document appears above this mark.

Another very handy feature is the *toolbar* near the top of the window:

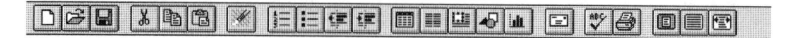

The toolbar has buttons that perform tasks such as opening files and printing. You can click these buttons instead of giving commands. You can even change the toolbar if you want to put on different buttons yourself; this is covered in Chapter 16.

## Entering Text

As soon as Word is loaded, it is ready for you to start entering text. Near the upper-left corner of the document window, the blinking vertical bar is where the first letters you type appear. This bar is called the *insertion point,* just as in other Windows programs. It indicates where you are in the text.

When you type text, you can correct typing mistakes by pressing the `BACKSPACE` key located in the upper-right corner of the main part of the keyboard (marked as `←`) to erase the character to the left of the insertion point.

You can type just as you would on a typewriter. To start experimenting, type **This is just like a typewriter**. If you make a mistake as you type, you can press `BACKSPACE` to erase the letter (or letters) you just typed. (In Chapter 2, you will learn other ways to delete text.)

## Selecting and Inserting Text

To tell Word to do something to some text in your document, you first indicate the text you want to work on and then indicate the action. To indicate the text on which you will work, you *select* the text with the mouse or the keyboard. If what you want to do is insert text, you set the insertion point to the position where you want to insert the new text.

While selecting and inserting text may sound easy, it is often one of the things that confuses beginning Word users, especially those who have not dealt much with computers. Even though selecting is basic to all Windows use, it requires you to use a few things at once and thus can be a bit daunting to beginners. Figure 1-3 shows the way your screen should look with the sentence that you just typed.

Note that there are two nontext items that appear as vertical bars. The blinking vertical bar that is at the end of your text is the insertion point that you were just introduced to. The other vertical bar, which moves when you move the mouse, is called the *I-beam*. The I-beam is one of a few shapes that the *mouse pointer* takes as you move it around the screen. The insertion point and the I-beam are very different and should not be confused.

**Chapter 1:** *Getting Started* 9

***Figure 1-3.***   *Screen after sentence is typed*

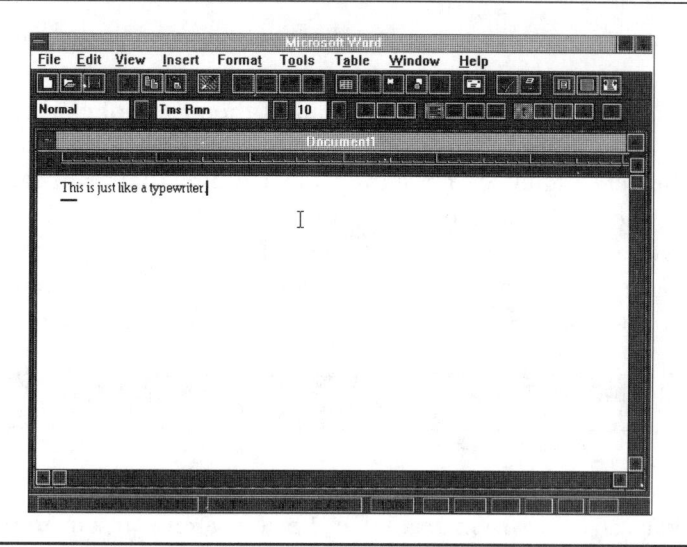

The *arrow pointer* and the I-beam are two different aspects of the mouse pointer. They look like this:

Arrow    I-beam

They are used to point at menus and parts of your document. The mouse pointer's shape is totally dependent on where you move the mouse. As you move from a command or window control area to the text area, the pointer changes from the arrow to the I-beam. The insertion point, however, is a specific location in your document that remains the same even when you move the mouse pointer. You can see this by moving the I-beam around and noting that the blinking insertion point remains stationary.

When you begin to type, Windows (not Word) makes the mouse pointer invisible. This makes it easier to type because it prevents the mouse pointer from obscuring the text you are typing. The mouse pointer becomes visible again when you move the mouse.

This chapter shows you the basics of selecting and inserting text. You will see more ways to select and insert text in the next chapter.

## Selecting Text with the Mouse

To select text with the mouse, you click the I-beam at the beginning of the group of characters you want to select, hold down the left button on the mouse, move the I-beam to the end of the group of characters, and release the mouse button. This is known as *dragging* the mouse across the text. As you select text, it becomes *highlighted,* meaning that it appears as white letters on a black or colored background.

For example, assume that you want to select the letter "j" in the word "just" in the sentence you typed. Move the I-beam to just before the "j", as shown here:

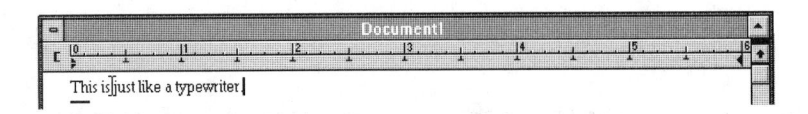

(If you see an arrow instead of an I-beam when you start to make a selection, you are pointing above the letters.) Hold down the mouse button; the blinking insertion point jumps to the location of the I-beam, but don't be concerned with that for now. While holding down the mouse button, drag the I-beam to the right until the "j" in "just" is highlighted, as shown here:

Release the mouse button, and you have selected the letter.

You have now created a selection. Whenever you give Word commands that have an effect on text in your file, the effect is only on the selected text. You can select from one character to the whole document at any time. The text that is highlighted is the text that is currently selected (in this case, the letter "j").

You have just seen how to select a single letter by dragging the mouse. You can also select more than one letter by using the same technique. For example, to select the word "like" in the sentence, move the I-beam to just

**Chapter 1:** *Getting Started* 11

before the "l", hold down the mouse button, drag the I-beam to the right until the "e" is highlighted, and release the mouse button. You have now selected the entire word.

You can use the mouse to quickly select specific amounts of text. A common task is to select a whole word. Instead of having to drag over the word as you just did, you can double-click the word you want. To see this, move the I-beam to anywhere on the word "just" and double-click. The result is shown here:

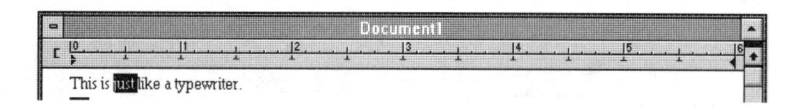

```
┌─────────────────────── Document1 ───────────────────────┐
  |0      |1      |2      |3      |4      |5      |6
  This is just like a typewriter.
```

Note that Word also selects the space after the word.

You can also select a whole sentence quickly. If you hold down the (CTRL) key at the same time as you click once anywhere on the sentence, Word selects the entire sentence, including the space after the period.

## Inserting Text with the Mouse

You may be wondering, "If the insertion point disappears when I select text, why have an insertion point at all?" The insertion point tells you where the next letter that you type will appear—in other words "where you are." As you can imagine, that can be pretty important. It allows you to quickly change the place where you insert text.

When you click the I-beam in the text area, Word puts the insertion point in the place where you click. If anything is selected when you click the I-beam, it becomes deselected when the insertion point is placed. You can now see that you will never have both a selection and an insertion point on the screen at the same time.

To see this, first select the word "just" by double-clicking it. Next, put the I-beam between the letter "r" and the period at the end of the sentence. When you click the mouse button, "just" becomes deselected and the insertion point appears between the "r" and the period:

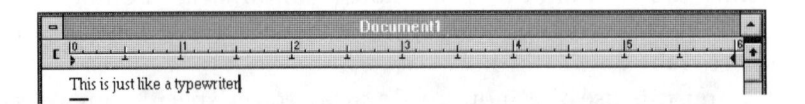

```
                              Document1
   [  |0        |1        |2        |3        |4        |5        |6
   This is just like a typewriter|
```

If you begin typing when the insertion point is between two characters, the text you type appears at that position. For example, type **but is much easier** and notice how these words appear between the "r" and the period. Every time you type a letter, the insertion point moves to the right:

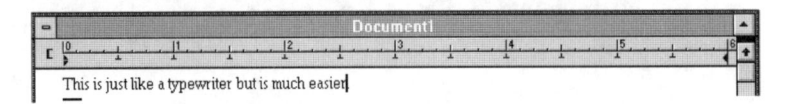

```
                              Document1
   [  |0        |1        |2        |3        |4        |5        |6
   This is just like a typewriter but is much easier|
```

It may take some practice to get used to pointing with the mouse. A common mistake is to click the mouse button so hard that you move the mouse, with the result that the pointer is no longer exactly where you want it on the screen. If you press the mouse hard and move it as you are pressing, you make a selection instead of placing the insertion point. When you point at information on the screen, Word uses either the tip of the arrow or the middle of the I-beam (not the whole pointer) to indicate what you are pointing at.

## Selecting and Inserting Text with the Keyboard

So far, you have only seen how to use the mouse to create selections or place the insertion point. Some people prefer to use the keyboard. Word lets you perform these tasks with the keyboard as easily as with the mouse.

To move the insertion point, use the arrow keys. These arrow keys, marked (←), (→), (↑), and (↓), almost always appear below the right (SHIFT) key or between the main part of the keyboard and the numeric keys on the far right. Experiment with these keys to see how the insertion point moves in the sentence you have typed.

Making selections with the keyboard is just as easy as using the mouse. You move the insertion point to the beginning of the desired selection, hold

**Chapter 1:** *Getting Started* 13

down the (SHIFT) key, and use the arrow keys to move to the end of the desired selection. The selection (as indicated by the highlighting) moves as you press the arrow keys. Release the (SHIFT) key when you have finished making the selection.

For example, to select the word "typewriter" in the sentence you typed, use the (←) or (→) key to move the insertion point to the left of the first "t". Hold down the (SHIFT) key and press the (→) key until the entire word is selected. If you go too far, keep the (SHIFT) key held down and press the (←) key.

## Using Word Commands

Just as there are two ways to give commands in Windows, there are two ways to give Word commands: with the mouse and with the keyboard. Almost every command can be given with the mouse, and most can also be given with the keyboard. Some people strongly prefer the mouse over the keyboard; others, the opposite. Most Word users, however, find that they use a mixture of mouse and keyboard to give commands.

All Word commands appear in the *menus,* which are grouped in the *menu bar* at the top of the Word program window. The menus contain groups of similar commands and look like this:

```
File  Edit  View  Insert  Format  Tools  Table  Window  Help
```

In this book, every command is identified by the command name and the menu name so that you can find it easily. For example, the Ribbon command appears in the View menu; in this book, you would be told to "give the Ribbon command from the View menu." Note that the first menu on the left, marked with a long horizontal line, is called the Word *program Control menu.* This is not to be confused with the menu marked with the short horizontal line in the document window, called the *document Control menu.*

To give a command with the mouse, you point at the desired menu, click and hold the mouse button, and then drag down to the desired command while still holding down the mouse button. When you release the button, the command executes. For example, give the Ruler command from the View menu. This command turns the *ruler* on and off. The ruler is a tool that helps you format your document, and is decribed in detail in Chapter 11.

Many Word commands also have *keyboard equivalents*—keystrokes you can press instead of having to use the mouse. The keyboard equivalents are various combinations of the (CTRL) key, the (ALT) key, and the (SHIFT) key with regular keyboard keys.

Keyboard equivalents of commands are sometimes listed on the menu, to the right of the name of the command. If a command does not have a keyboard equivalent listed in the menu, you can still access it by pressing the (ALT) key, then the letter that is underlined in the menu name, and then the letter that is underlined in the command name.

For example, here is the File menu:

```
File
 New...
 Open...        Ctrl+F12
 Close

 Save           Shift+F12
 Save As...          F12
 Save All

 Find File...
 Summary Info...
 Template...

 Print Preview
 Print...  Ctrl+Shift+F12
 Print Merge...
 Print Setup...

 Exit              Alt+F4
```

The keyboard equivalent for the Open command from the File menu is (CTRL)-(F12), the keyboard equivalent for the Save command is (SHIFT)-(F12), and so on. Another way to give the Open command is to press (ALT)-(F)-(O) (since "F" is underlined in the File menu name and "O" is underlined in the Open command). To press (ALT)-(F)-(O), hold down the (ALT) key, press (F), release both keys, and press (O).

To see how to use keyboard equivalents, press (ALT)-(V)-(B), the key combination for the Ribbon command. (Press (ALT)-(V)-(B) using the same technique that you used with (ALT)-(F)-(O).) This turns the *ribbon* on and off. The ribbon helps you format characters, and is described in Chapter 10. The top of your screen (without the ribbon and ruler) now looks like this:

**Chapter 1:** *Getting Started*

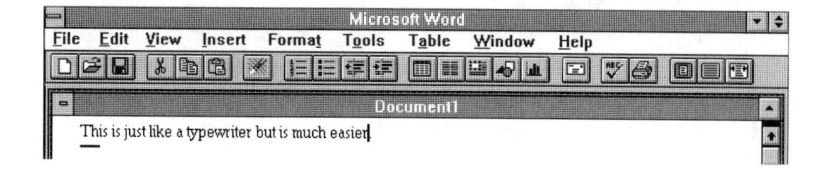

[screenshot of Microsoft Word window with text "This is just like a typewriter but is much easier"]

You can change the keys associated with any command, as you will see in Chapter 16. The keyboard equivalents discussed in this book are the ones that come assigned to the commands when you run Word for the first time. You can also add and remove commands from the menus. If you are using a copy of Word that someone else has used, the key equivalents and the commands you see in the menus may be somewhat different from what you see in this book.

Many Word commands act on a part of a document you specify. For example, you may want to make a word in your text bold. When you want a command to act on some specific text, you always select the text first and then give the command. This is true of all Windows programs: specify what you want to work on first and then give the command.

## Making Paragraphs in Word

In your text, each set of lines that is grouped as a unit is called a *paragraph*. Unfortunately, this is easy to confuse with the definition of a paragraph that you learned in grammar school, which is a group of sentences developing an idea. In Word, a paragraph is really just a line or a group of lines that ends with a press of the (ENTER) key. For instance, in a business letter, the line with the date, the lines that show the recipient's address, and the line with the salutation are all paragraphs, as is each group of sentences in the letter. When you see the word "paragraph" in this book and the Word reference manual, it refers to Word's definition.

Word identifies the end of a paragraph by a special mark that it puts in your text when you press the (ENTER) key. For this reason, you do not use the

**ENTER** key at the end of each line inside a paragraph, only at the end of the paragraph. One of Word's features that makes typing much easier is automatic *wordwrap*, which eliminates the need to decide where to end each line. As you type a paragraph, Word automatically figures out what will fit on a line and where to start a new line. You press **ENTER** only at the end of the paragraph.

For example, continue typing after the sentence you have already typed. Use the mouse or keyboard to move the insertion point to follow the period, and type a second sentence: **As I type in this second sentence, I notice that Word goes to the next line without my pressing the Enter key.** Now press **ENTER**, and notice that the insertion point moves to the beginning of the next line after the text.

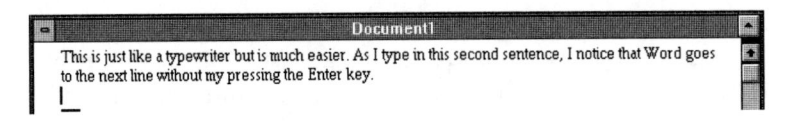

```
Document1
This is just like a typewriter but is much easier. As I type in this second sentence, I notice that Word goes
to the next line without my pressing the Enter key.
|
```

## Getting Help

The Help command is a quick way to get information about a Word command or to figure out what is happening in the program. Help has a list of choices that you can use to get information about any command and all of its options.

To get help, give the Help Index command from the Help menu, the menu that is at the far right side of the menu bar. You can select the topic you want help on from the dialog box, shown in Figure 1-4. When you are finished, give the Exit command from the File menu in the Help window to continue with Word. You can also just click anywhere in the main Word window, and the Help window will move behind the Word window.

*Figure 1-4.*   Help dialog box

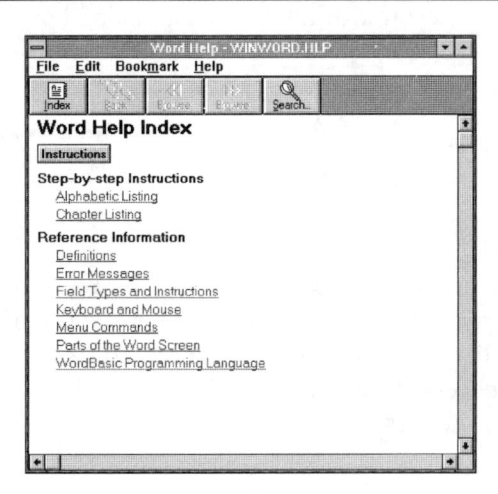

You can also get help on specific Word commands. To do this, press (F1) at any time. For example, to find out the features of the Open dialog box, give the Open command from the File menu and press (F1).

## Leaving Word

Since you have entered only practice text, it is unlikely that you want to save it in a file. (Don't worry; the real text comes at the beginning of the next chapter). When you leave Word, the program checks to see if you have saved your text in a file before it returns you to the Windows Program Manger. It is easy, however, to tell Word not to bother.

When you want to exit from Word and return to the Windows Program Manager, give the Exit command from the File menu. If there is text that you have not saved on disk (you will learn how to save text in the next chapter), Word prompts you with the following dialog box:

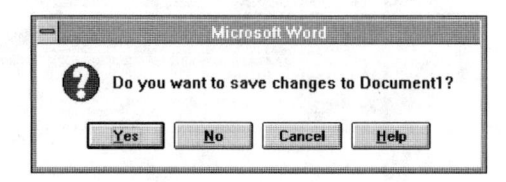

[Microsoft Word dialog: Do you want to save changes to Document1? Yes / No / Cancel / Help]

If you want to save your text, select the Yes button in the box. In this case, however, you can select the No button since the material is just for practice. If you realize that you want to do more editing or would like to save the file under a different name, select the Cancel button. You can also quit from Word with the (ALT)-(F4) key.

## Review

Start a new document and copy any two sentences from this book into the document. Select the first sentence by using the mouse. Then place the insertion point in the second sentence. Now select the first sentence by using the keyboard.

Type another sentence between the first and second sentence. Note how the text moves to the right as you do this.

# 2

# Basic Editing with Word

This and the next seven chapters show you how to enter and edit a variety of documents, from short memos to long reports. The lessons in this chapter use the sample business letter that you type in the first lesson.

## Lesson 1: Typing Your First File

Now that you know how to start Word, how to enter text, and a bit about giving Word commands, you are ready to type your first exercise, the business letter shown in Figure 2-1. Type it using the rules you have learned so far; if you make mistakes, correct them with the BACKSPACE key.

Note that this letter may be longer than one screen, depending on the size of your PC's monitor. If you reach the bottom of the screen as you are typing, just keep typing. Word scrolls the text up as you type.

Whenever you want to add text to the middle of text that you have already entered, simply move the I-beam to the desired location, click the mouse

***Figure 2-1.***   *Text of SAMPLE1 file*

> January 11, 1992
>
> Chris Richford, Vice President
> Manufacturer's Bank of the Northeast
> 1000 First Avenue
> Millerton, CT 06492
>
> Dear Ms. Richford:
>
> I am pleased to send you the latest update on the results of our expanded product line. The enclosed summary documents our increased profit margin (7%) for the fourth quarter of 1991, which is largely due to the successful introduction of our new model, the DC50. In 1992 we expect to continue increasing our profitable inroads into this new area.
>
> As you can see, we are well within the projections we outlined to you when you helped us obtain short-term financing. Thank you again for all your assistance. If you have any questions regarding this information, please feel free to call me.
>
> Sincerely,
>
> Thomas Mead, Controller
> National Generators
> 1275 Oak Glen Industrial Park
> Oak Glen, CT 06410

button to set the insertion point, and type. You can also move the insertion point with the keyboard.

The next section explains how to save the letter you have just typed in a file on disk. This file will be used in many of the chapters in this book.

## Lesson 2: Saving Your Text in a File

Now that you have text that you want to keep, you need to know how to tell Word to save it in a file. To do this, give the Save As command from the File menu. Word displays the dialog box shown in Figure 2-2. (Note that you may see a different dialog box if you use a different version of Windows.) Type **SAMPLE1** and press (ENTER) (or type **SAMPLE1** and select the OK button).

Word displays a dialog box for Summary Info. This contains any notes that you might want to make about the file for future reference. This optional information is not part of the letter itself, but it could be useful to you when,

**Figure 2-2.** *Save As dialog box*

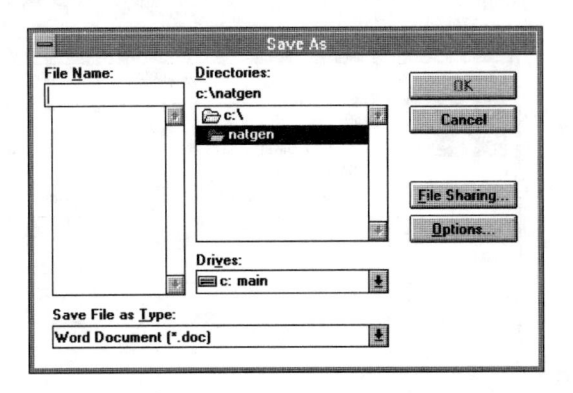

in a few years, you come across the file and wonder what is in it. Summary information is described in Chapter 21. For this example, select the Cancel button to save without a summary.

Word saves the file on disk. You can continue to edit the file if you wish, or you can leave Word with the Quit command from the File menu. If you are unfamiliar with dialog boxes, there is a lesson later in this chapter on that subject.

You have other choices in the Save As command that you will not use yet but that you should know about. You can see these choices by selecting the Options button. Figure 2-3 shows the dialog box that appears.

The list in the Save File as Type section of the Save As dialog box lets you select a type of file to save—for example, if you are creating a file to be read by another program. This is described in detail in Chapter 24.

The Directories and Drives lists are for changing where you will save the file. These are the same lists you see in many other Windows programs.

It is a good idea to save your file in a different directory than the one in which Word is saved. Although you may be tempted just to save all your Word files in the Word directory, this leads to difficulty later. It is best to create directories for your various projects and keep files for those projects in those directories.

***Figure 2-3.*** *Dialog box for Save options*

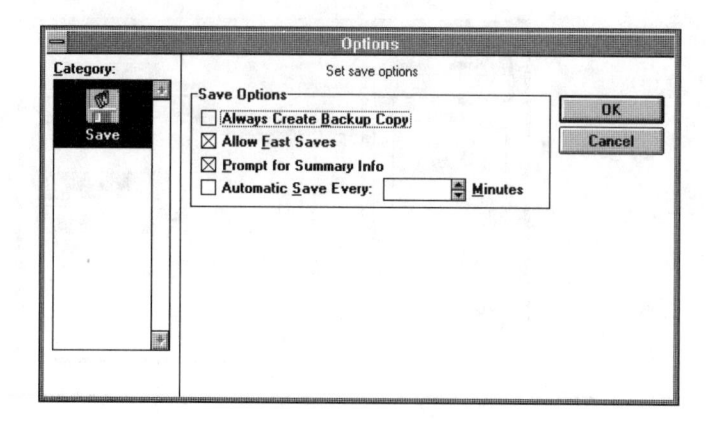

## Lesson 3: Opening a File

If you want to edit this file again later (which you will, since it is used for examples throughout this book), you open it with the Open command from the File menu. A list of files will appear. Either click the file you want (to select it) and select the OK button, or double-click the file you want.

If you make editing changes in a file and you do not want to save those changes (for example, if you are experimenting with some Word commands and do not want to change the file on disk), use the Close command from the File menu; when the command prompt asks if you want to save your changes, select the No button.

Word can open many types of files, not just ones that you created in Word. For instance, you can open graphics files, as described in Chapter 7. Chapter 24 gives more detail about the additional types of files you can open.

## Lesson 4: Scrolling Around in Your Document

Word gives you many ways to move around in a file when you are editing. Since your file can be much longer than a single screenful of text, you need a way to find text that you want to change or add to. As you saw before, you always have either an insertion point or a selection in your text. However, that insertion point or selection may not be visible if you are looking at a different part of your text.

To start this lesson, move to the beginning of the SAMPLE1 file, as shown in Figure 2-4. If you have closed the file, open it with the Open command. If you have quit from Word, start Word and open the file automatically by double-clicking the file's icon in the Program Manager. If the insertion point is not already there, move to the beginning of the text by dragging the *scroll box* (on the right side of the screen) up to the top of the scroll bar. Click the I-beam before the first letter of the file to place the insertion point there. To move to the beginning of the document with the keyboard, simply press (CTRL)-(HOME).

## Scrolling with the Mouse

To see different parts of your text, use the scroll bar on the right border of the window. For example, to scroll the screen down one line, click the arrow

*Figure 2-4.*   Top of SAMPLE1 document

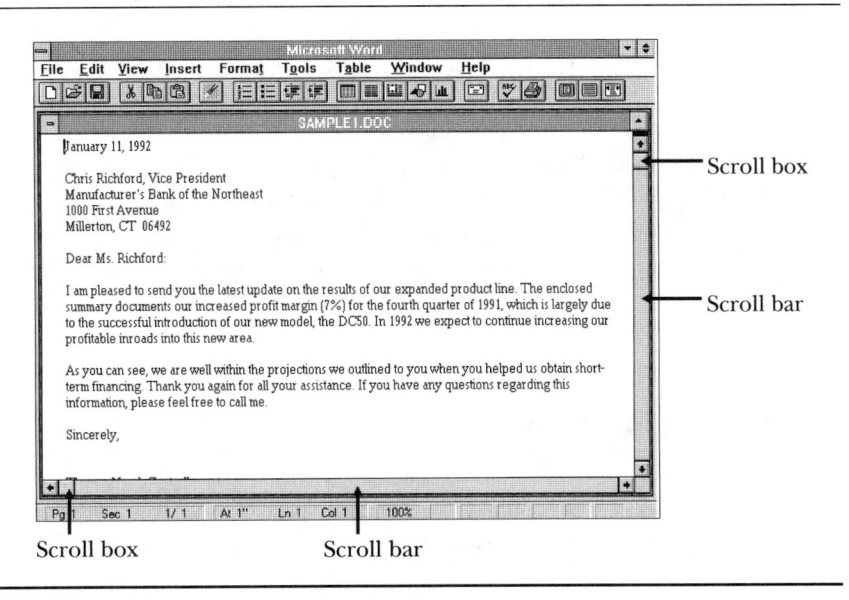

at the bottom right of the screen that is pointing down. If you point at this arrow and continue to hold down the button, the screen continues to scroll. The scroll bar on the bottom border of the window moves it left and right, which you rarely want to do.

To jump to a particular place in your text, you can drag the scroll box up and down the scroll bar and then release the mouse. This is sometimes called *thumbing*, since it is like thumbing through a book. To get to the end of a file, drag the box to the bottom of the bar; drag it to the top to get to the beginning of the file.

If you click above or below the scroll box in the scroll bar, Word jumps up or down by a full screen. In this case, that is not very useful, since the SAMPLE1 letter is quite short. In longer documents, it is very handy to click in the scroll bar if you are looking for particular information or skimming the information in a file.

When you scroll or jump by using the scroll box or the scroll bars, Word does not change the position of the insertion point or selection. You can see this by scrolling back to the top of the SAMPLE1 file. Notice that the insertion point is still blinking before the first letter. If you had made a selection and scrolled with the mouse, your selection would still be highlighted and in the same place.

## Scrolling with the Keyboard

To scroll up or down a line at a time with the keyboard, press (↑) or (↓). To move up or down by a full screen, press the (PAGE UP) or (PAGE DOWN) key on your keyboard. Scrolling with these keys differs from scrolling with the mouse because Word moves the insertion point when you scroll with the keyboard. When you give these keyboard scrolling commands, Word puts the insertion point at the top of the window that you see when you scroll.

## Lesson 5: Changing Text

You saw in Chapter 1 how to select text and how to insert text at the insertion point. As you were typing the text for the SAMPLE1 file earlier in

**Chapter 2:** *Basic Editing with Word* 25

this chapter, if you made a mistake, you had to correct it by pressing the BACKSPACE key, character by character. However, there are faster ways of deleting text than by backspacing over one character at a time. You can select all the text you want to delete (with either the mouse or keyboard) and press DEL.

Deleting text is a common practice, but replacing text with new text is even more common. For example, as you review what you have written, you often think of better words to use. To replace some text in a document with new words, simply select the text and begin typing. Word deletes the first text and starts inserting at that point.

To see this, assume that you want to replace the word "pleased" with the word "happy" in the first full sentence of the letter. Select "pleased" and type **happy**. Notice that when you type the "h", Word removes the selected text, replaces it with "h", and puts the insertion point at that spot. It is as if you had pressed DEL and started typing.

You can also delete text with some other keyboard commands. To delete the character after the insertion point (instead of the one before it), press DEL. (You do not have to select the character.) You can also delete whole words at a time. CTRL-BACKSPACE deletes the word before the insertion point, while CTRL-DEL deletes the word after it.

## Lesson 6: More Ways to Select Text

Most people prefer to use the mouse for moving the insertion point and selecting text. This is because using the mouse makes a very visual connection to the document; you do not have to remember which keys to use.

### Selecting Text with the Mouse

You can choose from six different kinds of selections of fixed lengths: a character, a word, a sentence, a line, a paragraph, and the entire document. If you want to select a portion of text that is not included in the six choices (such as several words but not a sentence, several sentences but not a paragraph, or several paragraphs, but not an entire document), you can also make selections of varying lengths.

You already saw in the last chapter how to select a character, a word, and a sentence by dragging, double-clicking, and clicking with the (CTRL) key, respectively. You also learned how to select varying amounts of text by clicking and dragging.

To review the steps, point at any letter in the word "update" in the first sentence. Click the button to set the insertion point, double-click to select the entire word, press the (CTRL) key, and hold down the mouse button to select the entire sentence. You can select a variable amount of text by clicking at the beginning of the desired selection and dragging to the end.

To select larger areas of text, move the mouse pointer into the *selection bar,* the blank column between the left window border and the text. When you point to the selection bar, the I-beam changes to an arrow that points up and to the right instead of to the left (as in the command area). For example, point to the selection bar on the third line of the body of the letter, which begins with "to the successful", as in Figure 2-5.

*Figure 2-5.*     Pointing in the selection bar

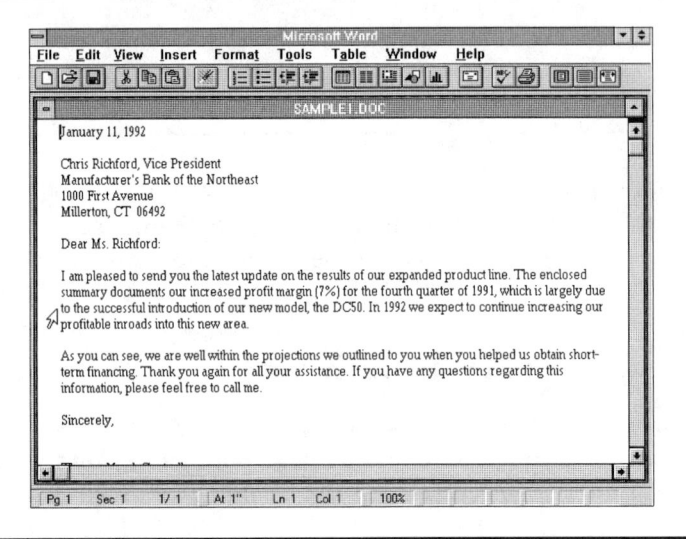

Clicking in the selection bar has a different effect than clicking in the text. Clicking once selects the entire line, double-clicking selects the entire paragraph, and pressing the (CTRL) key and then the mouse button selects the entire document. Experiment with each of these choices.

When selecting by dragging, if the text that you want to select is not completely on the screen, you can extend the selection by scrolling the screen. To do this, start your selection, hold down the mouse button, and briefly bring the pointer into the upper or lower screen border. Word then scrolls the screen, and you can continue to extend your selection. Sometimes Word scrolls more than you expect, so using this method takes a bit of practice. If you are still holding down the mouse button, you can back up to the proper spot and then release the button.

## Selecting Text with the Keyboard

Word has many keyboard commands that allow you to move the insertion point and select parts of your document. The keyboard commands for selecting text are the same as the keyboard commands for moving the insertion point, except that the (SHIFT) key is held down. For example, the (↓) key moves the insertion point down a line, while (SHIFT)-(↓) extends the selection down one line.

Table 2-1 shows the keys for moving the insertion point.

You may have noticed that many of these key combinations use the keypad. Of course, you may want to use the keypad for its most obvious use, namely to type numbers. To do so, you must put Word in *numeric lock* mode by pressing the (NUM LOCK) key at the top of the keypad. When you are in numeric lock mode, you see "NUM" appear near the bottom right of Word's window.

## Lesson 7: The Undo Command

Now that you know how to select any text you want, you can experiment with selecting different amounts of text and deleting or replacing them. You might hesitate to experiment with important information, fearing that when you delete information, it is gone forever. With Word, however, you can give

**Table 2-1.** *Insertion Point Movement with the Keyboard*

| Movement | Key |
| --- | --- |
| Right one character | → |
| Left one character | ← |
| Up one line | ↑ |
| Down one line | ↓ |
| To end of line | END |
| To beginning of line | HOME |
| Up one screen | PAGE UP |
| Down one screen | PAGE DOWN |
| Left one word | CTRL-← |
| Right one word | CTRL-→ |
| Up one paragraph | CTRL-↑ |
| Down one paragraph | CTRL-↓ |
| To top of window | CTRL-PAGE UP |
| To bottom of window | CTRL-PAGE DOWN |
| To beginning of document | CTRL-HOME |
| To end of document | CTRL-END |

the Undo command from the Edit menu to undo the last change and restore the text that you deleted, replaced, or changed.

The Undo command restores your text to the way it was before your last edit. For example, if you select a paragraph of text and then delete it by pressing DEL, you can use the Undo command from the Edit menu to bring the paragraph back, even if you have moved to a new selection. The Undo command restores only the last editing command that you have given, such as Cut or Copy or pressing BACKSPACE a few times (Cut and Copy are described in Chapter 4). It cannot restore earlier edits.

The Undo command can also undo your last Undo command. This may seem strange, but it is useful if you are not sure that you want to restore an edit you have made. For example, if you delete a sentence but are not sure that you deleted the correct sentence, you can undo the deletion; and if it turns out that you did delete the correct sentence, give the Undo command again to cause Word to delete it again.

To experiment with the Undo command, delete the date from the letter:

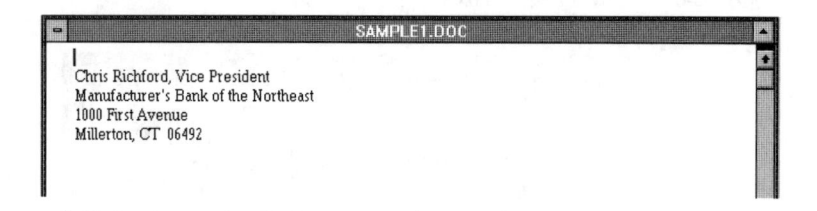

```
┌─────────────────── SAMPLE1.DOC ───────────────────┐
│ |                                                  │
│ Chris Richford, Vice President                     │
│ Manufacturer's Bank of the Northeast               │
│ 1000 First Avenue                                  │
│ Millerton, CT 06492                                │
└────────────────────────────────────────────────────┘
```

Now give the Undo command, and the date is restored.

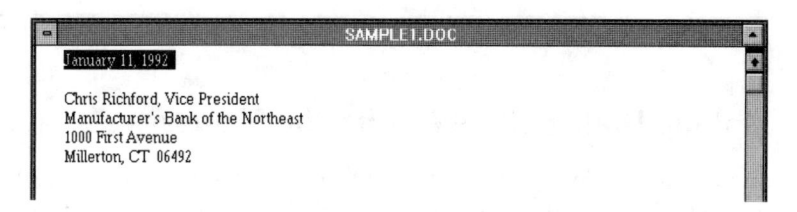

```
┌─────────────────── SAMPLE1.DOC ───────────────────┐
│ January 11, 1992                                   │
│                                                    │
│ Chris Richford, Vice President                     │
│ Manufacturer's Bank of the Northeast               │
│ 1000 First Avenue                                  │
│ Millerton, CT 06492                                │
└────────────────────────────────────────────────────┘
```

As you will see in later chapters, you can use the Undo command to reverse a number of different editing commands. You may well find it to be a safety net at a critical moment. Remember, however, that Undo can restore only your last edit; anything done before that cannot be undone.

## Lesson 8: Making Choices in Dialog Boxes

The Word commands introduced so far have been quite simple. When you give some commands, however, you are offered a *dialog box* of items to choose from. Dialog boxes are common to all Windows programs. This lesson is a quick refresher on how to use the mouse and the keyboard to make dialog box choices.

The Find command from the Edit menu is a good example of a command that has a dialog box with many choices. When you give the Find command, Word presents you with the dialog box shown in Figure 2-6. Many of the dialog boxes that you see in Windows have only one or two buttons, such as OK or Cancel. Here you have many sets of buttons.

***Figure 2-6.***   *Find dialog box*

## Making Dialog Choices with the Mouse

The Match Whole Word Only and Match Case buttons are on-off buttons that tell if you want a particular feature. If you click one of the square boxes (such as Match Case), an "X" appears in the box:

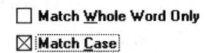

This indicates that the choice is selected. A list of square boxes, sometimes called *check boxes,* indicates that you can check more than one of the boxes at the same time. For example, the dialog box with both Match Whole Word Only and Match Case options selected looks like this:

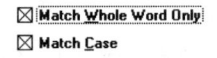

The round buttons (sometimes called *radio buttons*) under Direction indicate that only one of the choices in the group of buttons can be selected at a time. For example, if you click the Up button, the Down choice is deselected.

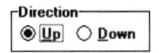

Some dialog boxes have *drop-down lists* that let you choose one item from a list. For example, Figure 2-7 shows the Character dialog box from the Format

**Figure 2-7.**   *Character dialog box*

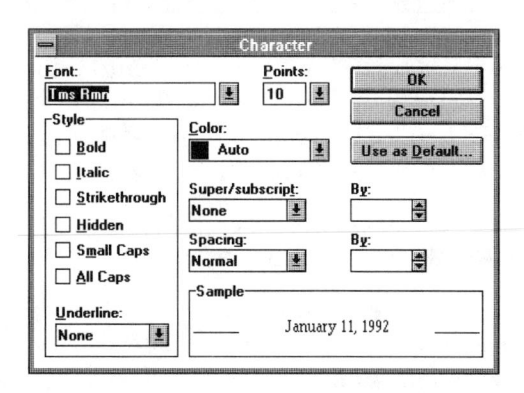

menu. This dialog box has six drop-down lists. You can select from the list by clicking the name or the arrow and scrolling up or down the list while holding down the mouse button.

Some dialog boxes allow you to enter text or numbers; you have already seen this in the Save As command. In the Find dialog box, you enter text by typing in the Find What box.

Many Word dialog boxes can be moved around on the screen while they are open. This lets you look at your document before you make your choices. You can click the title bar of any dialog box with a shaded title bar (like the Character dialog box shown in Figure 2-7) and drag it to a new location.

## Making Dialog Choices with the Keyboard

Word lets you make dialog box choices with the keyboard. Only die-hard keyboard enthusiasts will want to do so because the method is somewhat convoluted.

To move to the next option in a dialog box, press (TAB); to move to the previous option, press (SHIFT)-(TAB). You can jump directly to an option by pressing (ALT) and the underlined letter in that option's name. To select an option in a drop-down list, use the (↑) and (↓) keys, and then press (ALT)-(↓) to close the list.

## Lesson 9: Inserting Special Characters in Your Text

In Chapter 1, you saw how to type text into your document. You saw that to make paragraphs, you had to use the ENTER key and that Word inserted a special paragraph mark into your document. There are other special characters in Word for other purposes, which are described in this lesson.

### Line Breaks Within Paragraphs

If you want to force Word to start a new line within a paragraph but not start a new paragraph, hold down the SHIFT key while you press the ENTER key. This key combination is called a *newline,* and it lets you make lines of different lengths within a paragraph that are not like the lines of a paragraph made with wordwrap—you can start a new line without starting a new paragraph. You would use newline instead of starting a new paragraph because many Word formatting commands pertain to the whole paragraph. If you signal a paragraph with ENTER, you have to format it separately from the preceding lines; if you use newline, you only need to format the whole paragraph once.

A good example of using newline is in typing the recipient's address in a letter. You will learn in Chapter 16 how to see the difference between the end of a paragraph and newline; for now, it is not important.

Look again at the SAMPLE1 letter. You used ENTER characters at the end of each line. Instead, it is better to use a newline (the SHIFT-ENTER combination) in the two addresses since each address is really a single unit. You can change the ENTER characters to newline characters by selecting each one and pressing SHIFT-ENTER. You can select them even though you can't see them by dragging over the blank character at the end of the paragraph; you will see the selection extend by an extra space. You can see the difference after you have made the changes by giving the commands to select whole paragraphs and noticing that the whole address is selected.

### Nonbreaking Spaces

A *nonbreaking space* acts like a piece of glue between two words and prevents wordwrap from placing them on different lines. For example, it is common typing practice not to leave a short abbreviation at the end of a line. Instead of having text look like this:

> Please be sure that all of the samples are sent to Ms.
> Price as soon as possible.

you would want to move the abbreviation to the second line:

> Please be sure that all of the samples are sent to
> Ms. Price as soon as possible.

This is easy when you are typing on a typewriter. However, remember that Word wraps words for you automatically, sometimes splitting an abbreviation from what follows.

If you want to be sure that a space between words is never broken, use a nonbreaking space, which is typed as (CTRL)-(SHIFT)-(SPACEBAR). The space looks identical to a normal space on your screen, but Word never uses that word break as a line break.

## Inserting Other Characters

Your PC has many special characters that are directly accessible through the keypad at the right of the keyboard. For example, many European languages use umlauts on some vowels, as in "ö". To type this character, press the (NUM LOCK) key so that your keyboard indicates it is in "Num Lock" mode (a small light near the top right of the keyboard will show). Hold down the (ALT) key, press (0) on the keypad and, while still holding down the (ALT) key, type the number associated with the letter. In the case of "ö", that number is 246.

It is often difficult to remember all of the key combinations, since each font can have up to 255 characters. To make inserting these characters easier in Word, Microsoft includes the Symbol command from the Insert menu. This command shows you a table of all the characters in the current font, such as those in Figure 2-8. The table is in the order that the characters appear internally in the font.

To insert a particular character in your text, put the insertion point where you want the character, give the Symbol command, choose the font you want,

**Figure 2-8.**   *Symbol dialog box*

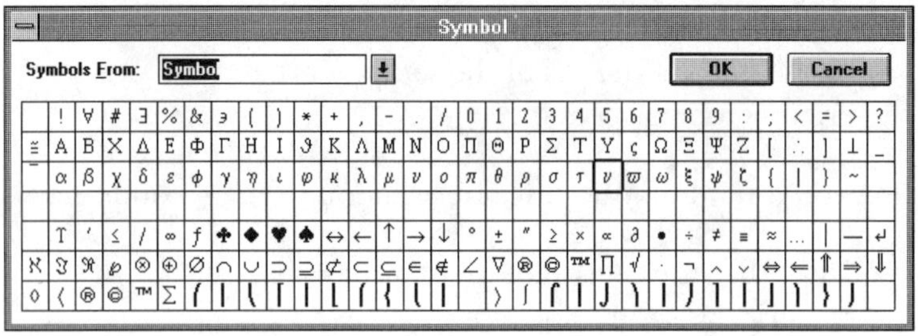

and click the desired character. You can insert as many characters as you want this way, since the Symbol window stays open until you close it by pressing (CTRL)-(F4) or selecting the Cancel button. You can change the font when the Symbol window is open by using the drop-down list near the top of the dialog box.

The Symbol command is particularly useful with the fonts that are not alphanumeric. As you can see, the Symbol font that is initially shown is made up of symbols that you might want to use in scientific or technical documents. Choosing the symbols with the Symbol command is much easier than looking them up in a table and pressing the corresponding keys.

Although the international characters can also be entered directly by using the (ALT) key and the keypad, the Symbol command is much more efficient and requires less memorization.

## Lesson 10: Printing Your Document

Normally, the primary purpose of word processing is to obtain a finished printed document. At this point you have learned the basics of using Word to input and edit a document. Now that you have edited your text, it is likely that you want to see it on a printed page.

To print the file that you are editing, use the Print command from the File menu. When you give this command, you see a dialog box that is explained in detail in Chapter 8. To print a single copy of your document, you simply select the OK button. You will also see in Chapter 8 how to use the Setup and Options buttons, which help you set up printing parameters. Before printing, be sure that your printer is turned on and that it is properly connected to your PC.

## Review

Start a new document and type a few paragraphs from a magazine article you have read recently. Make sure you type in more than one screenful of text, and don't worry about spelling. Save this text on disk as MAGAZINE. You will use this file in the review sections for many other chapters.

Practice moving the insertion point with the keyboard and practice scrolling with the mouse.

Change the first word in the second sentence to something else. Think about the many ways you can do this, and try them all. Each time you make a change, undo the change with the Undo command from the Edit menu.

# 3

# Using Word's Windows

Using Word's windows effectively will probably save you more time than any of its editing features. Until now you have used only one window in Word. However, you can split the large window into two smaller ones with little effort. You can also have many separate windows in different files open at once. This may seem like a feature that only advanced users would want. However, it is possible to use windows in your everyday editing to meet a number of different needs.

For example, if you are editing the top of a letter and want to look at some information near the bottom, you do not need to take your attention away from either part if you split your window into two. If you are writing a memo and need to look at a report you wrote earlier, you can use one window for the memo and another window for the report.

## Lesson 11: Splitting a Window in One File

To see how two windows can significantly help editing, start Word with the SAMPLE1 file in one window. In this lesson you learn how to split the window horizontally to get two views of the file. When you are looking at two parts of one file, it is common to make a split about halfway down the screen.

One feature of the Word window you may notice that is different from windows in most other Windows programs is the black bar near the top of the scroll bar, above the up scroll arrow on the right side of the window. This is called the *split bar* because you can use it to split a window.

Splitting a window is straightforward. Point at the split bar, and the mouse pointer becomes a *split icon*. Hold down the mouse button and drag the split bar down to where you want to divide the window; when you release the button, the window is split.

When you press the mouse button, notice that Word draws a gray bar across the screen. It may be hard to see the bar at first. Look right below the title bar:

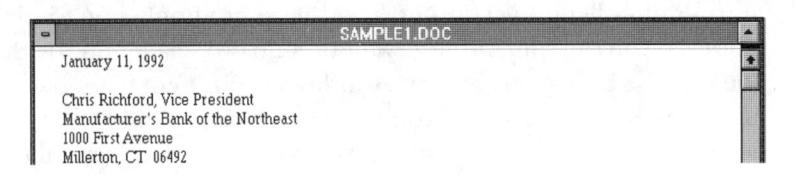

```
                        SAMPLE1.DOC
January 11, 1992

Chris Richford, Vice President
Manufacturer's Bank of the Northeast
1000 First Avenue
Millerton, CT  06492
```

Now drag the split bar down until the gray bar is below the line that begins "I am pleased...", as in Figure 3-1. When you release the button, Word creates the two halves of the window, each with its own separate vertical scroll bar, as shown in Figure 3-2. Notice that Word repeats one line of text in both windows.

You also can split a window by giving the Split command from the window's Control menu. With the keyboard, this would be (ALT)-(-)(T) (press (ALT), then (-), release both keys, and press (T)). The mouse pointer becomes a two-headed arrow that you can position with the mouse or the (↑) and (↓) keys. When the arrow is at the position where you want the split, press (ENTER).

You can change the position of the split at any time by dragging the split bar to a new location or by giving the Split command from the window's

**Chapter 3:** *Using Word's Windows* 39

*Figure 3-1.* Gray bar positioned at desired point

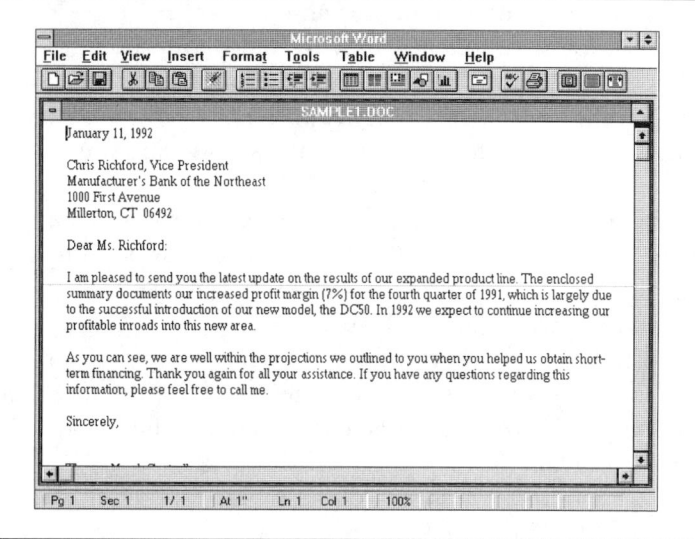

*Figure 3-2.* Window after splitting

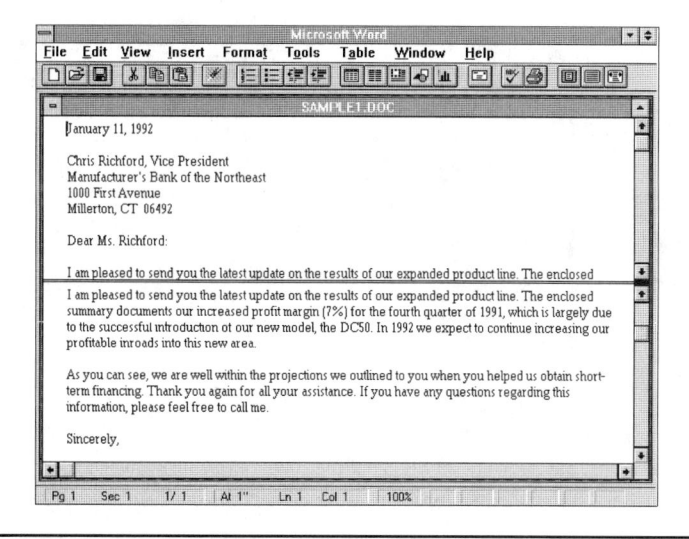

Control menu again. To go back to a single window, drag the split bar all the way to the top or bottom of the window.

Once you have split a window, you need only point to either part to move the insertion point from part to part. You can also move the insertion point between the parts by pressing F6. The text that you view in each part of a window can be scrolled independently. If you want, you can view the same text in both halves of the split window.

To see how you can view different parts of a document, split the window again (if you closed it) and move the insertion point to the bottom half by clicking in that part of the window or pressing F6. You can now scroll to the end of the file, as shown in Figure 3-3.

Now move the insertion point to the beginning of the file in the lower half, so both windows show the same text. After the line "1000 First Avenue" in the top half, type **Suite 120** and notice that the second window is updated almost simultaneously.

Each half of a window can be used independently. You can use the Find command to find specific information in one part of the window without

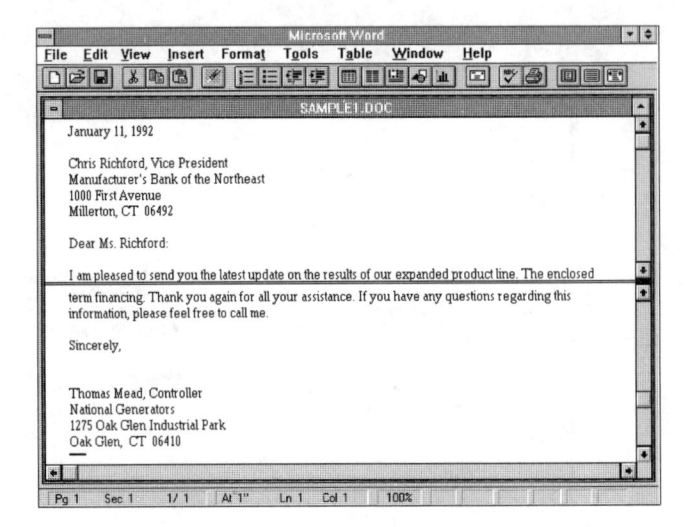

*Figure 3-3.* Top and bottom parts of file

losing your place in the other. This is useful in finding related text in a long document. Other good uses for split windows are moving text, which you will see in Chapter 4, and comparing similar text.

## Lesson 12: Moving and Sizing Windows

You can change the location of a document window by dragging the title bar and change the size of a window by dragging its size box or one of the edges of the window. Like all Windows programs, you can also change the location and size of the Word program window in the same fashion. As you will see in the next lesson, it is convenient to change the locations and sizes of document windows when you have more than one document open in Word's program window.

To move a window, click its *title bar*—the shaded area at the top of the window—and drag the window while still holding down the mouse button. This is exactly like moving windows in all Windows programs. Note that you can move a window so that part of the window disappears off the side or bottom of the screen. You cannot move a window that is maximized.

The easiest way to change the size of a window is to click and drag the *size box* in the lower-right corner of the window. This allows you to make the window narrow or short. You can also drag the horizontal or vertical border of any window. Again, this is like other Windows programs.

The keyboard commands to change the location and size of a window are in that window's Control menu. For all Windows programs, you use ALT-- to see the Control menu for a document window and ALT-SPACEBAR to see the Control menu for the program window.

You also can change the size of document windows by using the maximize or restore box that you saw in Chapter 1. Clicking this box causes the window to grow to the full size of Word's program window or, if it is already enlarged, to shrink to its previous size. Maximizing is handy if you have many windows that you open only occasionally. After you close these less-used windows, instead of having to drag down the size box of your main window, you can simply click its maximize box.

The restore box remembers the shape of the window that you last used. If you change a window, maximize it, and then click the restore box, your window is the same size and shape and in the same location as it was before you maximized it. For example, use the size box to shrink the SAMPLE1 window to the middle of the Word program window, as in Figure 3-4. Click the maximize and restore boxes a few times and you'll see how zoom remembers the last window size.

## Lesson 13: Using Two Windows for Two Files

You may have already guessed the next step in using windows: using one window to look at one file and a second window to look at a different file. To look at two different files, use the Open command from the File menu to open a window for a new file. You can have many windows open at a time. On PCs with larger screens, you can easily work with four or more windows open at the same time. Word allows you to have over 20 documents open at one time, but it is unlikely that you would want to do so.

*Figure 3-4.    SAMPLE1 window shrunk*

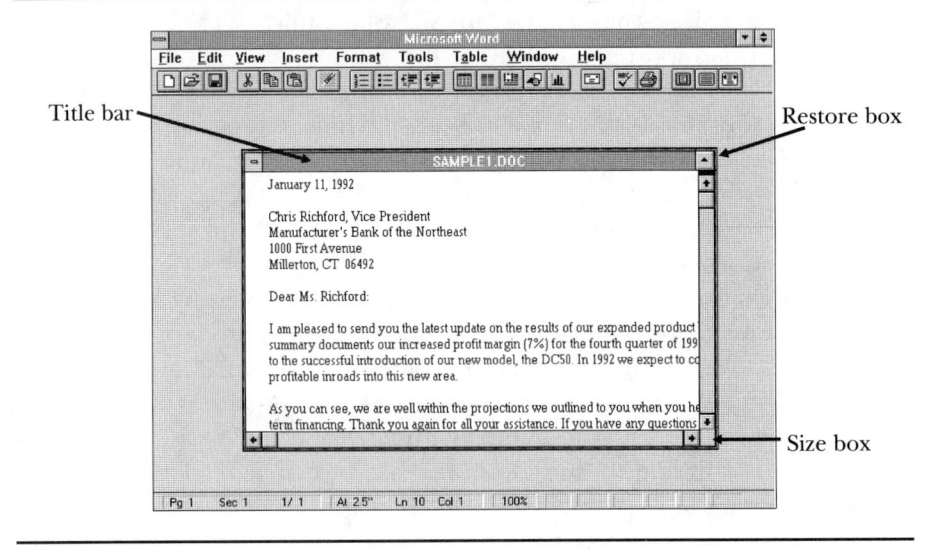

**Chapter 3:**  *Using Word's Windows*  43

To see how useful multiple windows are, close the SAMPLE1 window by giving the Close command from the File menu to clear your experimental modifications out of Word's memory (select No to the prompt of whether you want to save the changes). Give the New command from the File menu, and enter the short report shown in Figure 3-5. (Use the (TAB) key to line up the figures.) Save this on disk with the name REPORT1.

Use the Open command to open a window with the SAMPLE1 file. Word opens a document in the same location and with the same size as when you saved it, so the SAMPLE1 file hides the REPORT1 file.

Shrink both windows to about half the height of the screen by using their size boxes, and drag the SAMPLE1 window to the top of the screen and the REPORT1 window to the bottom. Your screen should look like the one in Figure 3-6.

You can now look at parts of each file independently. You can scroll each window so that you can see the relevant sections and compare the texts. In Chapter 4, you will see how you can quickly copy and move text from one window to another.

*Figure 3-5.*    Text of REPORT1

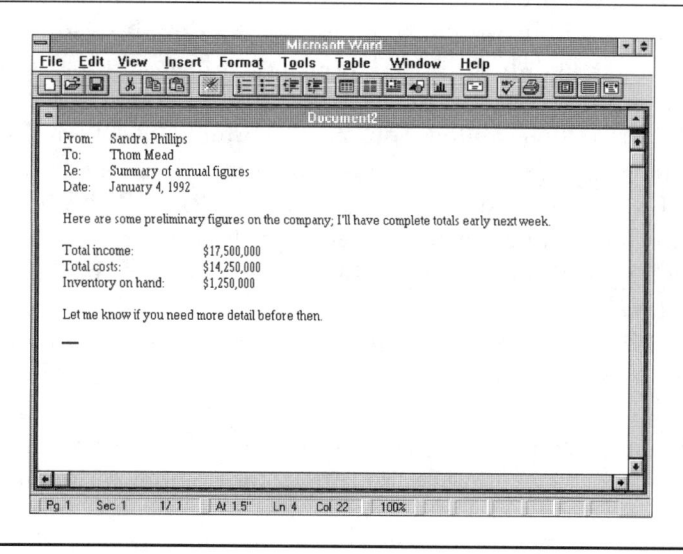

*Figure 3-6.*   *Both windows visible*

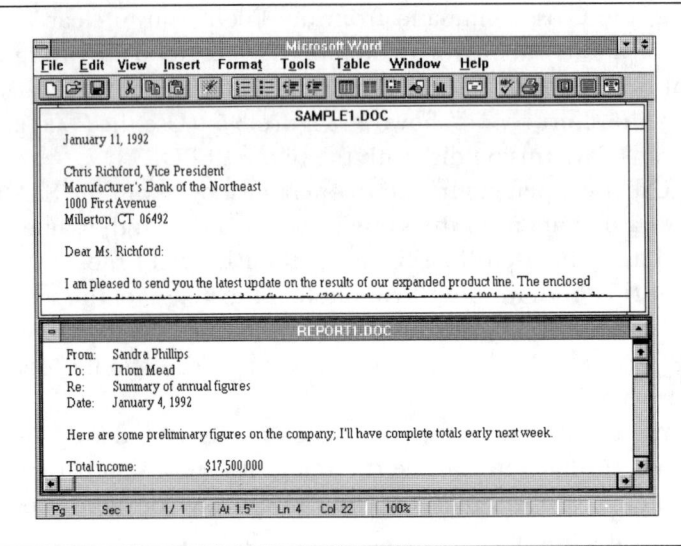

You may not want to have both windows fully showing since this reduces the amount of text you can see in each window. Instead, you may want both windows large, which forces you to switch from window to window. You can make a window come to the front and be completely visible by clicking anywhere in that window. You can also bring the back window to the front by pressing CTRL-F6 or by choosing the document name in the Window menu.

Use the size boxes of the SAMPLE1 and REPORT1 windows to make them almost the full size of the screen, and then move them so they are slightly offset, as in Figure 3-7. Experiment with switching back and forth between windows.

Of course, if you have more than two windows active, you can have that number of files open at the same time. If you have edited the text in a window and want to keep the changes, remember to save it with the Save or Save As command before closing the window. If you don't, Word reminds you that the window has been edited and prompts for whether you want to save the edits.

***Figure 3-7.*** *Two windows overlapping*

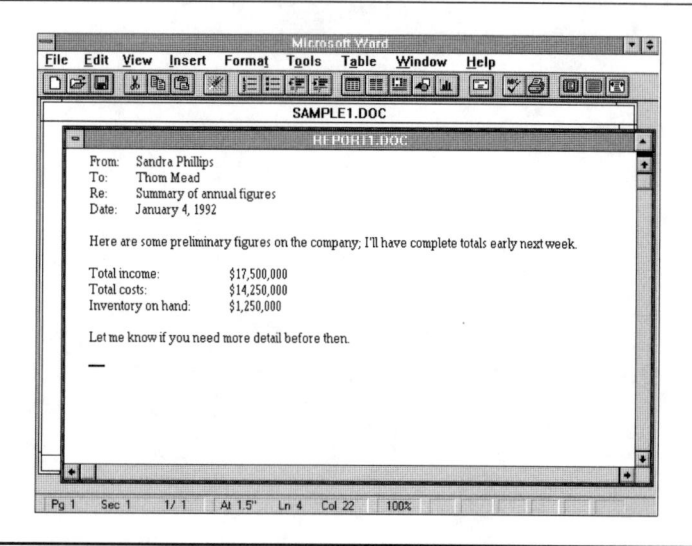

# Review

Open the MAGAZINE practice file that you made in the Review section of Chapter 2. Split the window in two. Show the beginning and end of that file at the same time.

# 4

# Moving and Copying Text

So far, the editing skills you have learned are how to enter text, how to move the insertion point and selection, and how to delete text from a document. This chapter explains how to use the Cut and Paste commands to move text from one part of a file to another, and how to copy text within a file with the Copy command. You will also see how to use the same procedures to move and copy text between files.

    The ability to move sections of text is one of the most useful features of word processing. For example, after writing a report you may decide you want to change the order of paragraphs or sentences. Since you can rearrange your ideas after seeing them on paper or on the screen, your finished writing will be much better organized. In this chapter, you will see that moving text is easy to do with Word.

## Lesson 14: Using the Clipboard

Word uses the Windows *Clipboard* to hold information. You can imagine the Clipboard as a holder for a single chunk of text or a single picture. Every time you use the Copy or Cut command from the Edit menu in a Windows program, the contents of the Clipboard are replaced with the selected text or picture.

The Clipboard acts as a temporary holder of a single piece of information. It is most useful for moving text: you select the text, move it from its current location into the Clipboard, put the insertion point at the desired location, and copy it there from the Clipboard.

Many Windows programs, including Word, interact with the Clipboard by using three commands from the Edit menu:

- The Copy command places a copy of the selected text into the Clipboard, replacing its previous contents.
- The Cut command does the same thing as the Copy command, except that it removes the selected text from the document. This is like giving the Copy command followed by pressing the `BACKSPACE` key.
- The Paste command inserts the contents of the Clipboard at the insertion point. If you have text selected when you give the Paste command, the contents of the Clipboard replaces the selected text; this is similar to replacing text, as you saw in Chapter 2. Note that this does not "empty" the Clipboard; instead, the contents remain there until you replace them with another Copy or Cut command.

Word includes an extremely useful command you can use when you are using the Clipboard. The Run command, found in Word's program Control menu, has the Clipboard option, which opens a window that lets you look at the contents of the Clipboard but not edit them. This is a handy way to check what you have in the Clipboard. Word is one of the few programs with a Run command.

For example, select the word "latest" in the first paragraph of the SAMPLE1 letter and copy it to the Clipboard with the Copy command from the Edit menu. Give the Run command from the program Control menu and select Clipboard. Word displays the Clipboard window:

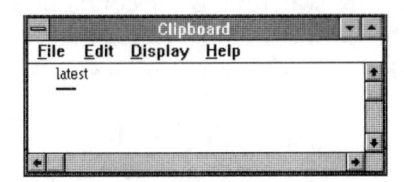

The Clipboard in Word acts just as it does in other Windows applications. Thus, if you now select another word from the file and give the Cut command, the Clipboard no longer contains the word "latest"—it contains the word you just selected. If you then give the Undo command from the Edit menu, you will find that the second word is back in the text, and if you then give the Show Clipboard command from the Window menu, you'll find "latest" back in the Clipboard.

When the text is no longer in the Clipboard (for example, three edits ago), you cannot use the Undo command to restore it. Notice that deleting characters with the (BACKSPACE) key does not put the characters into the Clipboard; only the Cut command and the Copy command do. However, you can still use the Undo command to restore text erased with the (BACKSPACE) key if that erasure is the last edit you made.

This chapter shows you the basic use of the Clipboard. You will also see the Clipboard used in Chapter 7 for importing pictures to your Word documents.

## Lesson 15: Moving and Copying Text Within a Document

As stated in the previous lesson, the basic method for moving text within a document is as follows:

1. Select the text that is to be moved.
2. Give the Cut command.
3. Set the insertion point at the desired location for the text.
4. Give the Paste command.

For example, try switching the second and third sentences of the second paragraph of the SAMPLE1 file. To do this, select the third sentence, then delete the sentence with the Cut command. Your screen now looks like the one in Figure 4-1.

Now set the insertion point at the beginning of the second sentence and give the Paste command. Press the (SPACEBAR) to separate the two sentences, as shown in Figure 4-2. Notice that Word automatically reformats the paragraph for you.

This is the way you most often use the Clipboard. Since it can hold any amount of information, you can use it to move large portions of your text. This is also a convenient method for moving phrases around in a sentence to see different effects on the sound and meaning. Practice moving text around in your file by using the Clipboard and the Cut and Paste commands.

The Clipboard is also useful for making copies of parts of your text. Although copying text is not as common as moving text, you may find that a sentence or a line of text is used over and over in your document. If you copy the text, you do not have to retype it each time it is used.

***Figure 4-1.***   Third sentence cut

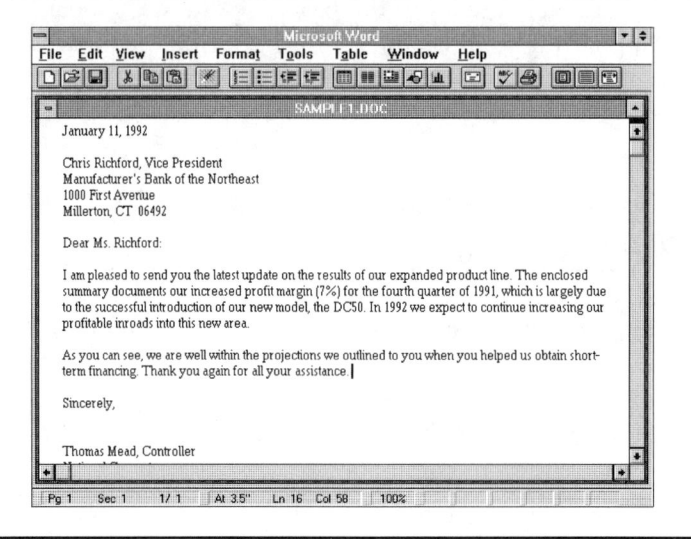

**Chapter 4:** *Moving and Copying Text* 51

To copy text, use the Copy command, which puts the contents of the selection in the Clipboard. The original text remains in your document, and a copy of it is placed in the Clipboard. This procedure is the same if you are copying text within a document (such as repeating a quotation in an academic paper) or copying information from one file to another. The contents even remain in the Clipboard when you leave Word and start another application.

The Copy, Cut, and Paste commands become even more powerful when they are used with split windows since you can use the Clipboard to move text from one part of the window to the other without losing your place in either part of the file. This lets you instantly see the results of moving text as you perform the commands.

For example, you might want to see the effect of adding "From:" and the sender's name to the top of the letter. You can do this easily by leaving the end of the letter in the bottom part and showing the beginning of the letter in the top part.

With the window split into halves, position the text as shown in Figure 4-3. Type **From:** before the salutation (on the line above Chris Richford's name),

*Figure 4-2.* Sentence inserted from Clipboard

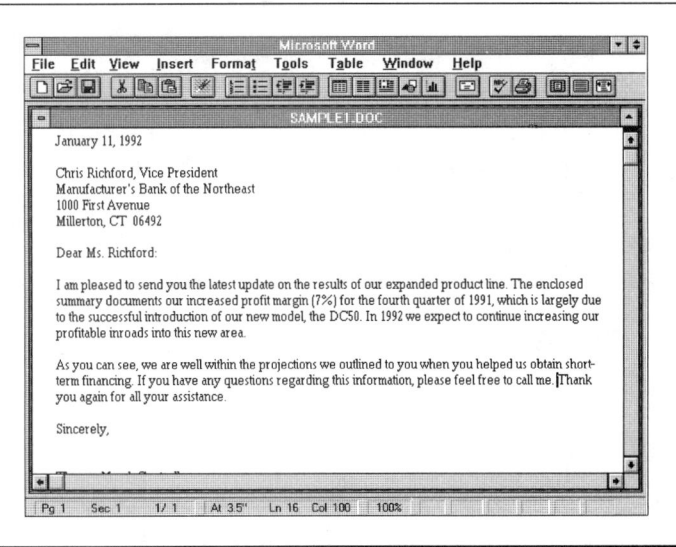

press the (ENTER) key, and move to the lower half. Select the line with Thomas Mead's name, and give the Copy command.

Now move to the top window, move the insertion point to the line beneath "From:", and then use the Paste command to place the line under "From:". Add another line after the name by pressing (ENTER).

## Lesson 16: Using the Clipboard with Two Files

In Chapter 3, you saw how to view two files at once (SAMPLE1 and REPORT1). As you are viewing two files, you can also copy or move information between them. (Be sure both SAMPLE1 and REPORT1 are open.) It is likely that you will want to move text from one file to another if you have documents that are made up of many files. Copying text is also common when you have multiple documents since you may want to repeat part of one document in another.

*Figure 4-3.*   Window split for moving

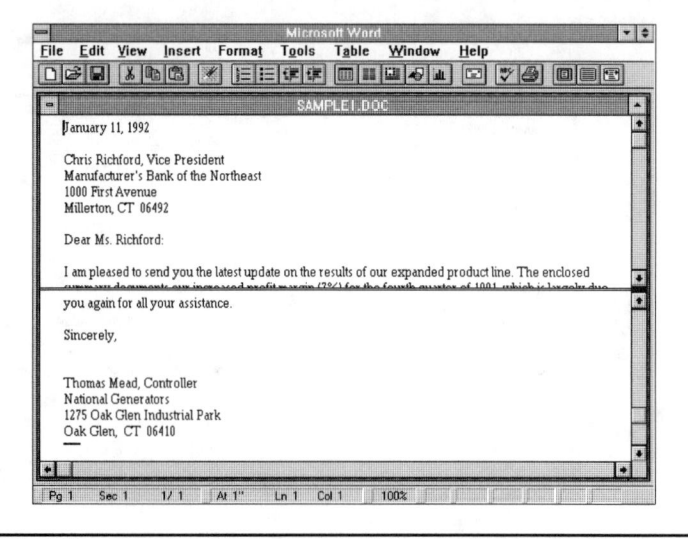

**Chapter 4:**  *Moving and Copying Text*　　　　　　　　　　　　　　　　　　　　　　**53**

As you are editing SAMPLE1, you may need some of the information in REPORT1—for example, if you want to include the table of numbers. You can see those numbers by scrolling through REPORT1, and you can even copy the whole table to SAMPLE1 with the Copy and Paste commands.

To do this, add text between the paragraphs of SAMPLE1:

> to the successful introduction of our new model, the DC50. In 1992 we expect to continue increasing our profitable inroads into this new area.
>
> Our current figures are|
>
> As you can see, we are well within the projections we outlined to you when you helped us obtain short-term financing. If you have any questions regarding this information, please feel free to call me. Thank you again for all your assistance.

Now move to the REPORT1 window and select the figures, as in Figure 4-4. Use the Copy command to copy these to the Clipboard, switch to the SAMPLE1 window, and use the Paste command to copy the text from the Clipboard after the new text, as in Figure 4-5.

When using two windows to copy or move information, some people prefer to leave the windows at full size (as shown in the preceding example)

*Figure 4-4.*　　*Figures selected*

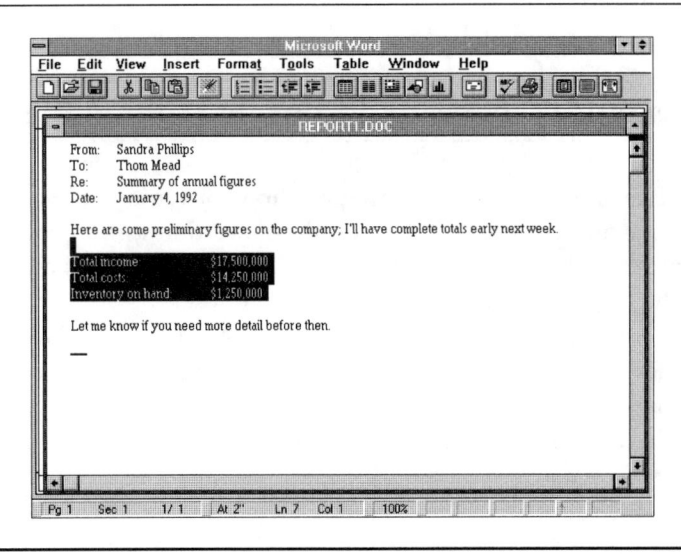

*Figure 4-5.*     *Figures pasted into SAMPLE1*

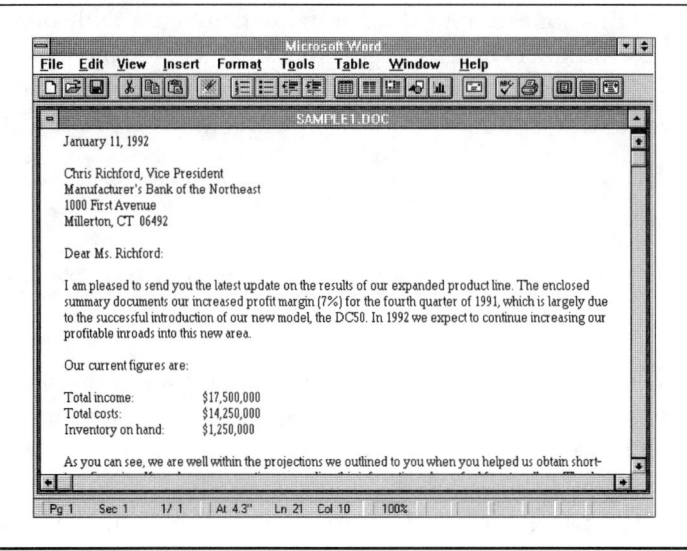

while others prefer to make the windows half size so they can see both windows. As you use Word, experiment with both options.

## Lesson 17: Moving and Copying Without the Clipboard

The previous lessons showed you how convenient it is to use the Clipboard to move and copy text. However, there are times when you want to move or copy text without using the Clipboard. For example, you may have something on the Clipboard that you do not want to lose.

To move text without using the Clipboard, you use Word's new *drag-and-drop* feature. This allows you to select text and drag it to a new location without cutting and pasting.

To move text with drag-and-drop:

1. Select the text.

**Chapter 4:** *Moving and Copying Text* 55

2. Point in the selected text and hold down the mouse button. The pointer changes shape to include a gray box at the bottom of the arrow:

3. While still holding down the mouse button, drag to the position where you want the text to move. Notice there is now a dotted insertion point that moves with the pointer.

4. When you release the mouse button, the text moves to the new location.

For example, assume you want to move the second sentence of the last paragraph of the letter to the end of that paragraph. First, select the sentence, including the space in front of it:

> As you can see, we are well within the projections we outlined to you when you helped us obtain short-term financing. If you have any questions regarding this information, please feel free to call me. Thank you again for all your assistance.

Now click the selected sentence so that the drag-and-drop pointer appears:

> As you can see, we are well within the projections we outlined to you when you helped us obtain short-term financing. If you have any questions regarding this information, please feel free to call me. Thank you again for all your assistance.

Drag the insertion point to just after the period in the third sentence:

> As you can see, we are well within the projections we outlined to you when you helped us obtain short-term financing. If you have any questions regarding this information, please feel free to call me. Thank you again for all your assistance.

Release the mouse button, and the sentence moves:

> As you can see, we are well within the projections we outlined to you when you helped us obtain short-term financing. If you have any questions regarding this information, please feel free to call me. Thank you again for all your assistance. **If you have any questions regarding this information, please feel free to call me.**

If you do not like this feature, you can turn it off by using the General options in the Options command from the Tools menu.

If you are using the keyboard, there is a feature similar to drag-and-drop that is not as direct. After selecting the text to move, press (F2). Word prompts "Move to where?" at the bottom of the window. Use the arrow keys to move the dotted insertion point to the desired location and press (ENTER).

## Review

Open the MAGAZINE and SAMPLE1 files at the same time. Copy the second sentence of the SAMPLE1 file (which starts "The enclosed...") to the beginning of the second paragraph in the MAGAZINE file.

# 5

# Searching and Replacing

As you have seen, you can easily move a selection around the screen and change the selection. If you know where you want to go—for example, about 20 lines down or to the end of the file—you can scroll through your text quickly. However, you often want to go to a specific word or phrase in a long document. Instead of searching visually for the phrase, you can move to its exact position with the Find command. The Find command searches for the word or phrase you specify.

Searching with the Find command has many uses other than simply moving to a certain word or phrase. For instance, you can find the first occurrence of a particular word by moving to the beginning of a document and then searching for the word. You can review your text to see whether you defined new terms when they first appeared. Since you can also search for groups of words, you can easily check for phrases that you may have overused.

Replacing text with the Replace command is not as common as searching for text, but it is still a very valuable feature. For example, you can use the Replace command to look for each occurrence of an overused phrase and replace it with another phrase on a case-by-case basis. You can also use Replace to quickly change every occurrence of something, such as a changed or misspelled name.

## Lesson 18: Searching for Text

The Find command quickly moves to the next instance of a word or phrase and selects it. The movement is always relative to your current position in a file; for example, if the insertion point is in the middle of a file and you search for the word "invoice", Word finds the next occurrence of "invoice" that appears in the text. If it does not find the word when it reaches the end of the file, it asks you if you want to search from the beginning. Choose Yes, and it does.

Move to the beginning of the SAMPLE1 file and give the Find command from the Edit menu. Word brings up the Find dialog box:

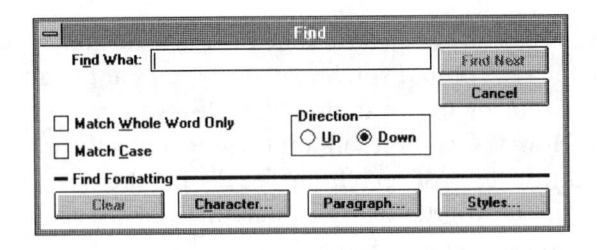

The blinking insertion point in the Find What box indicates that you should fill in the word or phrase you want to search for.

Type **please** and select the Find Next button (or press (ENTER)). You can enter up to 255 characters in this field. The first instance of the word "please" in the letter, which in this case is in the word "pleased", becomes selected, as shown in Figure 5-1.

If you want to search for the same word or phrase again, you do not need to retype it; the dialog box stays open. Simply select the Find Next button or press (ENTER), and Word searches again. Note the heavier outline around the Find Next button. This outline indicates that the button will be activated when you press (ENTER). When you are finished searching, select the Cancel button. If you close the Find dialog box and want to repeat the search, press (SHIFT)-(F4) to repeat the Find command.

**Chapter 5:** *Searching and Replacing*

The other options for the Find command are as follows:

- Choosing Match Whole Word Only indicates that you want Word to restrict your search to whole words and ignore words in which your selection is merely a part. If you choose this option, and the text you are searching for is "the", for example, Word does not stop if it finds "they". If you don't check the box, Word stops, even if the text you are searching for is part of another word, as in Figure 5-1.

- For Match Case, you must decide if Word should pay attention to whether the letters in the text are upper- or lowercase. If you do not choose this option, Word ignores case, meaning that Word does not differentiate between upper- and lowercase letters as it searches the text. Checking this box makes the search more restrictive: the text must be an exact match of the word or phrase you are searching for, including capital letters. Thus, if you check the box to match the case

*Figure 5-1.*   *"Please" selected*

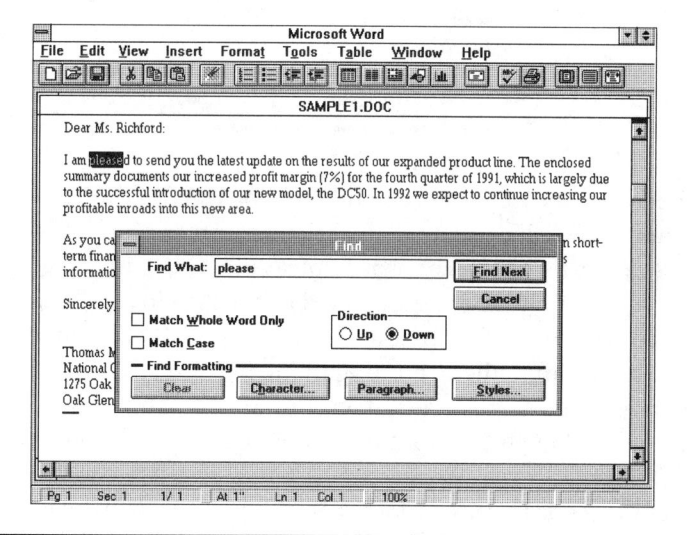

and you are searching for "the", Word does not stop when it finds "The".
- So far, you have used the Find command only to search forward in your document. The Direction options let you choose among Down (that is, forward) and Up (backward).

You can also search for specific text formatting, such as letters in italics. These options, in the Find Formatting area at the bottom of the dialog box, are covered in Chapter 9.

Word remembers the text in the Find What choice and the setting for each of the choices whenever you use the Find command. For example, if you change the setting of the case choice to check for case, that setting is still selected the next time you give the Find command.

To see how to use the choices, move the insertion point to the beginning of the first full paragraph of the SAMPLE1 file and give the Find command. Type **As** (with a capital "A") and check the Match Case option:

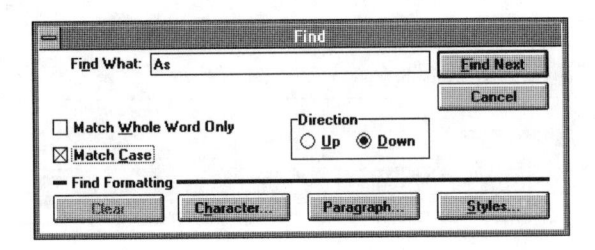

When you execute the command, the word "As" at the beginning of the second paragraph is selected; if you had not chosen to search for the matching case, the lowercase "as" in the word "pleased" in the first paragraph would have been found first. Select the Cancel button to close the dialog box.

To see the effect of the Match Whole Word Only option, move the insertion point to the beginning of the file and give the Find command again. Change Find What to **as**, check the Match Whole Word Only option, and choose the Match Case option to deselect it. Now, even though the search is not restricted to an uppercase "A", it is restricted to "as" only when it is a separate word. Thus, Word skips over the "as" in "Northeast" (and in "pleased", "increased", and "increasing"), going directly to the "As" in the second paragraph.

The text you search for can have as many as 255 characters. (You cannot see this much in the Find dialog box, but you can scroll left and right by selecting at the left and right ends of the text entry box.) If Word finds the text, the entire word or phrase is selected. If the text does not appear in the file, Word displays an alert box with "The search text is not found" and does not move the selection or insertion point. If you began the search at any location other than the beginning of the file, Word stops at the end and prompts "Continue search from beginning of document?" Select the No button to stop the search. You can also cancel a search by pressing (ESC).

## Lesson 19: Replacing Text

It is useful to be able to replace every instance of a particular word or phrase in a document with some other word or phrase. For example, you may want to change "pleased" to "happy" throughout a letter, or you may need to change many, but not all, instances of a person's name to another name. You may also want to replace a wordy or misused phrase with a more concise one throughout a document.

When you give the Replace command from the Edit menu, you automatically change all instances of one word or phrase to another. You can also have Word show you each instance of the phrase you want to change so you can choose whether or not to change it based on its context. You can undo changes with the Undo command.

The choices in the Replace dialog box are similar to those of the Find command. For example, go back to the top of the file, give the Replace command, and enter **pleased** for Find What and **happy** for Replace With, as shown in Figure 5-2. Note that the Replace command started with the Find What text from the previous Find command.

The dialog box has buttons labeled Find Next, Replace, Replace All, and Cancel. If you select the Replace All button, Word simply replaces each occurrence of the specified word or phrase throughout your document without asking for confirmation. If you select the Find Next button, Word stops at the first word to be replaced. Selecting the Replace button indicates that you want to make the replacement for the current selection, while selecting

***Figure 5-2.*** *Replace dialog box*

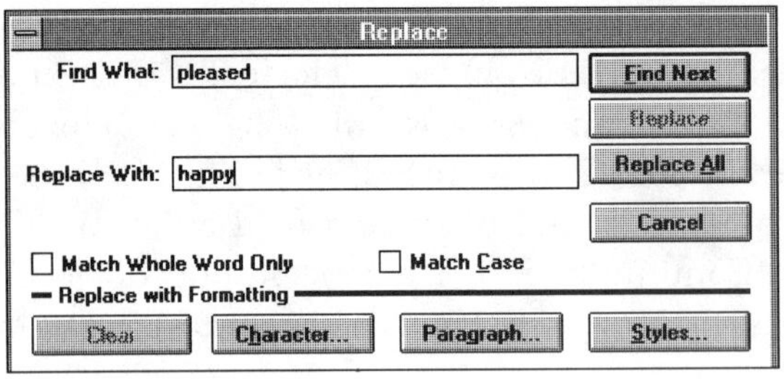

the Find Next button indicates that you do not. If you are finished replacing words, close the window or select Cancel.

As you might guess, the Replace command can ease the job of changing many items in a long file. For example, if one person is mentioned repeatedly throughout a long memo, and that person changes jobs within the company, you may have to change many instances of the person's name and title. The Replace command allows you to do this with just one command. If the person's name needs to be changed in many, but not all, instances, choosing to confirm each replacement lets you look through the file easily.

If you do not choose to match the case when replacing text, Word intelligently chooses how to replace the letters. For instance, if you choose to change "airplane" to "boat" with no case requirement and Word finds "Airplane", it replaces it with "Boat", because this is most likely what you would want. The rule is that words with initial- or all-capital letters ("Airplane" or "AIRPLANE") are replaced with corresponding capital letters ("Boat" or "BOAT").

In the Replace command, the Match Whole Word Only option acts like it does in the Find command. When Word searches for the text in the Find What field, it stops only when it finds that text as whole words.

## Lesson 20: Using Special Characters in Find and Replace

Word searches for the exact text you specify in the Find and Replace commands. However, there are times when you want Word to search for less specifically defined words. The Find and Replace commands allow you to include a question mark wildcard in order to broaden your search.

If Word sees a question mark in the text you tell it to search for, it assumes that any character can match it. (If you are familiar with "wildcard" characters in filenames on other computers, this is identical to the question mark used there; however, Word doesn't use the * wildcard.) For example, if you search for "f?r", Word stops when it finds "far", "for", "fur", and so on. The question mark indicates that any character at all (even numbers and punctuation marks) can be in the position you indicate.

Move to the beginning of the first paragraph and give the Find command. Enter **e?s** for the Find What text, and then press the (ENTER) key. Word selects the "eas" in "pleased":

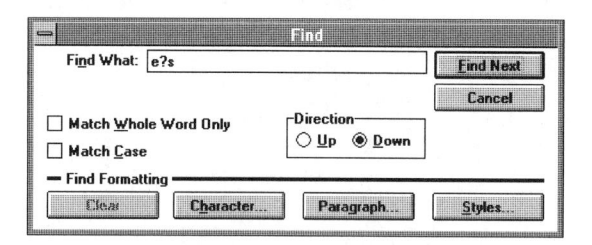

Now select the Find Next button, and Word selects the "eas" in "increased". Selecting the Find Next button again selects "ess" in "successful", and so on.

You may also want to search for characters that are special to Word but that you cannot normally enter in the Find or Replace command. For instance, you may want to find the word "The" preceded by a (TAB) character. Since you can't normally enter a (TAB) character as text to search for (Word moves to the next choice for the Find command), you need a way to indicate that you want to search for the (TAB) character. You represent many codes with caret characters.

*Caret characters* are special characters that you precede with a caret mark (^). The caret characters are shown in Table 5-1. Note that you use two characters, the caret and the character indicated. A caret character is not a control character.

*Table 5-1.*     *Caret Characters*

| Character | Meaning |
| --- | --- |
| ^t | (TAB) character |
| ^p | Paragraph marker |
| ^n | Newline character |
| ^d | Section marker or required page break (described in Chapter 12) |
| ^w | White space (this is any number of spaces, tabs, paragraph marks, newline characters, division markers, and page-break characters) |
| ^# | Any digit |
| ^* | Any letter |
| ^- | Optional hyphen |
| ^~ | Nonbreaking hyphen |
| ^s | Nonbreaking space |
| ^1 | Picture |
| ^2 | Footnote mark |
| ^5 | Annotation mark |
| ^14 | Column break |
| ^m | Contents of the Find What field (used in Replace only) |
| ^c | Contents of the Clipboard |
| ^^ | Caret character (^) |
| ^? | Question mark character (?) |
| ^*number* | Any character, where *number* is its ASCII value |

**Chapter 5:**  *Searching and Replacing*  65

For example, the dialog box to search for "me." followed by a paragraph marker and the word "Now" looks like this:

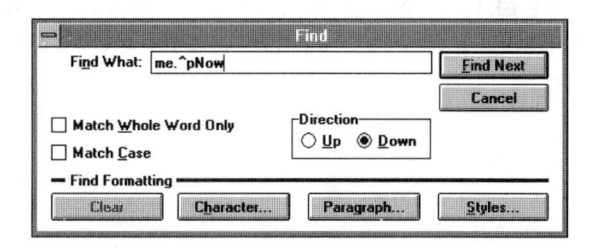

[Find dialog box: Find What: me.^pNow; Match Whole Word Only; Match Case; Direction: Up/Down; Find Formatting: Clear, Character, Paragraph, Styles; Find Next, Cancel]

In the Replace command, you can enter any of the special characters from the table for the Find What option. In addition, you can also use the same characters in the Replace With field, except the question mark, ^?, and ^w caret characters.

You can also indicate that you want the contents of the Clipboard inserted in place of the text found. To do this, use ^c in the Replace With field. For example, assume that you have copied the name of your company with formatting to the Clipboard. Figure 5-3 shows how you would replace the words "our company" with the contents of the Clipboard by using the Replace command.

***Figure 5-3.***   *Replacing with the contents of the Clipboard*

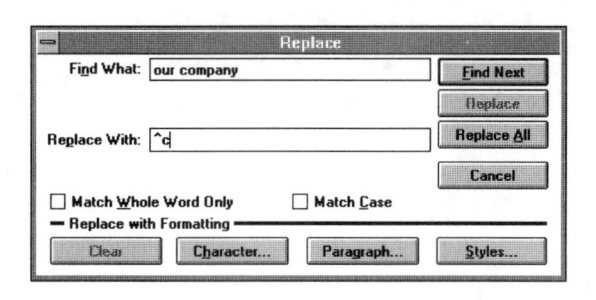

[Replace dialog box: Find What: our company; Replace With: ^c; Match Whole Word Only; Match Case; Replace with Formatting: Clear, Character, Paragraph, Styles; Find Next, Replace, Replace All, Cancel]

# Review

Use the MAGAZINE file to experiment with the Find and Replace commands and their options. Search for the paragraph markers by using a caret character.

# 6

# Using Glossaries

## Lesson 21: Introduction to Glossaries

As you work more with a word processor, you will probably find that particular phrases or blocks of text are used over and over, such as the name of a company or a long product name. Typing this text many times in a report or memo is tedious, and copying it from another file each time can take almost as long as typing it.

Word eliminates this problem by using glossaries. A *glossary* is a set of names that correspond to longer phrases. Instead of repeatedly typing the longer phrase in the text, you simply type the name followed by (F3). Any phrase or block of text can be abbreviated. The abbreviation can consist of as many as 31 letters or numbers, if necessary, but keeping the names short makes this feature more useful. The "global" glossary is automatically available when you run Word.

For example, in the SAMPLE1 file, Thomas Mead's name and address could be used as a name in the glossary for those occasions when he types his address at the bottom of a letter. Chris Richford's name and address and the name "National Generators" could also be used. Table 6-1 shows the suggested entries for this glossary.

Glossaries can be great time savers since they eliminate the necessity of having to type sections of text that you use often. They also prevent typing mistakes in commonly used terms and names. (It could be very embarrassing to misspell a client's company name in a letter.) You can also store graphics in the glossary by using the same methods you use to store text.

The rest of this chapter explains how to set up glossaries and how to use the entries in them. As you read the lessons, remember that glossaries are kept separate from documents, so the glossary entries you make as you create one document can be used elsewhere in your work.

## Lesson 22: Creating a Glossary

You can create a *glossary entry*—a name and its associated text—by giving the Glossary command from the Edit menu. While editing a file, select the phrase or block of text for which you want to use a name. Then give the Glossary command, enter the name, and select the Define button. This creates the entry.

*Table 6-1.*   *Glossary Entries for the SAMPLE1 File*

| Name | Expanded Text |
| --- | --- |
| ng | National Generators |
| thomaddr | Thomas Mead, Controller<br>National Generators<br>1275 Oak Glen Industrial Park<br>Oak Glen, CT 06401 |
| richford | Chris Richford, Vice President<br>Manufacturer's Bank of the Northeast<br>1000 First Avenue<br>Millerton, CT 06492 |

**Chapter 6:** *Using Glossaries*

Now use the SAMPLE1 letter to see how to create entries. To store Chris Richford's name and address under the name "richford", select the text in the letter and give the Glossary command from the Edit menu. The Glossary dialog box appears, as shown in Figure 6-1. In the Glossary Name box, type **richford**. The first few words of the text you selected appear at the bottom of the dialog box. Select the Define button to define the entry and close the dialog box.

Also notice that the name is now in the list of names that appears under the Glossary Name box. To see what a name stands for, select it from the list. Select the Cancel button to close the dialog box.

When you want to expand a name, set the insertion point at the place where you want the text. You then have two choices:

- Type the name of the entry and press F3.
- Give the Glossary command, select the desired name from the list, and select Insert or Insert as Plain Text. Use Insert if you want to keep any character formatting you applied to the text of the entry, and use Insert as Plain Text if you want the text to be entered in the current formatting.

To practice expanding names, enter the three entries in Table 6-1 in the glossary. (You have already created "richford".) Close the Glossary dialog box and the SAMPLE1 window, and give the New command from the File menu to start a new letter. Your finished text will look like the text in Figure 6-2, but you will use the names in the glossary instead of typing the names and addresses or the company name in the body of the text.

*Figure 6-1.*    *Glossary dialog box*

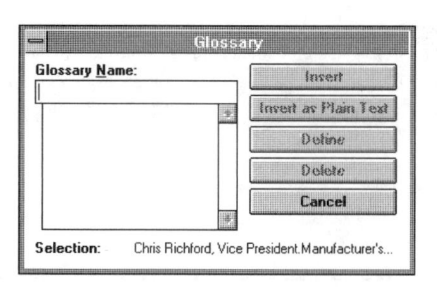

***Figure 6-2.*** *SAMPLE2 text*

```
January 22, 1992

Chris Richford, Vice President
Manufacturer's Bank of the Northeast
1000 First Avenue
Millerton, CT 06492

Dear Ms. Richford:

This is to confirm our conversation earlier today that National Generators will install a new payroll
program at the end of this month, and that all of National Generators' payroll checks will be drawn on the
new account we set up.

Sincerely,


Thomas Mead, Controller
National Generators
1275 Oak Glen Industrial Park
Oak Glen, CT 06410
```

Type **richford** and press (F3). As Figure 6-3 illustrates, the glossary name is expanded into the complete name and address. Continue the letter, using the glossary names when you can. Save this letter as SAMPLE2.

If you want to remove some of the entries in the glossary, give the Glossary command, select the entries, and select the Delete button. To replace the text of a glossary entry, type the new text that you want for the name in the document and select it. Give the Glossary command, select the name from the list, and select Define, then choose the Yes button to redefine the glossary entry.

***Figure 6-3.*** *Name expanded*

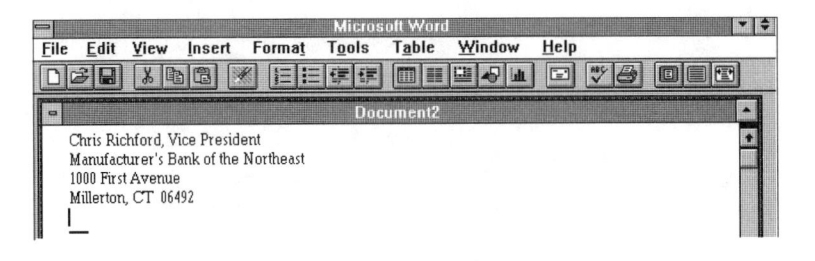

## Lesson 23: Storing, Opening, and Printing Glossaries

To save the new glossary entries on disk, give the Template command from the File menu. Use one of the three choices under Store New Macros And Glossaries As:

- Global makes the entries available to any document.
- With Document Template makes the entries available only to documents based on the same template as you are using. (Templates are described in Chapter 13.)
- Prompt For Each New specifies that Word prompt you each time you create a new glossary entry, unless you are using the NORMAL.DOT template. NORMAL.DOT is described in Chapter 13.

You will rarely want to keep glossaries other than the global one. The only reason you would want template-specific glossaries is if you work in a company and want to use a specialized glossary that someone else created.

As the glossary gets larger, you may forget what is in it. To print out the glossary to have it as a reference, give the Print command from the File menu, and select Glossary from the Print drop-down list.

## Lesson 24: Finding Other Uses for Glossaries

Glossaries can reduce typing and increase accuracy in many different applications. The following list should give you some ideas for using glossaries in your daily word processing.

- Complex scientific phrases, such as the names of chemicals, long theory names, process names, and the names of reactions
- Standard legal citations, case names, and legal jargon
- Long, nearly identical names, such as model numbers
- Phrases that are heavily used in a document

Table 6-2 shows examples of some of these uses.

*Table 6-2.*  *Suggested Glossary Entries for Various Uses*

| Name | Contents |
|---|---|
| 13cb | anhydrous 1,3-dichlorobenzene, U.S.P. |
| rsae | Rivest-Shamir-Abel encryption |
| mcatcom | methyl-selenium catalytic combustion |
| yrox | Youngblood-Roberts oxidation |
| fiduc | 34 N.E. 2d 68, 70 |
| rw | Roe v. Wade |
| eqpro | equal protection of the laws |
| cl12 | Colonial 12-422 Model S |

# Review

Look at some of the writing you are doing (or want to be doing) with Word. Determine which words and phrases would be good candidates for glossary entries. Add a few of them to the glossary. Start a new document and use these entries as you type some sample text.

# 7

# Pictures in Your Documents

There might be times when you want to include art and graphics in your text. Word allows you to use drawings from graphics programs such as CorelDraw in your text by pasting them from the Clipboard with the Paste command. You can also create graphics from within Word or open graphics files that you have stored on disk.

Word includes two advanced tools, Graph and Equation Editor, that also create pictures. These are beyond the scope of this book, but are described in additional manuals that come with Word.

## Lesson 25: Using Art in Your Text

There are two main purposes for including art in your text: to illustrate something that is being written about and to provide decoration. Informational images are useful if you are talking about a product, process, or a location where there are some salient features best described with a picture. Decorative art often makes an otherwise boring report more interesting to read.

The most common method for including art in your text is to create the art in another program, copy it to the Clipboard in that program, switch to

Word, and paste the image into your document by using the Paste command. As you will see in the next lesson, you can also create images directly in Word and use them in a similar fashion.

For example, suppose you want to include a product illustration in the SAMPLE1 file from a Windows drawing program you already use. First draw the product illustration in that program and copy it to the Clipboard with the program's Copy command. Switch from the graphics program to Word.

Open the SAMPLE1 file, put the insertion point at the end of the first paragraph, and add a new sentence, **Here is a picture of the DC50.** Now press (ENTER) twice and give the Paste command. Word puts the picture in the letter, as shown in Figure 7-1.

You can use Word to create simple graphics for your documents. If the graphic you want is a numerical chart (such as a bar chart or line chart) or an equation, you can use Word's Graph and Equation Editor programs for creating those.

*Figure 7-1.*   Picture inserted in document

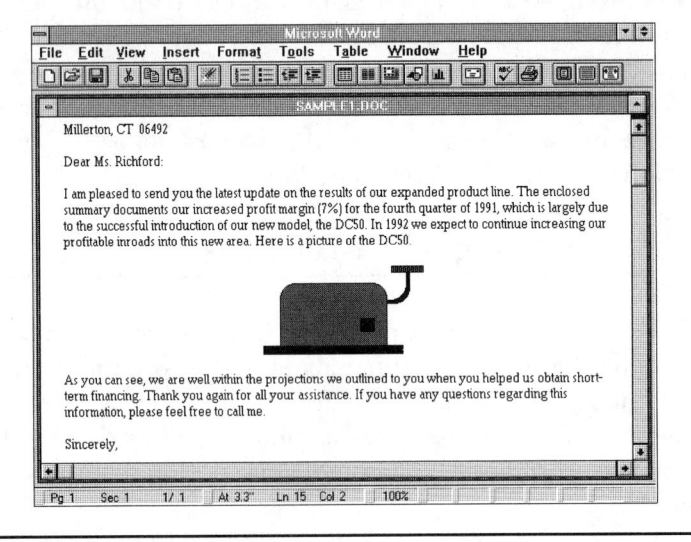

**Chapter 7:** *Pictures in Your Documents* 75

## Lesson 26: Creating Graphics in Word

Word comes with a simple drawing program so you can design graphics for use in Word without using another program. The drawing program, called Microsoft Draw, can create simple drawings but is not a substitute for a real drawing program if you need more advanced pictures.

To create your own graphic in Word, select the Insert Picture button on the toolbar:

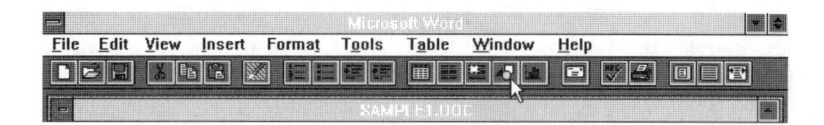

This opens the Microsoft Draw window, shown in Figure 7-2. The area on the left of the window holds the *drawing tools,* and the major portion in the middle of the window is the *drawing area.* There are also commands in menus.

*Figure 7-2.*   Microsoft Draw window

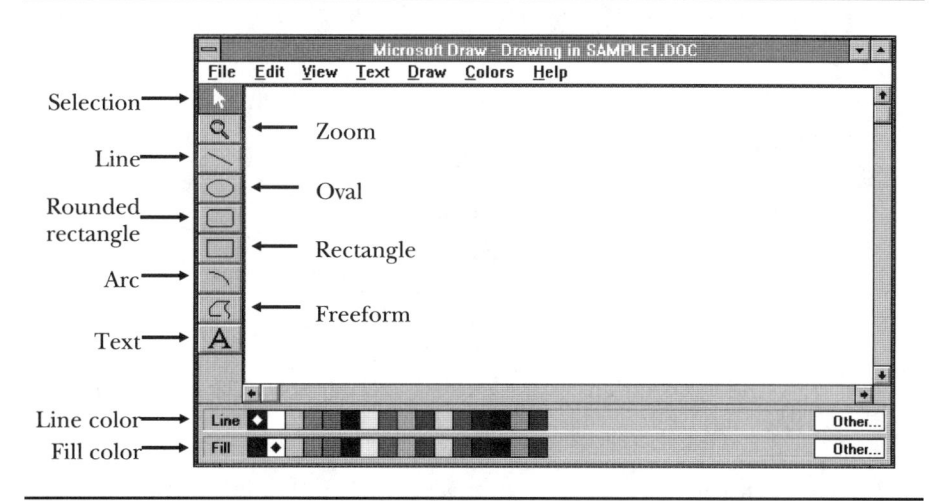

If you are familiar with other painting or drawing programs, you will probably be able to create pictures immediately. If not, you may need a bit of practice in order to get good graphics from the Microsoft Draw window.

Every picture drawn with the Microsoft Draw window consists of *elements* that make up the entire picture. For example, you might draw a square and put some text in it for a logo. The square is one element, and the text is another. You draw and edit elements by selecting drawing tools and using them in the drawing area. You can also Undo your last action.

Some of the tools and commands are for drawing, others are for editing, and others are for specifying parameters for elements. For example, Microsoft Draw has the Windows standard Cut, Copy, and Paste commands from the Edit menu. The tools are summarized in Table 7-1.

You use the line, freeform, rectangle, rounded rectangle, oval, and arc tools to draw elements. With these tools, you click in one corner of the desired element and drag to the diagonally opposite corner. For example, to draw an oval, click the oval tool, click in the drawing area at the upper-left corner of the desired oval, drag to the opposite corner, and release the mouse button. The element is automatically selected. Figure 7-3 shows the result.

With the drawing tools, holding down the (SHIFT) key while you drag restricts the motion of the tool. Restricting the oval tool causes you to draw perfect circles, restricting the rectangle tool causes you to draw perfect squares, and so on. Experiment with the drawing tools, with and without the (SHIFT) key.

*Table 7-1.*   *Tools in the Microsoft Draw Window*

| Tool | Action |
| --- | --- |
| Selection | Selects elements |
| Zoom | Magnifies the view |
| Line | Draws lines |
| Oval | Draws ovals |
| Rounded rectangle | Draws rectangles with rounded corners |
| Rectangle | Draws rectangles |
| Arc | Draws arcs |
| Freeform | Draws curves and polygons |
| Text | Inserts text |

**Chapter 7:** *Pictures in Your Documents* 77

The text tool allows you to type text into your drawing. Click the text tool, and then click in the drawing window where you want the text to go. Note that the commands from the Text menu change the text element, such as the alignment and character formatting.

Once you have drawn one or more elements in a drawing, you may want to modify them. To modify an element, it must be selected. If it is not already selected, you can select it with the selection tool. Click the selection tool, and then click the element you want to select. You must click directly on a line in the element to select it.

When you select with the selection tool, four boxes called *handles* appear, one at each corner. For example, here is an oval selected:

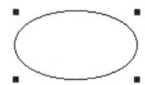

It is easy to move and resize an element in the Microsoft Draw window. To move an element, select it and drag its outline to another position. To resize an element, select it and drag any of the handles. Drag a corner handle of an element to change its width and height.

*Figure 7-3.*   Oval drawn

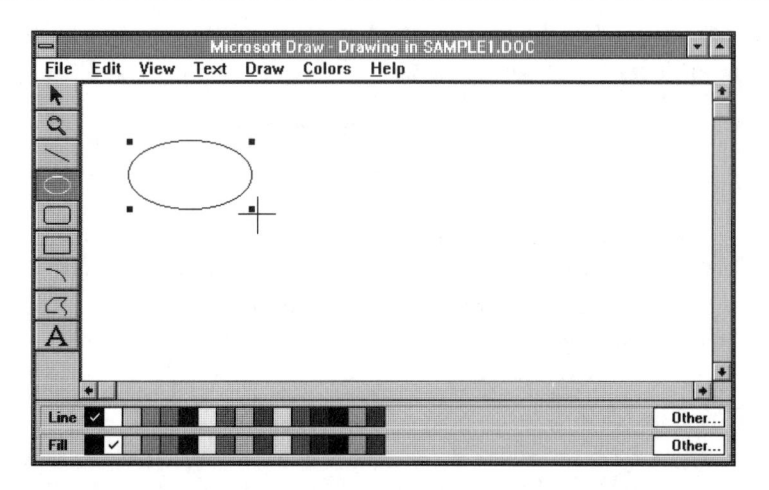

If you want to rotate or flip an element vertically or horizontally, select the element and choose one of the commands that appear when you click the Rotate/Flip command from the Draw menu. You can combine this with the result of the duplication tool to make interesting mirror images.

The Send to Back and Bring to Front commands from the Edit menu let you control how elements appear above and below each other. This lets you layer your elements so they appear in the proper order even if you move them.

You can change the magnification of the picture with the zoom tool or with the choices from the View menu. In that menu, Full Size is the normal magnification, and the other commands reduce or enlarge the drawing.

All elements consist of lines, fills, patterns, and styles. The *line* is the border of an element, and the *fill* is the interior. You can specify the color of the line and fill of an element with the lists at the bottom of the window. If you want no line around the element, give the Unframed command from the Draw menu.

You can specify that a *pattern* of lines be put over the fill, as shown in the Pattern command in the Draw menu. You can also specify that a *style* of line be used for the line, such as a broad line or dotted line. These are chosen from the Line Style command in the Draw menu.

For example, create a small rectangle:

Now give the Line Style command and select a 4-point border from the menu that appears.

You can also specify the color of the line.

The fill describes how the interior of the element looks. You can choose a color and pattern for the fill. For example, give the same rectangle a fancy fill with the Patterns command:

**Chapter 7:** *Pictures in Your Documents* 79

Once you have drawn your picture, give the Exit and Return command from the File menu. Word inserts the picture at the insertion point in your document.

Note that you can modify your picture (or any picture that you have included in your document) by double-clicking it. This opens the Microsoft Draw window with the picture in the drawing area. You can use this method to bring in art from other programs and modify them in Word.

## Lesson 27: Resizing and Cropping Graphics

Word treats a picture as if it were a character. When you select a picture, Word surrounds it in a border with eight boxes (called *handles*) on the corners and edges of the border, as in Figure 7-4. This border does not appear in the printout and disappears when you select any other text.

*Figure 7-4.*    Picture selected

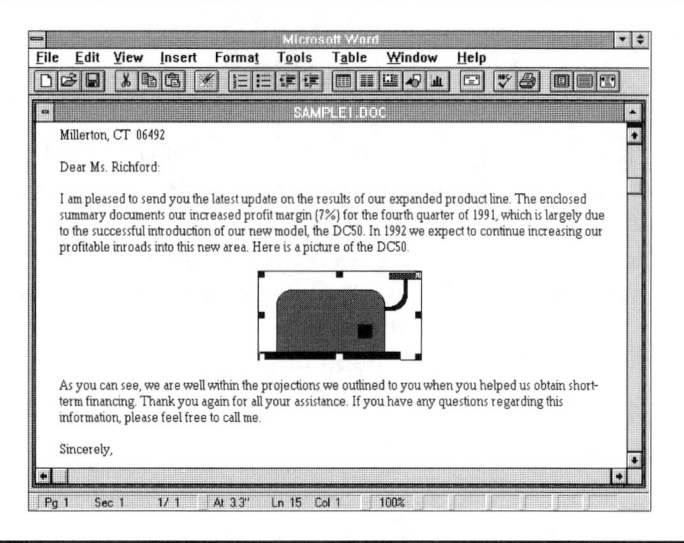

You can resize a picture in the main window by dragging on one of the handles. Dragging the handle on the bottom edge allows you to stretch or shrink the picture vertically:

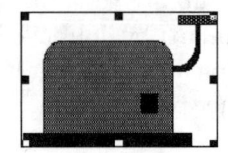

Dragging the handle on the right edge allows you to stretch or shrink the picture horizontally:

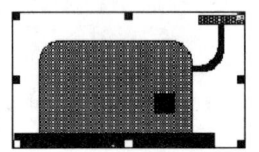

You can resize in both directions, keeping the picture proportionally sized, by dragging the handle in the lower-right corner. This is a good way to keep the vertical and horizontal dimensions the same.

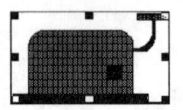

As you resize a picture, the bottom line of the Word window shows the percent of change if you drag the corner. This is useful if you want to resize by a specific amount, such as 50 percent.

If you hold down the (SHIFT) key while in the main window, Word *crops* the picture instead of resizing it. Cropping cuts the right side or bottom off the picture if you move the handles inward. If you move the handles outward, Word puts a blank border around the graphic. It is unlikely that you will use Word to crop pictures; resizing them is much more common.

## Lesson 28: Opening Graphics Files

Although transferring pictures through the Clipboard from a graphics program is easy, it is not always convenient. For example, if you want to transfer ten pictures into a particular document, you have to switch back and forth between the graphics program and Word. You may find it faster to open that program's graphics files directly in Word. You can also use this method if someone else has created the graphics files for you and you do not have the graphics program on your PC.

To open a picture document, give the Picture command from the Insert menu. In the List Files of Type drop-down list, select the type of file you want to import. This causes Word to list only those graphics files that match the type you indicate.

Word can open many types of Windows and MS-DOS graphics files, but not all. The types of files it can open are covered in depth in Chapter 24.

## Review

Open the MAGAZINE file and choose a spot to insert a graphic. Create that graphic by using Word's graphics capabilities. (Remember, this does not need to be a work of art.) Insert the graphic into the text. Select the graphic and make it twice as large.

# 8

# Printing Your Documents

Word and Microsoft Windows have many advanced features that make printing easy. When you edit and format text, for example, you do not need to know what type of printer your text will be printed on. Instead, when you are ready to print, you just give the Print command from the File menu, and it determines what it needs to do in order to use as many of the formats you specify as it can.

This is important because there is no standard method for instructing different printers how to perform certain tasks, such as printing superscripts. Most of the instructions are complex and involve strange character codes. Word does not require you to remember these codes. Instead, it stores the text formatting with your file, and when you print, it interacts with a special Windows file called a *printer driver* to determine how to use your printer's special features so they correspond to the format.

Different printers, of course, produce output of different quality. They also print at different speeds, have different special features, and range in cost from around $250 to over $10,000.

Although you learned a bit about printing in Chapter 2, this chapter gives you the rest of the information on how to tell Word what type of printer you have and how to use the options of the Print command.

## Lesson 29: Using the Print Setup Command

Before you give the Print command, you should tell Word about your printer with the Print Setup command from the File menu. This lets you set up your printer in the same way that you can from the Control Panel in Windows. The Print Setup dialog box is shown in Figure 8-1. See your Windows manual for more detailed information on choosing and setting up your printer.

Select the printer you want to set up and select the Setup button. The next dialog box you see depends on the type of printer you have. For example, Figure 8-2 shows the setup dialog box for the Apple LaserWriter II NT.

*Figure 8-1.*   *Print Setup dialog box*

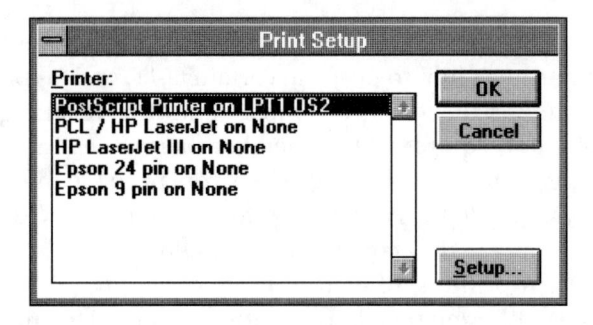

**Chapter 8:**  *Printing Your Documents*  85

*Figure 8-2.*     *Setup dialog box for Apple LaserWriter II NT*

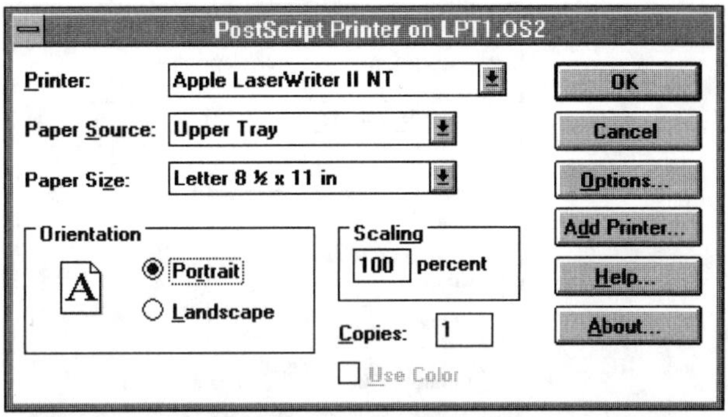

## Lesson 30: Giving the Print Command

The last set of print options that Word offers is in the Print command from the File menu. You use the Print command when you are ready to print your document. Figure 8-3 shows a typical Print dialog box.

You can choose to print only certain pages from your document by using the Range options. You can instruct Word to print

- The entire document (All is the default choice.)
- Just the selection or the current page (If there is a selection, the choice is Selection; otherwise it is Current Page.)
- Particular pages you specify in the From and To choices.

If you want to print more than one copy of a file, use the Copies option. This is a convenient way to print many copies of a letter or memo without having to give the Print command over and over.

***Figure 8-3.*** *Print dialog box*

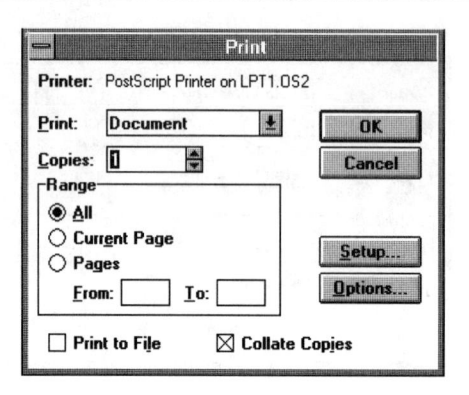

[Print dialog box showing: Printer: PostScript Printer on LPT1.OS2; Print: Document; Copies: 1; Range: All, Current Page, Pages, From/To; Print to File; Collate Copies; OK, Cancel, Setup..., Options... buttons]

You can specify what to print in the Print drop-down list. The choices are shown here:

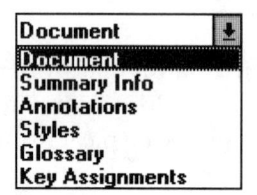

[Drop-down list showing: Document, Document, Summary Info, Annotations, Styles, Glossary, Key Assignments]

Document, the choice you will use most often, causes Word to print the document. The other choices are discussed in chapters that cover the related topic: Summary Info is described in Chapter 21, Annotations in Chapter 22, Styles in Chapter 13, Glossary in Chapter 6, and Key Assignments in Chapter 16.

The Options button in the Print dialog box brings up the Options dialog box for printers, as shown in Figure 8-4. The options allow you to change the way that Word prints your document. The choices are as follows:

| Option | Description |
| --- | --- |
| Draft Output | Uses the printer's draft mode, if it has one. This is usually faster but lower quality than normal printing. |
| Reverse Print Order | Prints the document in reverse order, last page first. |
| Update Fields | Updates all fields (an advanced feature) before starting to print. |
| Summary Info | Prints a separate page with the summary information (described in Chapter 21). |
| Field Codes | Prints the field codes in the text (described in Chapter 22). |
| Annotations | Prints the annotations (described in Chapter 22) at the end of the text on a separate page. |
| Hidden Text | Includes the hidden text in the printed output. |
| Envelope Options | Tells Word to use the printer's special envelope feeder for envelopes. |
| Widow/Orphan Control | Prevents widows and orphans, as described in the following text. |
| Use TrueType Fonts | Tells Word to use TrueType fonts as the defaults if you have TrueType print drivers installed in Windows. |

When you write memos and reports that are longer than one page, you may find that Word breaks the last paragraph on the page in an inappropriate place. Word automatically prevents *widows* (only the last line of a paragraph on the top of a page) and *orphans* (only the first line of a paragraph on the bottom of a page) by moving lines to or from a page as necessary. Word never leaves one line of a paragraph stranded on a page unless you deselect the Widow/Orphan Control option.

***Figure 8-4.***   *Options dialog box*

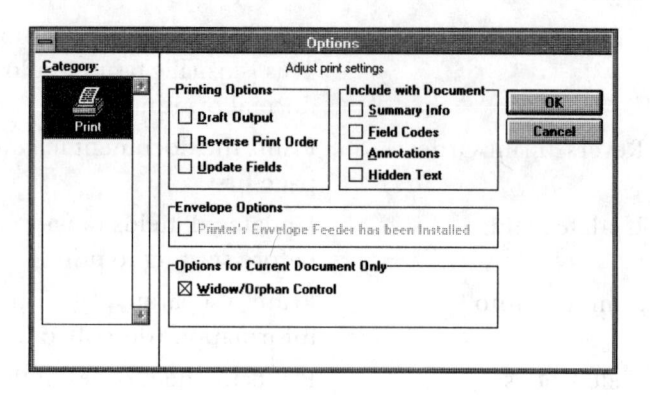

## Review

Experiment with the choices in the Print dialog box by selecting them and printing the MAGAZINE document. If you have more than one type of printer available, try different choices on each type of printer.

# II

## Using Word to Format

# 9

# Basic Formatting with Word

As part of the editing process, you will probably want to alter the way your text looks in order to present the information in an interesting form and to help your reader understand your meaning. Word's formatting capabilities let you choose exactly how your text looks when it is printed out.

Adding a formatting characteristic to text is called *direct formatting.* Direct formatting is actually what you normally do when typing or editing text. For example, when you make changes on a first draft, you might decide to underline a phrase or change the size of the text. In doing this, you are adding characteristics directly to text.

## Lesson 31: Introducing Formatting

The basic concept behind formatting with Word is that all text has certain characteristics associated with it. After you have specified the characteristics (such as underlining or indentation), Word automatically displays the text with those attributes. If you move the text to some other place in your document, the characteristics move with it.

You can enter an entire document without worrying about the formatting and then go back over it to add formatting, or if you wish, you can format text as you enter it. Each time you add a characteristic, you see it instantly on the screen. Both formatting methods work equally well. You can experiment with different formats, seeing which one best fits the meaning of the text.

Word gives you three units to apply formatting to: characters, paragraphs, and sections. At the level of the smallest unit (character), Word lets you change the format of each character or groups of letters (such as words or phrases). For example, you can underline, boldface, or italicize characters, as well as change type font and size, with different formatting commands. Character formatting is most often used to make certain words stand out in your text.

You have already learned to use the (ENTER) key to make paragraphs in Word. Paragraphs are the second formatting unit. The paragraph is important to Word because Word stores formatting information for each paragraph when you press (ENTER). In fact, all of the characteristics of a paragraph are stored in a bit of white space that is placed at the end of the paragraph. (This white space is actually a paragraph mark.)

For instance, many people like to indent the first line of every paragraph five spaces. Some word processing programs require you to press the (TAB) key at the beginning of each paragraph. Word, however, remembers this format once you have specified it, and inserts the spaces for you in succeeding paragraphs unless you tell it otherwise. Other paragraph formats you can specify include the indentation of the entire paragraph, line spacing, borders, and alignment with the margin.

You often may want to set different formatting characteristics for a particular paragraph. For example, when you include a long quotation in text, you usually indent the whole quotation a few spaces from the margin.

Since Word stores paragraph formatting characteristics in the paragraph mark, you can use the Copy and Paste commands to copy the formatting characteristics of one paragraph to another paragraph in a different location in your document. You do not need to do this as you type since Word uses the paragraph formatting of the previous paragraph when you start a new paragraph. Copy to the Clipboard the paragraph mark you want to transfer. Then select the paragraph mark you want to replace and give the Paste command. All of the formatting characteristics are then applied to the new paragraph.

Word lets you set up different characteristics for each *section*, which is the third formatting unit. These are characteristics such as page headings and margin size that do not change from paragraph to paragraph. You might have many sections in a document if you have many chapters or if you have many different page layouts within one document, such as in a brochure. You can see the section formatting by using different views of your Word document.

It is important to remember that each element of text, whether it is a character, a paragraph, or a section, has a set of formatting instructions attached to it. The end result is that formatting documents is easy with Word since you can copy the specifications from one formatting unit to another.

You may be wondering what all of these characteristics are. They are discussed in the next three chapters. For now, think of a direct formatting characteristic as a description of how the text looks or its position on the page.

## Lesson 32: Giving Formatting Commands

You can give formatting commands in Word in three ways:

- Give commands from the Format menu
- Press special key combinations
- Click icons in the ribbon and ruler

The formatting commands are much like the editing commands you have already learned. You apply formatting commands to selected text. If you give a formatting command when the insertion point is in a document (no text selected), the text you type at the insertion point has that formatting applied to it.

You do not need to use the menus to enter every formatting command. There are some character and paragraph formatting commands that can be entered by pressing the (CTRL) key and a letter, such as (CTRL)-(B) for boldface characters. These key sequences are described in the next two chapters.

If you have Word display the ribbon and the ruler, you can give character and paragraph formatting commands by clicking icons. These actions are described in the next two chapters.

Many of Word's dialog boxes for formatting include a sample that shows how the changes you are making will look. As you make settings in the dialog box, the Sample box changes so you can see the results before selecting OK. This helps you if you are not sure how some formatting will look.

The most common type of formatting you use is character formatting. For instance, book and magazine publishers commonly use italics for emphasis, foreign words, and book titles. They use underlining and boldface in different kinds of headings. Chapter 10 discusses character formatting, Chapter 11 discusses paragraph formatting, and Chapter 12 discusses section formatting.

## Lesson 33: Searching for and Replacing Formatting

In Chapter 5, you saw how the Find command looks for text. The Find command normally ignores formatting when looking for text. However, you can specify in the Find dialog box that the command look only for text that has particular formatting by using the buttons in the Find Formatting section at the bottom of the dialog box:

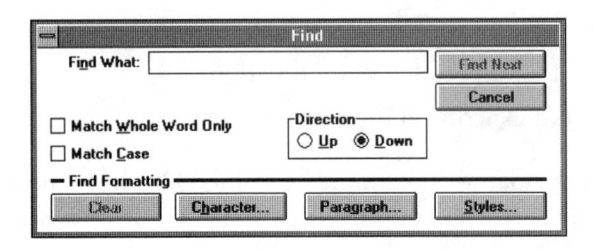

The Clear button clears any formatting specifications you may have already made. The Character, Paragraph, and Styles buttons bring up dialog boxes similar to those you will learn about in the next three chapters. In those dialog boxes, you choose the type of formatting you want to search for.

If you use the Format buttons, you can either search for all text with the specified formatting or only for specific text that has that formatting. To search for the next text that has particular formatting, leave the Find What choice blank, select the formatting choice button, and choose the desired format from the dialog box. You can choose many types of simultaneous formatting, such as bold and italic text.

**Chapter 9:** *Basic Formatting with Word* 95

When you select formatting from the dialog boxes, the choices are shown below the Find What box:

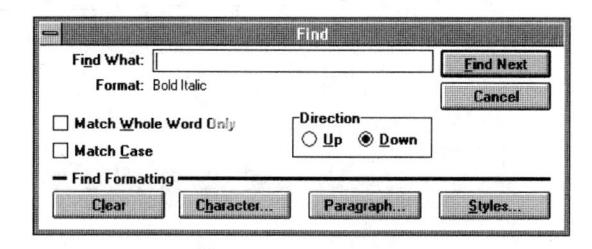

When you select the Find Next button after specifying the formatting, the next text that has that formatting is selected, regardless of the specific text.

To select specific text with specific formatting, enter that text in the Find What choice. Thus, to find the words "timely fashion" in italics, the dialog box would look like this:

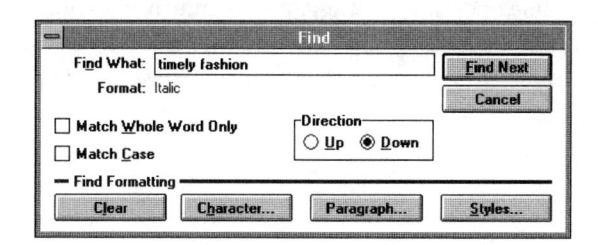

The Replace command works in a similar fashion to the Find command. In addition to finding text with particular formatting, you can also specify the formatting of the replaced text. Normally, Word replaces text with the same formatting as that on the first character that was found. With the Replace with Formatting buttons in the Replace command, you can specify the same text with different formatting without having to put the text in the Replace With choice. For example, the following illustrates how you can quickly replace all instances of "Annual Report" in italics with the same words in bold:

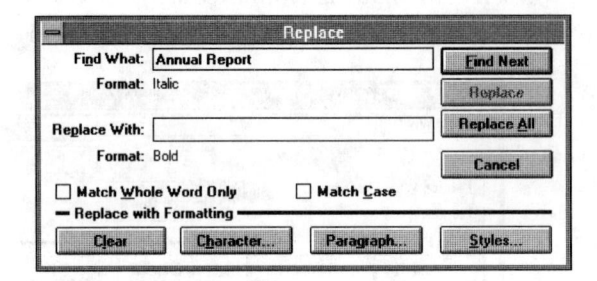

## Review

Look in books and magazines you normally read and pay attention to how they use character and paragraph formatting. Note how much formatting there is on title pages of books and in magazine articles. Think about how you would implement that type of formatting in your work.

# 10

# Formatting Characters

The purpose of character formatting is to make the reader notice a group of characters or words. This is often useful for emphasis, but common publishing practices also require it; for instance, book titles should generally be shown in italics. Examples of some character formats are shown here:

**bold characters**
underlined characters
*italicized characters*
**combinations**
characters with different fonts

## Lesson 34: Common Character Formatting

Type the text shown in Figure 10-1, which you will use to experiment with character formatting. Save this on disk with the name CHARACT. If you want to change the formatting of a group of characters, first select the group, and then give the Character command from the Format menu. The Character dialog box, shown in Figure 10-2, appears.

***Figure 10-1.*** *CHARACT file*

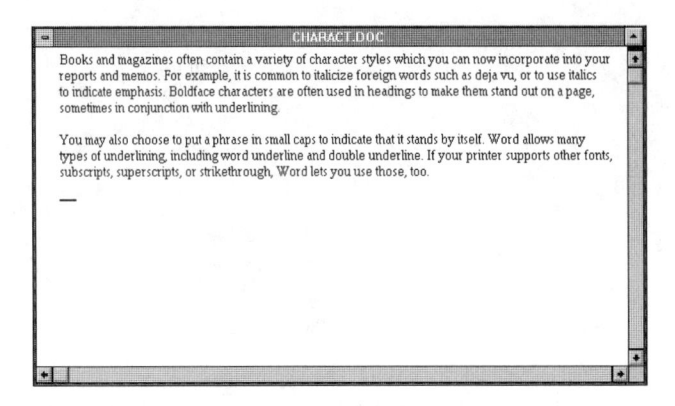

The standard character formatting, such as for bold, is either on or off. This type of formatting is called a *toggle* because it acts like a toggle switch. Choose it once and it's on; choose it again and it's off. You can change any of the toggles to indicate the formatting you want. In fact, you can choose more than one type of formatting for your text. For example, you might want a title on a report to be both underlined and bold.

You may have noticed the Sample box in the Character menu. This shows an example of the results of your formatting before you select OK. As you add

***Figure 10-2.*** *Character dialog box*

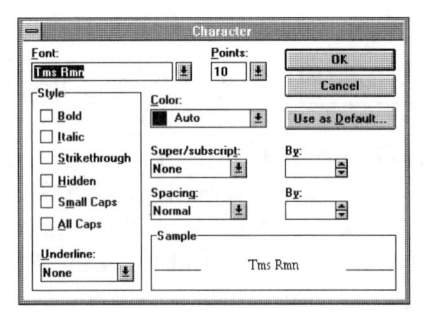

**Chapter 10:** *Formatting Characters* 99

or remove formatting options, the characters in the Sample box change to reflect the new formatting.

You can also set a format toggle from the ribbon, shown here:

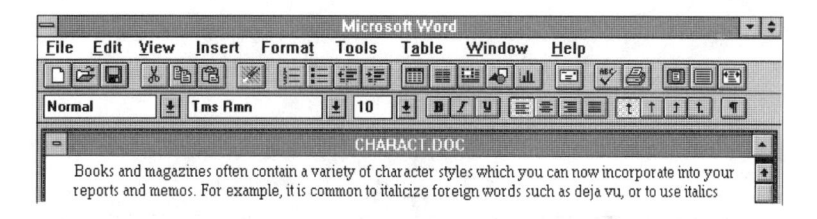

![Microsoft Word ribbon screenshot showing menu bar with File, Edit, View, Insert, Format, Tools, Table, Window, Help, toolbar icons, and a document CHARACT.DOC containing text: "Books and magazines often contain a variety of character styles which you can now incorporate into your reports and memos. For example, it is common to italicize foreign words such as deja vu, or to use italics"]

Turn the ribbon on by choosing Ribbon from the View menu. Then click any of the icons for boldface, italics, or underline.

The icons near the middle of the ribbon, marked **B**, *I*, and U, are used to make text bold, italic, or underlined. Just select the desired text and click the icon. When a toggle is set on, the button looks like it is pressed in.

The formats that most people use in their writing are plain (no emphasis), italics, bold, and underlining. Now, as an experiment, select the words "deja vu" in the text and give the Character command from the Format menu. Select the Italic option and then the OK button. When the dialog box disappears, the words "deja vu" become italic:

> Books and magazines often contain a variety of character styles which you can now incorporate into your reports and memos. For example, it is common to italicize foreign words such as *deja vu*, or to use italics to indicate emphasis. Boldface characters are often used in headings to make them stand out on a page, sometimes in conjunction with underlining.

Click once in the text or press the (→) key to remove the selection so you can see the italics more clearly.

Choosing bold and underline formatting is similar to choosing italics. Select the words "stand out" and then make them bold by clicking the **B** icon in the ribbon, or press (CTRL)-(B). Select the word "underlining" and click the U icon, or press (CTRL)-(U). (If you wish, you can also underline the period after the word.) The results look like this:

> Books and magazines often contain a variety of character styles which you can now incorporate into your reports and memos. For example, it is common to italicize foreign words such as *deja vu*, or to use italics to indicate emphasis. Boldface characters are often used in headings to make them **stand out** on a page, sometimes in conjunction with underlining.

As mentioned before, you can apply more than one format to a section of text. To practice this, select "in conjunction" and give the Character command. Now select both Bold and Italic and select the OK button.

> Books and magazines often contain a variety of character styles which you can now incorporate into your reports and memos. For example, it is common to italicize foreign words such as *deja vu*, or to use italics to indicate emphasis. Boldface characters are often used in headings to make them **stand out** on a page, sometimes ***in conjunction*** with underlining.

## Lesson 35: Other Character Formats

Word also lets you specify other types of formatting in the Character dialog box. In the area labeled Style (which you should think of as "characteristics"), the other choices are Strikethrough, Hidden, Small Caps, and All Caps. (Don't worry about Hidden; hidden text is covered in Chapter 18.) You can experiment with these to see what they look like.

As you can see from the mixture of formatting in Figure 10-3, it is easy to overuse character formatting. Most book and magazine publishers avoid using too many formats to prevent the text from looking like an old-time circus poster.

In the Underline drop-down list in the Character dialog box, you can choose from several types of underlining: single (regular), words only, and double. Here are examples of each:

single underlining
words only underlining
double underlining

*Figure 10-3.*   Text with many formats applied

Subscripts and superscripts are often useful in scientific or technical papers. You choose these from the Super/subscript drop-down list in the Character dialog box. You define how high or low you want your superscripts and subscripts by entering an amount in the By option.

To experiment with superscripts and subscripts, select the word "superscripts" in the CHARACT file, give the Character command, and select Superscript in the Super/subscript drop-down list. Notice that Word fills in "3 pt" (3 points) for the amount in the By option; you can change this to an amount between 0 and 63 points. (Points are described in the next two sections in this chapter.) Subscripts work the same way as superscripts. Note that Word may not show characters that are superscripted or subscripted past the top or bottom of the line.

If you have a color monitor or color printer, you can take advantage of Word's color formatting for characters. Choose a color from the drop-down list. The colors you can choose are black, blue, cyan, green, magenta, red, yellow, and white. The Auto choice uses the color you assigned for window text in the Control Panel program for Windows.

You can assign colors even if you do not have a color monitor or printer. Simply add the formatting to any text in your document. Word remembers the formatting, even if it cannot show it on the screen or printer. This way, if you later have access to a color device, your document will display and print in color.

The Spacing option lets you expand or condense the space between characters in the selection. You may want to change the space in headings to make them stand out or to get more information on a line. The choices are Normal, Expanded, and Condensed.

## Lesson 36: Introduction to Fonts

Windows has many different alphabet sets you can use in your writing. Each different alphabet set is called a *font*; in other words, each font is a consistent text design. There are many ways to draw the standard alphabet. For instance, you may have very curly letters, very blocky ones, or letters with many intricate details. Actually, a font contains more than just the letters of the alphabet: it contains all the numerals, punctuation marks, and special symbols as well.

If you have not experimented with fonts before, you will find that using different fonts creates different moods for your letters and reports. This section covers the basics of type and fonts; if you are already familiar with fonts, feel free to skim through it.

Each font can have variations within it. The two major types of variations are characteristics and size. You have already seen the different formatting characteristics that Word can produce, such as underline, italics, and bold. You may have noticed that when you applied a format with the Character command from the Format menu, the letters still appeared on the screen in much the way they were before. That is because using characteristics allows the letters to retain the basic feeling of a font (such as the character widths).

The *size* of a font is defined as the amount of vertical space the letters take on a line. This amount includes the distance the letter goes above and below the *baseline*, which is where the bottoms of most letters line up, as well as the *leading*, which is the space between the very bottom of a letter and the very top of the letter on the next line. Here is an example that shows the elements that make up the size of a font:

Font size is measured in *points*; one point is 1/72 of an inch. For instance, the characters in a 12-point font are 1/6 of an inch high (including the leading that Windows automatically uses).

Each font has many different design characteristics that help define it. For instance, some fonts have *serifs,* which are little decorative lines used to finish off the stroke of a letter. Fonts without serifs are called *sans serif.* Here you can see the difference between serif and sans serif:

**Chapter 10:** *Formatting Characters* 103

Serif
**Sans serif**

    A font can also have proportional spacing or monospacing. In a *proportional font,* the letters have different widths; for example, the "m" is much wider than the "i". In a *monospace font,* the letters and punctuation are all given the same amount of horizontal space, regardless of width. It is easy to see the difference:

       `This is a monospaced font.`

       This is a proportional font.

    Other design characteristics include whether the type has wide or thin lines, whether the characters are chubby or narrow, what kinds of embellishments are used in the letters, and whether the letters can connect (as in a *cursive,* or script, font).

    Each font has a name. The following illustration shows some of the fonts available for Windows:

       `Courier`
       **Helv**
       Modern
       *Script*
       Σψμβολ
       Tms Rmn

**10**

You may not have all of these installed, or you may have more, depending on your version of Windows or whether you have installed other Windows programs. There are thousands of fonts available for Windows from many sources. See your Windows documentation for information on installing additional fonts.

## Lesson 37: Changing Fonts

You can easily change the font of selected text with the Character command. The Character dialog box has two choices that relate to fonts: one for the font name and the other for the font size. For each font, Word lists only the sizes that are installed with the font, but you can enter any size you want between 4 and 16383 points (although you must enter whole numbers).

Note that Word will show only the fonts that apply to the current printer. Thus, it is important to have the desired printer chosen before you start Word.

You can also change the font and size in the ribbon. The drop-down lists in the ribbon act the same as those in the Character dialog box.

For practice, select the first sentence of the text in the CHARACT file and give the Character command. Select the Modern font and a size of 9 points. The selected paragraph now looks like this:

> Books and magazines often contain a variety of character styles which you can now incorporate into your reports and memos. For example, it is common to italicize foreign words such as *deja vu*, or to use italics to indicate emphasis. Boldface characters are often used in headings to make them **stand out** on a page, sometimes *in conjunction* with underlining.

You can enter a font size that is not listed by typing a number for your size choice. However, using font sizes that are not listed often causes the text to look jagged and poorly formed on the screen. Depending on the type of font you have chosen and the type of printer you have, the text may look fine or terrible when printed. Some fonts also look strange on the screen when bold or outlined. If you are using an alternate font manager like Adobe Type Manager, you will have fewer font problems.

Once you have experimented with all of the available character formatting and some of the fonts, print out the file on your printer to see how it looks.

**Chapter 10:** *Formatting Characters*

## Lesson 38: Selecting Character Formatting with the [CTRL] Key

Using the Character command or the ribbon to change character formatting, fonts, and font sizes can be tedious and slow if you need to give the command over and over. Word allows you to select character formatting and fonts with key combinations to make formatting faster.

Table 10-1 shows the key combinations used to select character formatting, fonts, and font sizes. As before, select the text you want to change, and then use the appropriate key combination.

For example, select the words "Books and magazines" in the CHARACT file; then press [CTRL]-[I] to put the words in italics. To add underlining, press [CTRL]-[U]. The result looks like this:

*Books and magazines* often contain a variety of character styles which you can now incorporate into your reports and memos. For example, it is common to italicize foreign words such as *deja vu* , or to use italics to indicate emphasis. Boldface characters are often used in headings to make them **stand out** on a page, sometimes *in conjunction* with underlining.

To make the words normal again, press [CTRL]-[SPACEBAR]. This key combination removes all formatting that is different from the standard for the current paragraph style (described in Chapter 13).

## Lesson 39: Copying Character Formats

Now that you know how to apply a format to a character, you may be inclined to go back and add character formats to other files you have created with Word. Giving the commands from the Character menu, the ribbon, or entering [CTRL]-key sequences can get tedious, however, so Word allows you to copy the format of one set of characters to another without having to specify the actual format.

When you want to do this, you begin with one set of characters formatted the way you want. The steps are as follows:

1. Select the characters you want to copy the formatting to.
2. Point at the characters that are already formatted.

***Table 10-1.*** *Character Formatting with* [CTRL]*-Key Combinations*

| Format | Key Combination |
|---|---|
| Normal for style | [CTRL]-[SPACEBAR] |
| Italic | [CTRL]-[I] |
| Bold | [CTRL]-[B] |
| Underline | [CTRL]-[U] |
| Word underline | [CTRL]-[W] |
| Double underline | [CTRL]-[D] |
| Small caps | [CTRL]-[K] |
| All caps | [CTRL]-[A] |
| Subscript | [CTRL]-[=] |
| Superscript | [CTRL]-[SHIFT]-[=] |
| Change font | [CTRL]-[F] |
| Change font size | [CTRL]-[P] |
| Increase font size | [CTRL]-[F2] |
| Decrease font size | [CTRL]-[SHIFT]-[F2] |

3. Hold down the [CTRL] and [SHIFT] keys and click the left mouse button.

The characters you selected will be formatted and the selection will move to them.

These steps are best explained by example. Suppose you want to change the first word in each sentence in the CHARACT file to Modern 9-point, underlined. (This is admittedly strange, but it is a good exercise.) Notice that the word "Books" already has this formatting. Select the word "For" in the second sentence:

*Books and magazines* often contain a variety of character styles which you can now incorporate into your reports and memos. **For** example, it is common to italicize foreign words such as *deja vu* , or to use italics to indicate emphasis. Boldface characters are often used in headings to make them **stand out** on a page, sometimes *in conjunction* with underlining.

Point at "Books", hold down the [CTRL] and [SHIFT] keys, and then click the left mouse button. The word "For" is changed to the new formatting:

**Chapter 10:** *Formatting Characters* 107

*Books and magazines* often contain a variety of character styles which you can now incorporate into your reports and memos. *For* example, it is common to italicize foreign words such as *deja vu* , or to use italics to indicate emphasis. Boldface characters are often used in headings to make them **stand out** on a page, sometimes ***in conjunction*** with underlining.

# Review

Open the MAGAZINE file and add character formatting to various words and phrases. Add more than one type of formatting to some words and notice how the formats combine.

# 11
# Formatting Paragraphs

One of the best ways to make letters and reports look professional is to use consistent formatting throughout the document. For example, if you indent your paragraphs, all paragraphs should probably be indented the same amount.

All headings should also be formatted consistently so the reader can quickly determine what you are saying. In a report, it is often important to see section headings and topics quickly. If your document is organized around an outline, consistently formatting each level of information helps the reader to understand the meaning of the whole document.

Formatting paragraphs in Word is quite easy because Word associates a format with each paragraph. You can specify paragraph formatting when you enter the paragraph, and you can change the formatting later if you change your mind (just as you can with character formatting, described in Chapter 10). Word automatically uses the same format for each paragraph until you tell it otherwise. As a result, all of your text paragraphs will look the same until you give different formatting commands.

Tab stops are a format characteristic that you can set for a paragraph. Word's tab stops work just like those on a typewriter, but with one additional feature: if your writing includes figures and columns, you can use one set of tab stops for one set of columns and a different set for another set of columns.

There are many other interesting paragraph formatting features. For example, you can tell Word that you want a border (such as a solid line) around a paragraph to make headings stand out. Paragraphs can be formatted by using buttons in the ruler and ribbon, commands from the menus, and CTRL-key combinations. This chapter includes instructions for all of these methods.

## Lesson 40: Basic Formatting for Paragraphs

Word stores a paragraph's format in the mark at the end of the paragraph. You may have noticed that an extra blank character is inserted at the end of each paragraph after the period; this is the paragraph mark that is inserted when you press the ENTER key. You can see the paragraph mark by clicking the far right icon on the ribbon:

[ribbon image with "Show all" label pointing to far right icon]

This also shows other characters, as described in Chapter 16. If you do not have the ruler showing, you can show these characters by choosing the All option in the View choices, in the Options command from the Tools menu.

You can choose from a variety of paragraph formatting options. To see a list of them from which you can make your choices, select any text in the paragraph or place the insertion point anywhere in the paragraph and give the Paragraph command from the Format menu. For example, load the SAMPLE1 file into Word and put the insertion point in the first text paragraph. Now give the Paragraph command. The dialog box is shown in Figure 11-1.

In the Paragraph dialog box, as in other Word dialog boxes, you simply choose the characteristics that you want the selected text to have. Since

**Chapter 11:** *Formatting Paragraphs* 111

*Figure 11-1.* Paragraph dialog box

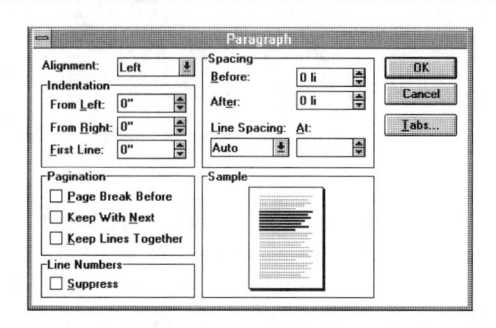

paragraph formatting applies to whole paragraphs, if you have selected only part of a paragraph or the insertion point placed in it, Word applies the formatting to that entire paragraph.

Many of the paragraph formatting commands can also be executed with CTRL-key sequences, like those used in character formatting, instead of from the menu (see the section "Selecting Paragraph Formatting with the CTRL Key" later in this chapter).

You can set two types of formatting from the ribbon. The buttons to the right of the character formatting buttons let you change the alignment and tab stops. These are both described in lessons later in this chapter. The ribbon looks like this:

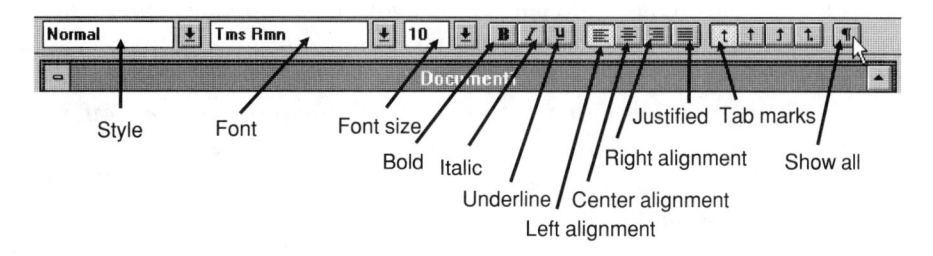

Another way of setting many paragraph formats is directly on the ruler. You can show the ruler with the Ruler command from the View menu:

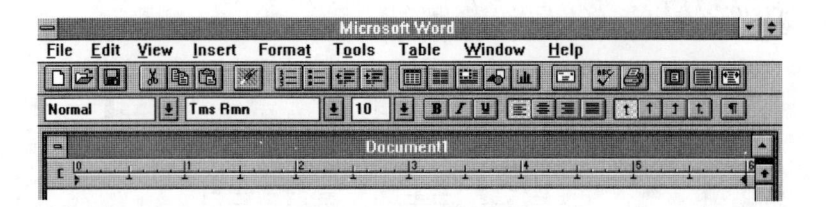

The ruler sets your paragraph indentations and shows where each tab stop is in the selected paragraph. The numbers on the ruler are incremented by inches. When you enter the settings for paragraph indentations, you normally give the position in inches, but you can change this with the Options command described in Chapter 16.

Remember that you can change the formatting of a paragraph at any time. Word has default settings for all of the paragraph formatting choices (sometimes called the *normal* choices), but it is likely that these will not be the best choices at all times. For example, you may enter some text in a memo with normal paragraph formatting and then decide later to indent the paragraph from both margins to make it stand out on the page. You can change the margins, see how the paragraph looks, and decide whether to keep the new format. You can, of course, change it back at any time as well.

## Lesson 41: Indenting Paragraphs

The most common changes that you make to paragraph formats are to the indentation of the whole paragraph and of the first line. These can be changed in the Paragraph dialog box or with the markers for the left indent, first line, and right indent on the ruler. Throughout this section, remember that paragraph indentation is always relative to page indentation, which is covered in Chapter 12.

In common business letters and memos, the first line of each paragraph is indented from the margin by five spaces, or about half an inch. To do this, give the Paragraph command from the Format menu and enter .5" in the First Line option:

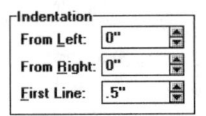

```
┌Indentation──────────────┐
│ From Left:  0"    ⬍    │
│ From Right: 0"    ⬍    │
│ First Line: .5"   ⬍    │
└─────────────────────────┘
```

When you change the indentation, the text is automatically wrapped around, just as it is when you enter text by typing.

Instead of using the Paragraph dialog box, you can drag the indicators on the ruler. Using the Paragraph dialog box lets you specify more exact values than you can by dragging the indicators on the ruler. Also, many users find that manipulating the ruler is difficult because it is so small. It is, however, useful to leave the ruler on the screen as you work with paragraph formats so you can see the formats for the selected paragraphs.

Sometimes you may want to indent an entire paragraph from the left and right margins. This is common for direct quotations in reports. Indenting is also used a great deal in letters, especially for the date and closing. (Remember that these are considered paragraphs in Word.) On a normal typewriter, you use the (TAB) key or (SPACEBAR) to move to the place you want. In Word, you indicate the indentation from the left margin, and every new line (unless you've selected a different first-line indent) starts there.

To see how this is done, select the date at the beginning of the SAMPLE1 letter, give the Paragraph command, and set the From Left option to 3 inches. Figure 11-2 shows the new position of the date. If you move the date, you will probably also indent the closing and the name and address.

The measurement indicated by the first-line indicator is relative to that in the left indent indicator. For example, if you want to indent the entire first paragraph 1 inch (from the page margin) and indent the first line 1/2 inch beyond that, set the From Left option to 1 inch and the First Line option to .5 inch. Note the result in the Sample box shown here:

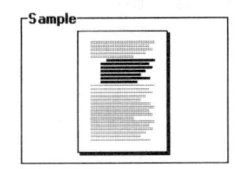

***Figure 11-2.*** *Date indented three inches*

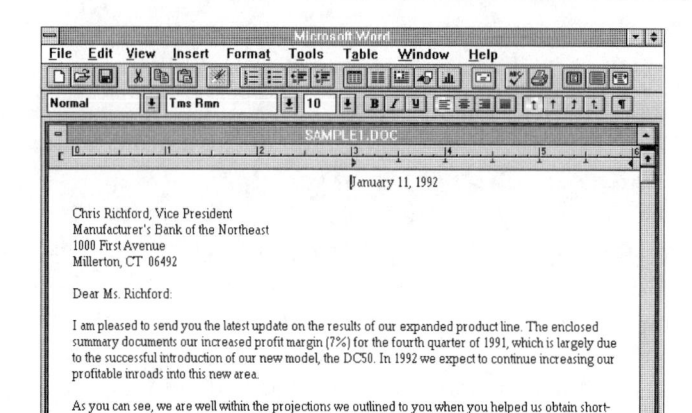

If you do not want to indent the first line but want to move the entire paragraph 1 inch from the margin, you set the left indent to 1 inch and the first line to 0 inches.

This brings up an interesting situation. What if you want the first line to start to the left of the rest of the paragraph? This format is called a *hanging indent* or an *outdent*. To see how this is formatted, select any part of the first full paragraph, give the Paragraph command, and set the From Left option to 1 inch and the First Line option to -0.5 (negative 1/2) inch. You can also do this on the ruler. The result is shown here:

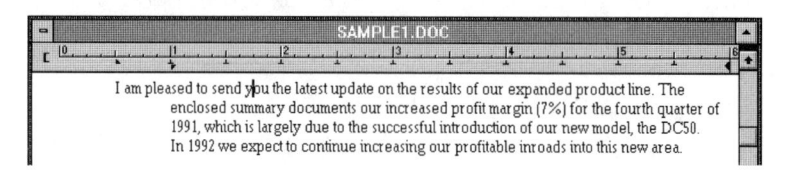

**Chapter 11:** *Formatting Paragraphs* 115

It is unlikely that you will change a paragraph's right margin unless you are also changing the left margin. Experiment by changing the right indent on the first full paragraph to 1 inch:

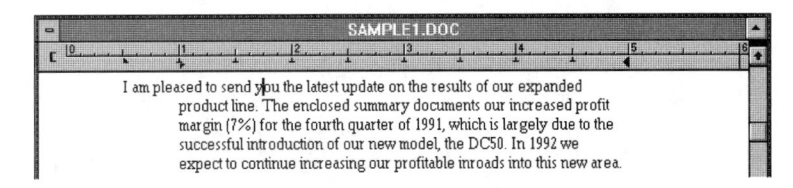

```
┌─────────────────── SAMPLE1.DOC ───────────────────┐
  |0    |1    |2    |3    |4    |5    |6
      I am pleased to send you the latest update on the results of our expanded
          product line. The enclosed summary documents our increased profit
          margin (7%) for the fourth quarter of 1991, which is largely due to the
          successful introduction of our new model, the DC50. In 1992 we
          expect to continue increasing our profitable inroads into this new area.
```

As always, the Undo command removes the effects of the last changes.

These indentation choices illustrate the reason that you want to treat related text (like an address) as one paragraph by using newline instead of `ENTER`. Remember that you use newline (`SHIFT`-`ENTER`) to go to a new line without starting a new paragraph. When you change the margin with the Paragraph command, all the lines are formatted together since they are in one paragraph.

For example, assume you want to move the lines with Thomas Mead's name, company, and address 3 inches from the left margin. If each line ends in a newline character, you can give just one command for the set of four lines, instead of having to format each line. To see how this works, change the paragraph's breaks to newline characters (if you did not use newline originally) by selecting the blank character at the end of each line:

```
¶
Thomas Mead, Controller¶
National Generators¶
1275 Oak Glen Industrial Park¶
Oak Glen, CT 06410¶
```

Replace the paragraph mark with the newline character (`SHIFT`-`ENTER`). Notice that the screen looks the same. Do this for all lines in the address except for the last. Then select or leave the insertion point in any part of this paragraph, give the Paragraph command, and set the left indent to 3 inches. All of the lines move.

## Lesson 42: Line Spacing for Paragraphs

In Word you can modify the number of lines above, below, and inside a paragraph. In the examples you have typed up to this point, you have inserted blank lines between paragraphs as if you were doing so on a typewriter—by pressing the (ENTER) key an extra time. Now you will see how to have Word do this automatically with the Paragraph command.

Although this method is not much easier than pressing the (ENTER) key a particular number of times after each paragraph, it allows you to enter text more consistently. Remember that one of the goals of using Word's formatting features is to make your documents look as consistent as possible. Instead of your having to remember how many lines you want after each paragraph and pressing the (ENTER) key that many times, Word remembers to do this for you in the paragraph format.

To see the utility of using automatic spacing in your document, first eliminate all of the extra blank lines. You can do this by selecting the paragraph mark at the end of each blank line and deleting them. An easier method, however, is to move the insertion point to the beginning of the document, give the Replace command from the Edit menu, enter **^p^p** in the Find What option (to indicate two consecutive paragraph marks), and enter **^p** in the Replace With option (to indicate a single paragraph mark). This is shown in Figure 11-3. Select the Replace All button to change all the instances of the double paragraph mark. Note that you had more than a single paragraph mark after the closing ("Sincerely") so there will still be an extra line. Your document now looks like the one in Figure 11-4.

*Figure 11-3.*   *Replacing doubled paragraph marks with single ones to eliminate blank lines*

**Chapter 11:** *Formatting Paragraphs* 117

If you want to insert blank lines between paragraphs, it is usually better to specify them as space after the paragraph, not before. Thus, you should change the After option in the Paragraph dialog box to "1 li" (one line in the current font size) for the first text paragraph in SAMPLE1.

You can enter the Before or After measurements in many ways. The simplest is to enter the number of lines since you usually want the space to be related to the size of the characters in the paragraph. You can also enter the number of points, such as **12 pt**. For example, to keep a blank line after a paragraph that is in a 12-point font, you would enter **1 li** or **12 pt** for the After option. In this case, type **1 li** into the box. You can see the result in the Sample box after pressing the (TAB) key.

Reformat each paragraph in the letter by selecting the entire document, giving the Paragraph command, and specifying **1 li**. The result looks just like the letter with the extra blank paragraphs. However, the lines between the closing and Thomas Mead's name should be specified as two lines before the name.

The Line Spacing option in the Paragraph command allows you to specify that a particular paragraph be double or triple spaced. To double-space a paragraph, select any part of it and select Double from the Line Spacing drop-down list. The result is shown in Figure 11-5.

*Figure 11-4.*    Blank lines removed

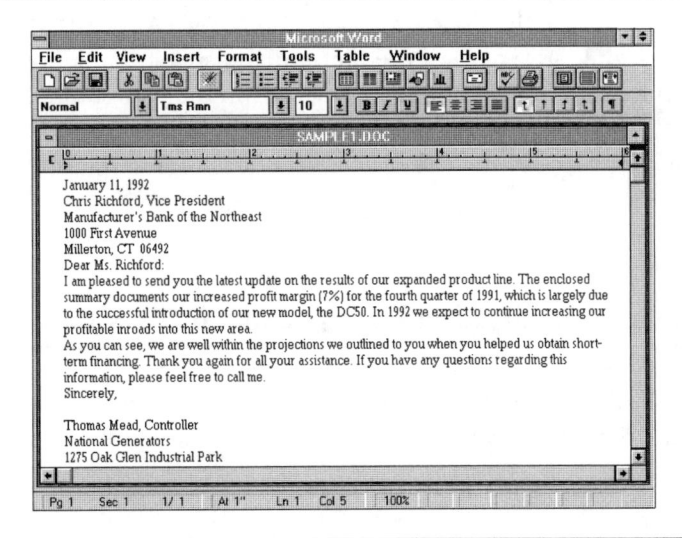

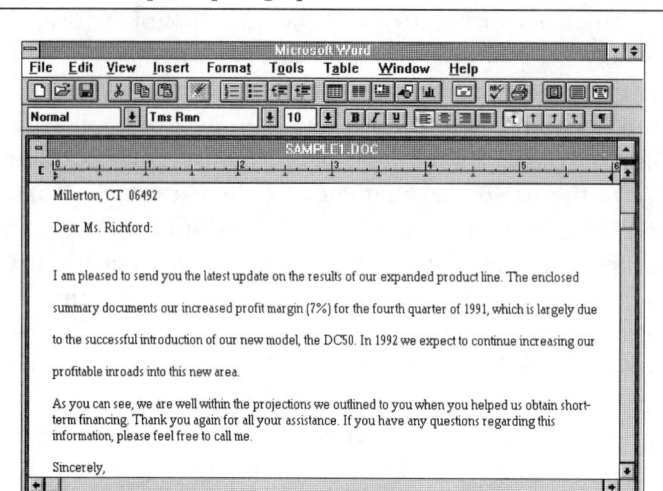

***Figure 11-5.***     Double-spaced paragraph

Word normally starts with the Line Spacing choice set to Auto. This setting lets Word adjust the line height for you if you change font sizes and gives your text a generally open look. The drop-down list under the Line Spacing option lets you change this. The two other choices are At Least, which indicates that Word should give at least the amount you specify if the font sizes change or you have superscripts and subscripts within the paragraph, and Exactly, which means that the amount you specify is used regardless of font size and placement. Type in the amount in the At choice next to the Line Spacing option.

# Lesson 43: Aligning Paragraphs and Using Keeps

All of the paragraphs you have typed so far have been *left-aligned*. This means that each line begins all the way at the left margin (unless you have indented the paragraph) and is formatted with wordwrap, but the right margin is *ragged,* which means that if a word falls a little short of the right margin, it stays there. Books and magazines often use *justified* margins, which means that, in addition to beginning at the left margin, the lines are filled with spaces so that each one ends on the right margin. (For example, this book uses justified margins.) Justified text is not only easy to read, it gives a professional look to your reports.

Almost all of your writing will be either left-aligned or justified; however, Word also lets you center each line of text in a paragraph, which is often useful for headings or for text that needs to stand out on a page, such as warnings. For a trendy look, you can even format right-aligned text, which makes the left margin ragged and aligns the right margin. The four types of paragraphs (left-aligned, justified, centered, and right-aligned) are illustrated in Figure 11-6.

Clear the SAMPLE1 file from your screen and enter the text for each example paragraph in Figure 11-6. Then set the alignment by selecting part of the paragraph and either clicking the desired alignment button in the ribbon or choosing from the Paragraph dialog box. For example, to center-align a paragraph with the ribbon, you would click the second icon:

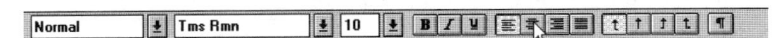

```
| Normal      | ± | Tms Rmn | ± | 10 | ± | B | I | U | ≡ | ≣ | ≡ | ↑ | ↑ | ↑ | ↑ | ¶ |
```

Note that regardless of how you change the alignment, the ribbon will show the alignment by making the appropriate button look pressed down. Exper-

*Figure 11-6.*     *Examples of alignment*

> This is a left-aligned paragraph. Notice that the right margin is ragged but that each line begins against the left margin. This is Word's normal paragraph style.
>
> This paragraph is justified. When you finish typing each line, Word puts extra space on the line to make it line up with the right margin. Most magazines and books are published with justified margins.
>
> A centered paragraph has white space to make each line an equal distance from the two margins. This is usually only used for headings or special information that needs to stand out.
>
> This paragraph is right-aligned. As you can see, each line ends against the right margin, but the left margin is ragged. This is an interesting, but rarely used, format.

iment by adding text to the centered and right-aligned paragraphs to see how Word shuffles the characters as you type them.

Remember that you can use the newline character to start a new line without starting a new paragraph. You can use newline together with the centered format to make text stand out on a page. For example, enter the following text as a single paragraph with newline characters:

```
WARNING!
Do not use this product
without first consulting your physician.
```

Now center the paragraph from the ribbon or by choosing Centered from the Paragraph dialog box. The result should look like this:

```
                    WARNING!
               Do not use this product
        without first consulting your physician.
```

There are times when you want to keep a whole paragraph together—in tables or figures, for instance, where blank space at the bottom of a page is preferable to splitting up the information. To keep a paragraph together, select the paragraph and choose the Keep Lines Together option in the Pagination part of the Paragraph dialog box:

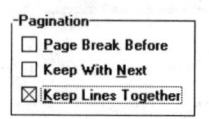

```
-Pagination-
 ☐ Page Break Before
 ☐ Keep With Next
 ☒ Keep Lines Together
```

If you want to keep the selected paragraph with the paragraph that follows it, select Keep With Next in the Paragraph dialog box. This tells Word that the two paragraphs must stay on the same page, which can be useful for keeping a heading with the text that follows it or a caption under a table.

The Page Break Before option is not used frequently. It causes Word to force a page break before the paragraph without your having to put in a page break character. This is described in more detail in Chapter 12.

**Chapter 11:** *Formatting Paragraphs* 121

# Lesson 44: Selecting Paragraph Formatting with the CTRL Key

With direct formatting, you can choose many of the paragraph formats with CTRL-key combinations, just as you did in Chapter 10 with character formatting. Table 11-1 shows the formats available.

As you can see, some of these key combinations, such as CTRL-M and CTRL-N, do not set an absolute format. Instead, they change the current settings of the paragraph by a small relative amount. You can use these key combinations repeatedly to move the margins.

For example, clear the example text file and open the SAMPLE1 file. Select or move the insertion point into any part of the first text paragraph of the letter; then press CTRL-N. If you check the ruler, you will notice that the paragraph moves one-half inch:

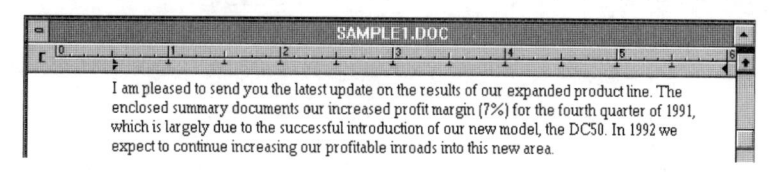

```
                    SAMPLE1.DOC
  |0      |1      |2      |3      |4      |5      |6
  I am pleased to send you the latest update on the results of our expanded product line. The
  enclosed summary documents our increased profit margin (7%) for the fourth quarter of 1991,
  which is largely due to the successful introduction of our new model, the DC50. In 1992 we
  expect to continue increasing our profitable inroads into this new area.
```

If you press CTRL-N again, the paragraph moves farther to the right:

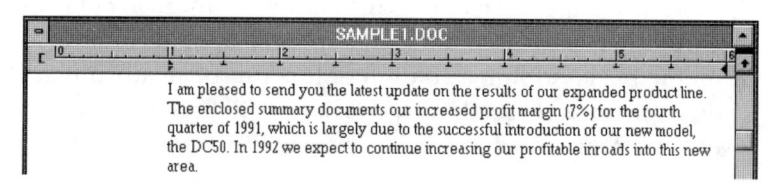

```
                    SAMPLE1.DOC
  |0      |1      |2      |3      |4      |5      |6
  I am pleased to send you the latest update on the results of our expanded product line.
  The enclosed summary documents our increased profit margin (7%) for the fourth
  quarter of 1991, which is largely due to the successful introduction of our new model,
  the DC50. In 1992 we expect to continue increasing our profitable inroads into this new
  area.
```

To move it back, you can use CTRL-M.

*Table 11-1.  Paragraph Formatting with* CTRL *-Key Combinations*

| Format | Key Combination |
| --- | --- |
| Normal | CTRL-Q |
| Indent first line 1/2 inch | CTRL-G |
| Decrease left indent 1/2 inch | CTRL-M |
| Increase left indent 1/2 inch | CTRL-N |
| 1/2-inch hanging indent | CTRL-T |
| 1 line before | CTRL-O |
| Left-aligned | CTRL-L |
| Justified | CTRL-J |
| Centered | CTRL-E |
| Right-aligned | CTRL-R |
| Double-spaced | CTRL-2 |

## Lesson 45: Using Tabs

Setting up aligned columns in your text is often one of the hardest chores in word processing. Even if the tabs are set just right, your data often does not fit on the page. Adding a column of text can be nearly impossible. However, if you set the tabs correctly with Word, you will find that making columnar text is very easy. You can set your tab positions either before or after you enter your tabbed text.

There are two methods for creating tables in Word. You can set up tables with tab stops, similar to the way you might on a typewriter, or you can use the table feature. For a short columnar table, using tab stops is quick and easy. However, there are disadvantages to tabs that the table feature overcomes. For example, if you use tab stops, only the far-right column can have text automatically wrap in the column. Also, changing the width of a column is more

**Chapter 11:** *Formatting Paragraphs* 123

difficult with tab stops. This chapter shows you how to use tab stops to align columns since they are easier to learn than the table feature. Tables are covered in Chapter 15.

You set and move tabs with the ruler. In your text, you skip to the tab stop the same way you do on a typewriter—by pressing the (TAB) key.

Word comes with a set of tabs defined as the default. These are set to every half inch. This is useful when you are typing letters and memos that don't require any special tab stops. You can change the setting for the default tab distance in the Tabs command from the Format menu. When you enter a new tab stop, Word automatically erases all the default tabs to the left of that new tab.

Word has four different types of tabs: *left, center, right,* and *decimal.* The type of tab indicates where the text lines up against it. A left tab is like a tab stop on a typewriter: the text begins at the tab stop and continues to the right. A right tab is the opposite of a left tab: the text starts to the left of the tab stop and ends at the tab stop.

The following example should clear up any confusion between these two types of tabs:

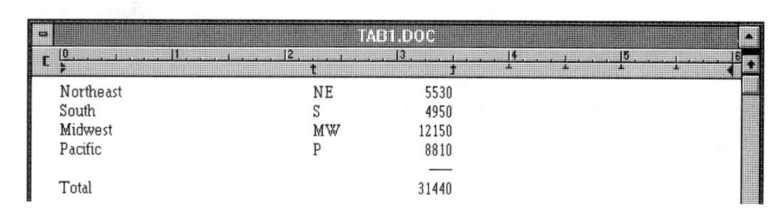

```
                    TAB1.DOC
|0........|1........|2........|3........|4........|5........|6
[                   ↱         ↰
    Northeast           NE         5530
    South               S          4950
    Midwest             MW        12150
    Pacific             P          8810
                                   ──
    Total                         31440
```

The first tab (at 2 1/4 inches) is a left (normal) tab stop, and the second (at 3 1/2 inches) is a right tab stop. Notice that the numbers in the third column (that is, after the second (TAB) character) all end at the tab. In general, left tabs are used for text and right tabs are used for numbers. Right tabs are especially useful if you include a sum for the group of numbers because numbers of different lengths then line up correctly.

A center tab causes the text to be centered around the tab stop, much like a centered paragraph; this tab is useful for headings of columns. A decimal tab causes numbers with decimal points to line up with the decimal point on the tab. These two types of tabs are shown here:

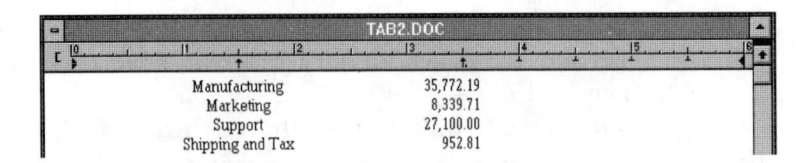

```
                          TAB2.DOC
  |10........|1........|2........|3........|4........|5........|6
                 ↑                    ↑
         Manufacturing         35,772.19
         Marketing              8,339.71
         Support               27,100.00
         Shipping and Tax         952.81
```

The tab stop at 1.5 inches is a center tab and the tab stop at 3.5 inches is a decimal tab. These two types of tabs are used much less frequently than left and right tabs.

## Lesson 46: Setting Tabs

Setting tabs on the ruler is fairly easy. You can select the type of tab you want from the icons on the ribbon:

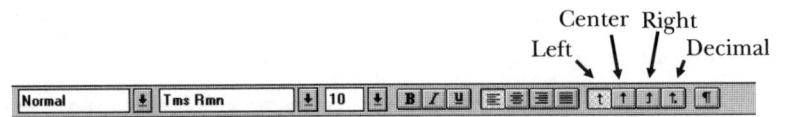

```
                                        Center  Right
                                    Left  \  |  /  Decimal
  | Normal  | | Tms Rmn | | 10 | | B I U | ≡ ≡ ≡ ≡ | t ↑ ↓ t | ¶ |
```

Then you point to the lower part of the ruler and click where you want the tab to be set. You can repeat this for as many tabs as you want. You can also drag the icons down to the ruler.

For example, to set a left tab at 2 1/4 inches, click the icon for the right tab stop in the ribbon and then point to the space between 2 and 2 1/2 inches in the ruler:

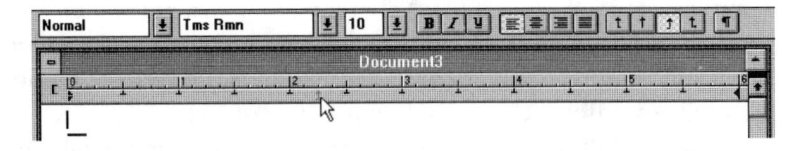

```
  | Normal  | | Tms Rmn | | 10 | | B I U | ≡ ≡ ≡ ≡ | t ↑ ↓ t | ¶ |
                          Document3
  |10........|1........|2........|3........|4........|5........|6
                              ↖
  L
```

You can move a tab setting on the ruler line by dragging it around. For example, drag the tab you just set to 2 1/2 inches. To delete a tab stop, drag it down off the ruler.

**Chapter 11:** *Formatting Paragraphs*

Set up the columns shown here for practice:

```
                    TAB3.DOC
  0        1        2        3        4        5       6
  Terrence          88       Regular           88.00
  Connors          150       Senior           125.00
  Long             130       Regular          130.00
  Yee               50       New               67.50
```

The second column is right-aligned, the third column is left-aligned, and the fourth column is decimal-aligned. (If you need help setting this up, the three tab stops are a right-aligned tab at 2 1/8 inches, a left-aligned tab at 3 inches, and a decimal-aligned tab at 4 1/2 inches.)

You can also specify a tab by giving the Tabs command from the Format menu or selecting the Tabs button in the Paragraph dialog box. Double-clicking a tab stop in the ruler also brings up this dialog box. The Tabs dialog box looks like this:

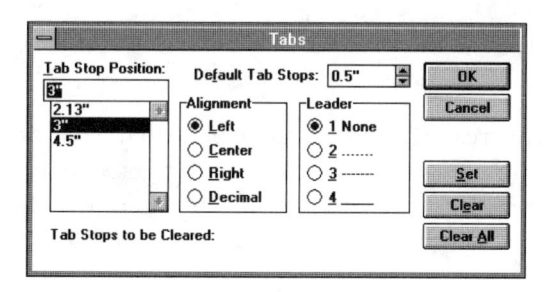

```
                          Tabs
  Tab Stop Position:    Default Tab Stops: 0.5"        OK
  3"
  2.13"                 ┌Alignment─┐  ┌Leader──┐      Cancel
  3"                    │ ● Left   │  │ ● 1 None│
  4.5"                  │ ○ Center │  │ ○ 2 .....│
                        │ ○ Right  │  │ ○ 3 -----│      Set
                        │ ○ Decimal│  │ ○ 4 ____│      Clear
  Tab Stops to be Cleared:                           Clear All
```

In the Tabs dialog box, select a type of tab, and then enter the desired location in the Tab Stop Position choice. You can use this choice to fine-tune the position of a tab. For example, if you have a tab set at 1 inch and you want it at 1 1/8 inches, select the tab stop on the ruler and type **1.125** in the Position choice.

To change the type of a tab, select it from the list at the left of the Tabs dialog box and select a different button in the Alignment choices. If you wish, you can clear all the tabs you have set for this paragraph by opening the Tabs dialog box and selecting the Clear All button. Be sure to select all the paragraphs you want to work on before changing the tabs.

## Lesson 47: Using Leader Characters

You may have noticed the Leader choice in the Tabs dialog box. Many columnar lists, such as financial summaries and tables of contents, often use characters to connect the columns of information across the page. These characters, usually dots, are called *leader characters* because they lead to the text at the next tab stop. Unless you specify otherwise, Word does not use a leader character.

For practice, change the first tab stop in the previous example to include a dot leader character. With the Tabs dialog box open, click the tab stop on the ruler, and then choose "...." from the Leader section. The columns then look like this:

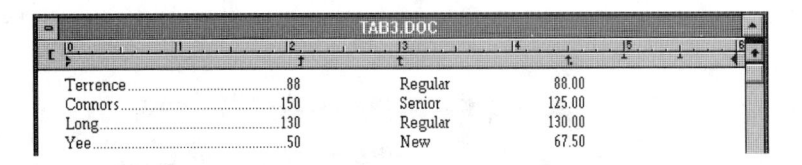

```
                                TAB3.DOC
  |0.........|1.........|2.........|3.........|4.........|5.........|6
                ↑              ↑              ↑
   Terrence...................88    Regular      88.00
   Connors....................150   Senior      125.00
   Long.......................130   Regular     130.00
   Yee........................50    New          67.50
```

This is a great deal easier than typing all the periods yourself. It is also easy to change to another type of leader character in a column since you don't have to erase the old characters and type the new characters for each entry. For example, try changing the leader character to dashes or underscores.

## Lesson 48: Working with Columns of Tabs

If you are editing a columnar list, you may want to move or delete a column of information. For example, you may want to switch two columns or remove a column in the middle of your list. To make such a move you need a way of selecting a single column.

There may be other times when you want to add a column in the middle of some other columns. In this case, you need to add a new column of tab characters.

The procedure for selecting a column of text with the mouse is as follows:

1. Put the insertion point at one corner of the column. Usually, you should select a character in the upper-left corner:

```
                    TAB3.DOC
|0        |1        |2        |3        |4        |5        |6

Terrence..............88       Regular     88.00
Connors...............150      Senior      125.00
Long..................130      Regular     130.00
Yee....................50      New          67.50
```

2. Press the right mouse button (not the left button, as you normally do) to activate the column selection feature.

3. Extend your selection by holding down the right mouse button and dragging to the lower-right corner of the column:

```
                    TAB3.DOC
|0        |1        |2        |3        |4        |5        |6

Terrence..............88       Regular     88.00
Connors...............150      Senior      125.00
Long..................130      Regular     130.00
Yee....................50      New          67.50
```

If you are editing a column made with tabs, be sure to include the tab characters that are before or after the column in your selection.

You can select more than one column at a time with this method. Word simply treats everything you select as a single column. (Note that you can select any text, not just text that is arranged in columns, in this method.)

Once you have selected a column of text, you can treat it as you would any other text. You can cut it, copy it to the Clipboard, delete it, add character formatting to it, and so on.

To select a column with the keyboard, put the insertion point at one corner of the desired selection, press `CTRL`-`SHIFT`-`F8`, and use the regular insertion point moving keys to extend the selection.

For example, to switch the positions of two columns, use the steps you would to move columns. First select the desired column, give the Cut command, move the insertion point to the first character of the column you want to paste in front of, and give the Paste command. If you want to move one column of several over to the far right, you must first make sure that in each line, the right column has a (TAB) pressed before the (ENTER) or newline. If you are showing formatting characters, the (TAB) looks like a small right arrow. Then (having already cut the column you want to move) move the insertion point in front of the top paragraph or newline mark and give the Paste command.

## Lesson 49: Copying Paragraph Formats

In Chapter 10 you learned how to copy character formats from one set of characters to other sets; here you learn the similar process for copying paragraph formats. Remember that you copy character formats by selecting the text you want to format, putting the insertion point above a character with the format you want, and holding down (CTRL) and (SHIFT) as you click the mouse button.

Paragraph formats are copied in much the same way, except that you point in the selection bar (to the left of the text) of the paragraph with the format you want instead of pointing at the characters. Thus, the steps are as follows:

1. Select the paragraph you want to copy the formatting to.
2. Point at the selection bar of the paragraph that is already formatted.
3. Hold down the (CTRL) and (SHIFT) keys and click the left mouse button.

## Lesson 50: Highlighting Paragraphs with Borders

Word lets you emphasize a paragraph by surrounding it with a border or by placing a bar above it, below it, or next to it. You have a wide selection of borders and bars. To add a border to a paragraph, select any part of the paragraph and give the Border command from the Format menu. Word displays the Border Paragraphs dialog box, shown in Figure 11-7, which lets you place lines and select the distance from the text, the line type, and shading.

**Chapter 11:** *Formatting Paragraphs* 129

*Figure 11-7.* Border Paragraphs dialog box

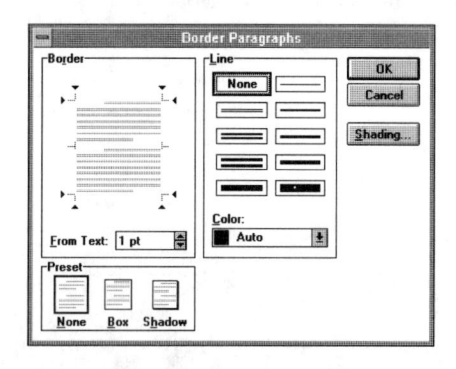

You can add lines to the top, bottom, left, and right of a paragraph; if you select all four, you put the paragraph in a box. To select a line to add, click between the appropriate guides in the Border box. To deselect a line, click None in the Preset box. You can also choose from the three preset border types (no border, a simple box, or a shadowed box) from the lower-left corner of the dialog box.

You can also add lines between paragraphs. If you select two paragraphs and double-click outside the guides, Word puts both paragraphs in a single box. However, if you want a line between the boxes, click between the center guides, as shown in Figure 11-8.

*Figure 11-8.* Specifying a line between paragraphs

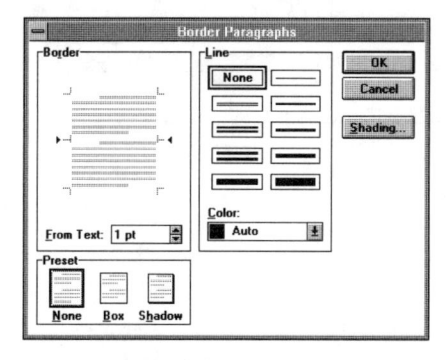

Each line can have a line style, selected from the choices in the Line options. The choices are shown here:

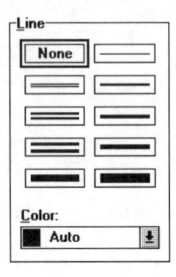

You can also specify a color for the lines from the Color choices.

The Shading button in the Border Paragraphs dialog box lets you select an amount of shading to put behind the paragraph. The Shading dialog box is shown in Figure 11-9.

To specify a shading, select the Custom button, and then choose a pattern from the drop-down list. You can also specify shading colors.

Shading is rarely used since almost any level of shading makes it hard to read the text when it is printed. Because of the way most laser printers are designed, any choice other than 10 or 12.5 percent comes out much too dark.

*Figure 11-9.*   Shading dialog box

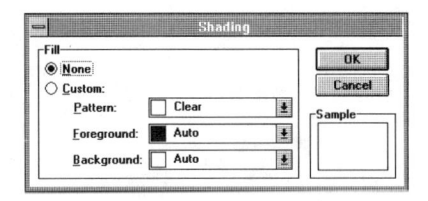

**Chapter 11:** *Formatting Paragraphs*

## Review

Add paragraph formatting to your MAGAZINE file. Experiment with combinations of first-line and left indentations.

Add a numbered list of steps you perform in a task in your job to the bottom of the Magazine file. Type **1.**, press (TAB), and then type the first step. Press (ENTER), type **2.**, press (TAB), and so on. Make sure at least one step takes more than one line. Select the steps and give them hanging indent formatting so the numbers appear to the left of the steps and all lines in the steps line up vertically.

# 12

# Formatting Sections

This chapter describes the remaining type of formatting: section formatting. A *section* can be thought of as one chapter in a larger document, but it can also refer to the entire document. *Section formatting* lets you specify such things as newspaper columns, headers and footers, page numbers, page margins, and footnote placement.

## Lesson 51: Using Word's View Modes

Word has several viewing modes. Section and page formatting are visible in only some of the modes. Except for the section mark, none of the section formats appear in normal mode. There are three main view modes:

- *Normal mode* is the view you have seen so far. You can edit in this mode, but, with the exception of the section mark, you do not see section formatting. This is sometimes called *galley mode*.

- *Page layout mode* also lets you edit your document, and you can also see section formatting.
- *Print preview mode* lets you see how your pages will look with all their formatting when printed, but you cannot edit in this mode.

(There is another mode, outline mode, described in Chapter 17.)

The page layout and print preview modes let you see exactly how your document will look when it is printed. Even though what you see on the screen in normal mode is generally what your document will look like when printed, it is not exact. For instance, you cannot see where the margins are positioned or how absolutely positioned paragraphs will appear when you are viewing in normal mode. If you specify the placement of a page number at the bottom of each page, you won't see the number on the screen in normal mode; it will appear only on the printed page.

Using the page layout and print preview modes is faster than printing out your documents, and it doesn't waste paper. You can use these modes at any time. The difference between the two modes is that page layout mode lets you edit your document, while print preview mode only lets you look at it and change the margins.

## Page Layout Mode

If you need to see how a page will look as you edit it, page layout mode is very useful, although it reduces Word's performance a bit. This is because Word has to make many more calculations about placement of text as you edit or scroll. On fast PCs, this is not very noticeable, but page layout mode is often difficult to use on slower PCs.

To switch from normal mode to page layout mode, give the Page Layout command from the View menu. This Page Layout window is similar to the normal mode window. However, the few differences help you navigate easily around the pages in your document.

In page layout mode, you can edit your text as well as other parts of the page that you cannot see in normal mode. For example, you can edit the headers and page numbers, which are described later in this chapter. In addition, you can see where absolutely positioned paragraphs will appear

**Chapter 12:** *Formatting Sections* 135

when printed. This helps you place these paragraphs exactly where you want them.

One major difference in page layout mode is the addition of two double arrows near the bottom of the vertical scroll bar:

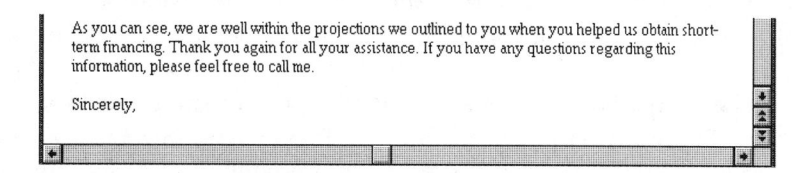

> As you can see, we are well within the projections we outlined to you when you helped us obtain short-term financing. Thank you again for all your assistance. If you have any questions regarding this information, please feel free to call me.
>
> Sincerely,

The double arrows let you quickly scroll up and down a full page.

You can also show boundary lines around text items by choosing the View option in the Options command from the Tools menu. Note that these do not print; they are only so you can see where each block of text is. The boundaries can surround such parts of text as headers, tables, positioned paragraphs, and so on.

If you have a large screen, you may find it useful to split the window into two panes—one in normal mode and the other in page layout mode. Splitting the window is covered in detail in Chapter 3. This can help you enter text quickly in normal mode but still see the exact results in page layout mode. To split the window, drag the split bar down the window, select some text in one part of the window, and give the Page Layout command.

In page layout mode, you can use the `ALT`-`↓` and `ALT`-`↑` key combinations to move quickly around the text areas on the screen. If you have only one text area (that is, no positioned paragraphs or headings), these key combinations have no effect.

The Draft command in the View menu can speed up page layout mode by reducing the amount of time it takes Word to display text. However, you will probably want to view your document in draft mode only if your PC is very slow.

## Print Preview Mode

The print preview mode has a much more limited use than the page layout mode. You enter print preview mode by giving the Print Preview command from the File menu. Generally, you use it only if you want to check the positioning on one or a few pages. When you give the Print Preview command, Word opens a new window, as shown in Figure 12-1. To close the Print Preview window, select the Cancel button to go to the previous mode. You can double-click in the text to go directly to page layout mode.

To scroll through the pages of your document while in print preview mode, click the scroll bar on the right of this window or press the (PAGE UP) or (PAGE DOWN) key. You can also drag the scroll box to go to a specific page.

The Print button lets you print directly from the Print Preview window. Selecting this button brings up the Print command dialog box, as described in Chapter 8.

You use the Margins button to change the location of the margins. It turns on and off the view of the margin lines. You can change the margins by selecting the Margins button and dragging the squares at the end of the margin lines. As you drag, Word tells you the measurement to which you are dragging at the top of the window. To see the effect of your changes, click anywhere off the page. Margins are discussed more thoroughly later in this chapter.

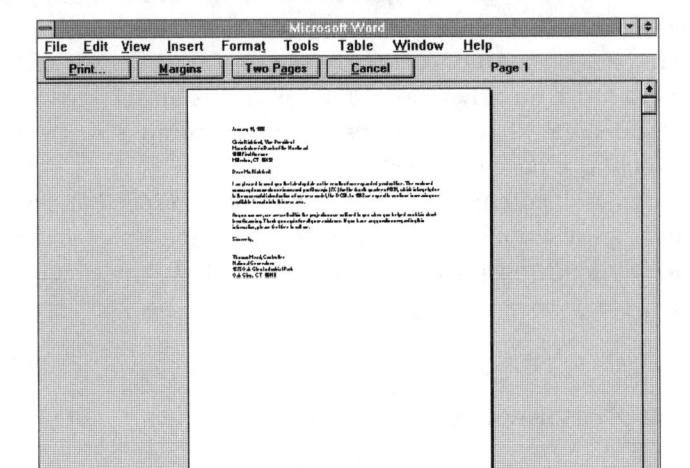

*Figure 12-1.*    Print Preview window

**Chapter 12:** *Formatting Sections* 137

If the paper you are using is larger than 8 1/2 x 11 inches, or if you are using a large screen with Windows, you may want to use the single-page display mode instead of the double-page display. This lets you see the text on the page more clearly. To switch, select the button labeled Two Pages or One Page.

## Zooming in Normal and Page Layout Modes

You can zoom in or out of the text in either normal or page layout mode. Zooming in lets you see exact placement of items near each other. It can also be used by people with visual disabilities to read the text they are editing more easily. Zooming out gives you a view similar to print preview mode but still allows you to edit your text. Note that you cannot zoom in print preview mode.

You can use the buttons on the toolbar to quickly zoom in and out of your document. The buttons are shown here:

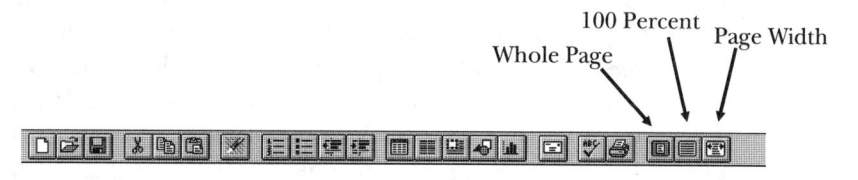

The Whole Page button shows you the whole page in your window, the 100 Percent button shows your document at the normal percentage, and the Page Width button shows the entire width of the page.

You can also zoom with the Zoom command in the View menu. The Zoom dialog box is shown here:

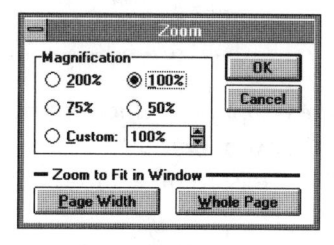

Choose a percentage from the Magnification choices or one of the buttons at the bottom of the dialog box. If there is a magnification you use often, enter it in the Custom choice; Word will remember it each time you give the Zoom command.

## Lesson 52: Introduction to Sections

So far you have learned how to format characters and paragraphs to improve their appearance. The third unit of formatting is the section, which allows you to specify the page formatting of your text when it is printed out. Page formatting, often called *page layout*, generally consists of setting the page margins and the position of the *headers* and *footers* (the text at the top and bottom of each page, such as the chapter name and the page number).

Most often you will use the same page layout throughout a section or document. Sometimes, however, you may use a few different page layouts. For example, the preface of a report may have different page number formatting than the main text. Word lets you change the page layout for each section.

If you want your document to be one long section, you do not need to do anything special. To split a document into two sections, put the insertion point where you want the section break and give the Break command from the Insert menu:

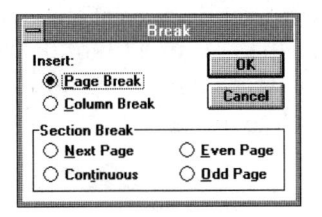

The four section break options, which specify where to start the the section, let you choose whether you want the section to continue on the same page as the previous section or to start on a different page. These choices are defined in Table 12-1.

If you are in normal mode (but not if you're in page layout mode), Word displays a double dotted line:

**Chapter 12:** *Formatting Sections* 139

```
┌─────────────────────── Document1 ───────────────────────┐
│ This is a section break:                                │
│ ▪                                                       │
│ |                                                       │
└─────────────────────────────────────────────────────────┘
```

You can delete the section mark with Undo, if you've just added it, or you can put the insertion point in front of the first text that follows the double dotted line and press the (BACKSPACE) key to remove it.

Many commands from the Format menu change the format for a section. The formatting characteristics of each section are kept in the section mark at the end of the section, just as paragraph characteristics are stored in the mark at the end of a paragraph. You can also bring up the Section command by double-clicking the section mark. A section mark holds the section formatting for the section preceding the mark.

There are five commands that affect the section formatting:

- Header/Footer in the View menu lets you enter headers and footers for the pages in the section.

- Page Numbers in the Insert menu enters a page number on the pages in the section.

- Columns from the Format menu specifies the number of columns of text in the section.

- Page Setup from the Format menu sets the margins and the description of the paper you are using.

*Table 12-1.*    *Choices for Beginning a New Section*

| Choice | Result |
| --- | --- |
| Next Page | Starts section on the next page |
| Continuous | Continues from previous section without break |
| Even Page | Starts section on the next even page |
| Odd Page | Starts section on the next odd page |

- Section Layout from the Format menu tells where the section starts and how pages are aligned with the top and bottom margins.

These commands are described throughout this chapter.

Figure 12-2 shows the beginning of a summary for a funding proposal. It is used to illustrate formatting throughout this chapter and the next one. You do not need to type the report into Word; however, you may want to type sections when trying out the examples.

## Lesson 53: Using Headers and Footers

Word allows you to put headers and footers at both the top and bottom of each page and to change their text as often as you want. Your headers and footers can be more than one paragraph, or they can be just a page number on the page.

The concept of odd and even pages is basic to many choices in section and document formatting, particularly in headers and footers. If you examine books and magazines, you find that they always begin on the right page. (For

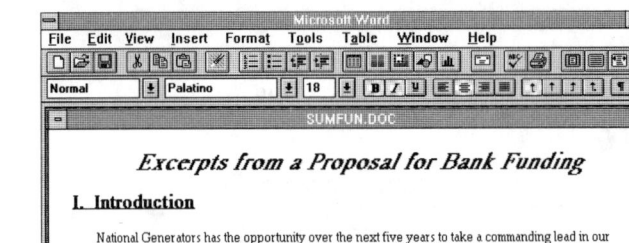

*Figure 12-2.*   *Funding proposal summary*

**Chapter 12:** *Formatting Sections*

example, look at the beginning of this book.) This means that all right-hand pages have odd numbers (1, 3, 5, and so on) and all left-hand pages have even numbers (2, 4, 6, and so on).

Knowing whether a page is odd or even often helps in formatting your pages, as you will see in this chapter. You need to specify a difference between even and odd pages only if your document will eventually be printed *back-to-back*, or *double-sided*, meaning on both sides of a piece of paper. If your document will be on only one side of the paper, you can ignore the difference between even and odd pages. If you use margin page numbers, you cannot differentiate between odd and even pages for the page number placement.

You can choose to have a header or footer appear on odd or even pages. You can also specify that the first page of a section have a unique header and footer. Depending on your requirements, you can have up to six different headers and footers in a document. Often, however, you will have similar or identical text at the top or bottom of even or odd pages or no text at all.

Creating headers and footers is fairly easy. First, decide what information you want to present; then decide which part of that information should be at the top and which part at the bottom of the page. If all you want is a page number, see the next lesson.

To open the header or footer dialog box, give the Header/Footer command in the View menu. The dialog box is shown in Figure 12-3. The two choices at the bottom left of the dialog box, Different First Page and Different Odd and Even Pages, determines how many headers and footers you have in the section.

If you are in normal mode, Word splits the screen and opens a pane into the header or footer you choose. If you are in page layout mode, Word moves

*Figure 12-3.*    *Header/Footer dialog box*

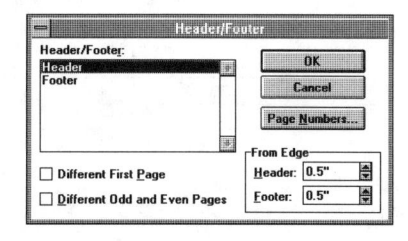

the insertion point into the header or footer you choose. In general, it is easier and more convenient to add and change headers and footers in normal mode.

Within the paragraphs that are headers and footers, you can use any character or paragraph formatting you want. For instance, you might have a chapter name in bold and the page number in italics. You can use paragraph formatting to line up the parts of the header or footer with the margins or to center them between the margins. Tab stops, described in Chapter 11, are especially helpful here.

Figure 12-4 shows a typical footer pane. The three icons at the left of the top of the pane let you enter the page number, date of printing, and time of printing, respectively, in your header or footer. For instance, to have a footer that says "Page " and the page number, type **Page**, type a space, and click the page number icon.

Header and footer panes also include a Link to Previous button. This feature can be confusing since it is sometimes not available. You use the Link to Previous button if you want to change the header or footer you are editing to be the same as the one in the previous section. When you create a new section in a document, Word automatically copies all the headers and footers to that new section, so this button does not normally need to be used. If the

*Figure 12-4.*     *Footer pane*

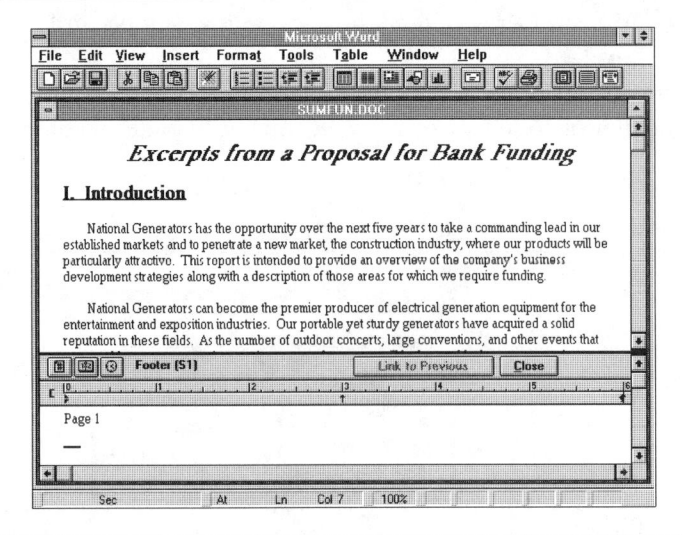

header that you are viewing is already the same as that in the previous section, the button is dimmed, indicating that you cannot select it.

As an example of headers and footers, you may want to show just the page number and chapter name on a page, with the chapter name centered at the top and the page number centered at the bottom. Figure 12-5 shows this format for the second page of the report in print preview mode.

You can specify the header and footer positions in the Header/Footer command, or you can modify them visually in print preview mode. In the Header/Footer command, enter values in the From Edge options to place the header and footer.

In the Print Preview window, you change the header and footer positions by dragging the header and footer text area around. Give the Print Preview command, select the Margins button, select the header or footer text area as shown in Figure 12-6, drag it up or down to the new position you want, and click in the gray area to reformat the document.

Next, decide if there should be a distinction between even and odd pages. If you will have different headers on even and odd pages, you should put the headers and footers on the right side of odd-numbered pages and the left side

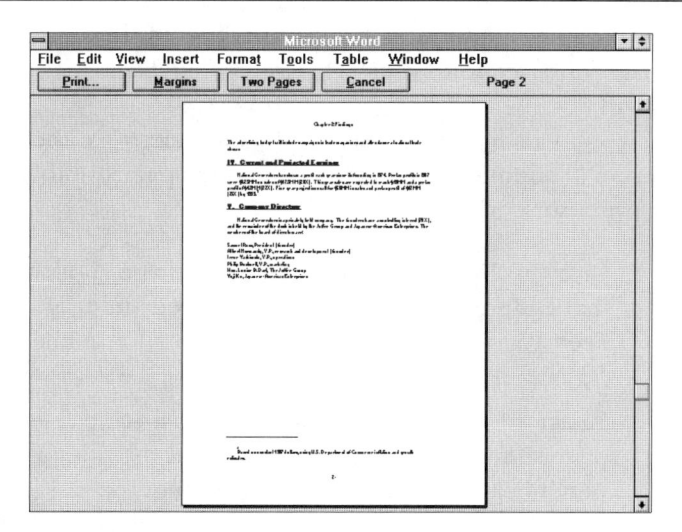

*Figure 12-5.*   *Header and footer centered on page*

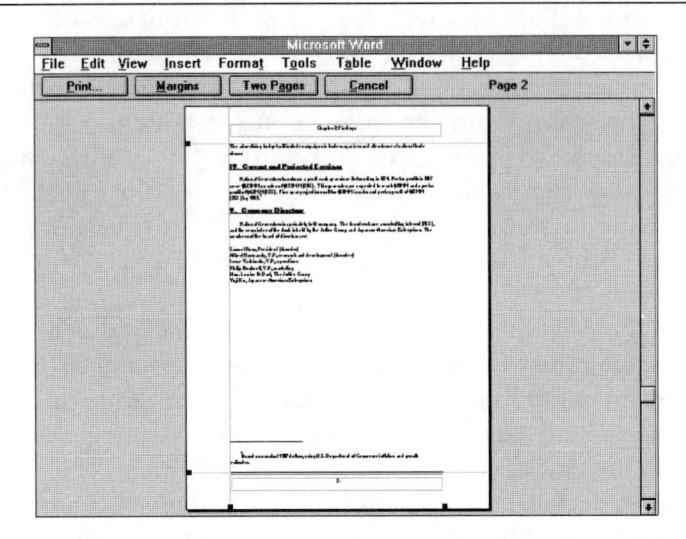

***Figure 12-6.*** *Header selected in print preview mode*

of even-numbered pages so that the information appears on the outside edge of the printed document. Again, look at a few books to see how this is done.

Finally, decide whether you want headers and footers on the first page of the section. You usually do not want a header since a header distracts the reader from the chapter title. If you want different headers and footers on the first page of a section, select Different First Page in the Header/Footer command.

Now you can actually create the header. Here are the steps for creating the header "Funding Proposal, page " and the page number on the right side of the page (for odd pages):

1. Give the Header/Footer command from the View menu. Be sure that Different First Page is not selected and that Different Odd and Even Pages is selected. The dialog box looks like the one in Figure 12-7.

2. Select the Odd Header choice in the list and select OK to open the pane shown in Figure 12-8. Note that the title of the pane tells you which header or footer you are editing.

**Chapter 12:** *Formatting Sections* 145

*Figure 12-7.*   *Header/Footer dialog box with Different Odd and Even Pages selected*

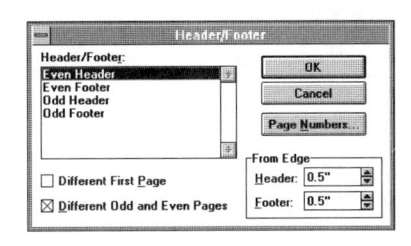

3. Add the text **Funding Proposal, page** followed by a space.
4. Click the page number icon at the left near the top of the Odd Header pane. Word inserts the page number in the heading. Don't worry that it shows an actual page number; the real page number will appear when you print.
5. Select the Close button of the Header pane.

Enter other headers and footers in the same way.

You can change the text of the headers and footers in page layout mode simply by editing the text. Remember that headers and footers are the same throughout a section, so changing the text of a header or footer on one page in page layout mode changes that text for the entire section as well.

*Figure 12-8.*   *Odd Header pane*

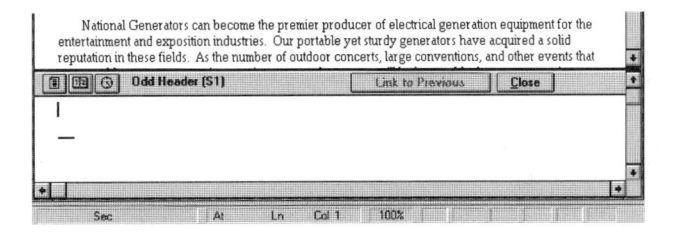

## Lesson 54: Page Numbering

If all you want in the header or footer of a section is a page number, you can give the Page Numbers command from the Insert menu. This creates a header or footer containing just the page number. If you followed the directions in the previous lesson, you do not need to use this command.

The Page Numbers dialog box looks like this:

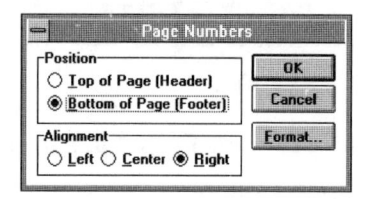

As you can see, your two choices in the Position section will create a header or a footer. The choices in the Alignment section tell Word what type of paragraph formatting to use when it creates the header or footer.

Whether you used the Header/Footer command or the Page Numbers command, you can modify the way page numbers appear in your document. Give the Header/Footer command and select the Page Numbers button in that dialog box. You see the following:

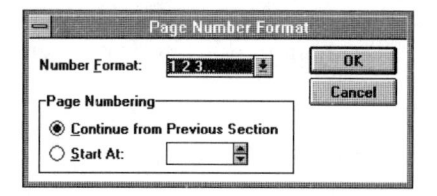

Page numbering can start at 1 in each section or at the number after the last page of the previous section. If you choose the Continue from Previous Section option, Word continues numbering from the previous section in the file; if this is the first section, it starts at 1. If you choose Start At and fill in a number, it will start there.

You can use this option to restart the page numbering to 1 in a book with two numbering sequences. For example, this book has front matter numbered with lowercase Roman numerals. The first page of the first chapter starts again at 1. If this were a Word document, the front matter would be a different section from Chapter 1.

You can also choose a format for page numbers. This is extremely useful when you submit articles and reports for publication because many publishers have guidelines about the format of page numbers. Table 12-2 shows the formats for the page numbers that are available on Word.

## Lesson 55: Creating Text with Newspaper Columns

You can use Word to print out newsletters and other material formatted with two or more columns on a page. These columns are called *newspaper columns* since they snake on the page as in newspapers. When you use more than one column, Word adjusts whatever formatting commands you have given so that they work within the columns.

It is usually convenient to edit in page layout mode if you are editing a section or document that has two or more columns and many headings. Using this mode lets you see if a heading is falling near the bottom of a column and how the columns balance out.

The Columns command in the Format menu has the choices for producing multicolumn text. Figure 12-9 shows the dialog box. Number of Columns is the number of columns you want and Space Between is the amount of white space between two columns. You can also specify whether you want a line between the columns.

*Table 12-2.    Page Number Formats*

| Format | Choice |
| --- | --- |
| Numeric | 1 2 3 |
| Roman (upper) | I II III |
| Roman (lower) | i ii iii |
| Alphabetic (upper) | A B C |
| Alphabetic (lower) | a b c |

***Figure 12-9.***   *Columns dialog box*

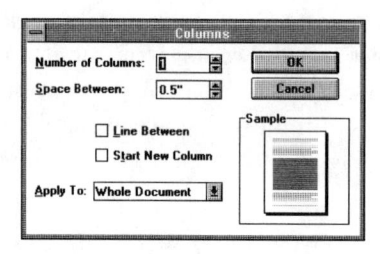

The Start New Column option tells Word to insert a column break at the insertion point when you execute the command. You can also insert a column break at any time with the Break command from the Insert menu.

Word will calculate the column widths. Columns are always the same width within a section. The width of the column is based on the margins of the section and the space between the columns.

Remember that you will not see the multiple columns on the screen in normal mode; you will see them only in page layout or print preview mode.

You can also change the number of columns from the toolbar. Select the Text Columns button:

Drag the mouse pointer to the right until you have chosen the number of columns you want.

Splitting a page into columns greatly reduces the number of words per line, so you may want to format the paragraphs as left aligned rather than as justified unless you are using a small font. Justifying narrow columns usually results in a great deal of white space between words. For example, compare the paragraphs shown in Figure 12-10.

**Chapter 12:** *Formatting Sections*  149

***Figure 12-10.***   *Justification in the left column leaves too much white space between words*

<pre>
National   Generators     National Generators
has   the   opportunity   has the opportunity
over  the   next  five    over the next five
years  to    take   a     years to take a
commanding  lead  in      commanding lead in
our         established   our established
markets     and     to    markets and to
penetrate    a    new     penetrate a new
market,           the     market, the
construction industry,    construction industry,
where  our  products      where our products
will  be  particularly    will be particularly
attractive.               attractive.
</pre>

You will also want to use as many nonrequired hyphens as possible to make the lines more even. Automatic hyphenation is described more fully in Chapter 19.

Even though multicolumn text is not often used in business documents, you may find that it enhances the appearance of some reports.

## Lesson 56: Numbering Lines in Your Document

The legal profession often requires that line numbers be printed on documents such as pleadings and depositions. One method is to use forms with line numbers already printed on them. However, this limits the kind of text you can include, and it is difficult to line up the text and the paper in many printers. For example, footnotes (which are common in pleadings) do not line up with the numbers on preprinted forms. You can only see the line numbers in print preview mode and when you print your document.

Word's line-numbering capability enables lawyers (and anyone else who requires numbered lines) to edit and print documents easily. Line numbers appear only on the printed document and in print preview mode (not in normal or page layout mode).

To turn on line numbering, simply select the Line Numbers button in the Section Layout command from the Format menu. This brings up the following dialog box:

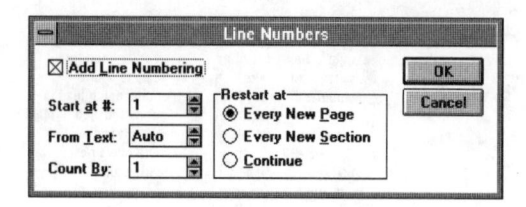

[Line Numbers dialog box showing: Add Line Numbering checkbox (checked), Start at #: 1, From Text: Auto, Count By: 1, Restart at: Every New Page (selected), Every New Section, Continue, with OK and Cancel buttons]

Select the Add Line Numbering option to start numbering.

You can specify what number to start at, how far from the text the numbers should appear, and whether to show every line number or only a few. For example, if you enter **5** for Count By, Word only prints every fifth line number.

The choices for the Restart at option tell Word how often to start the numbers. Generally, you want the numbering on each page to begin with 1, so you should select Every New Page. If, instead, you want the lines of your document numbered from beginning to end, choose Every New Section (for numbering in each section) or Continue (for the whole document).

## Lesson 57: Positioning with Frames

In a normal Word document, each paragraph appears on the page after the one that is before it. However, there are many times when you want a paragraph or a group of paragraphs to appear in a particular spot on the page and want other paragraphs to flow around this. That is, you want to specify the position for the paragraph (such as "in the middle of the page, 3 inches from the left margin and 4 inches from the top margin" or "at the bottom of this column"). To do this in Word, you insert a *frame* on your page and fill it with text, pictures, and so on. You can then move the frame to a desired location or specify the location exactly by using dialog boxes.

Frames are often used to add interesting layout elements, such as pictures or excerpts from your text. Figure 12-11 shows how a text excerpt in a two-column document can make the page look more interesting.

**Chapter 12:** *Formatting Sections* 151

Few people use frames in their daily work. Frames are mostly used by people doing desktop publishing or preparing highly designed documents such as sales brochures. Word's advanced framing features can match those of expensive desktop publishing programs such as Aldus PageMaker. These features are beyond the scope of this book but are covered briefly here so you can see their power in case you have need for them in the future.

You create a frame on a page by clicking the Insert Frame button in the toolbar:

You can also create a frame by giving the Frame command from the Insert menu. When you start a frame, Word prompts you at the bottom of the screen to draw the frame where you want it. Don't be concerned about the exact position or size of the frame because they are easy to change. Click one corner of the location you want and drag to the diagonally opposite corner. Word makes room for the frame by moving your text around.

*Figure 12-11.*    *Two-column document with frame added*

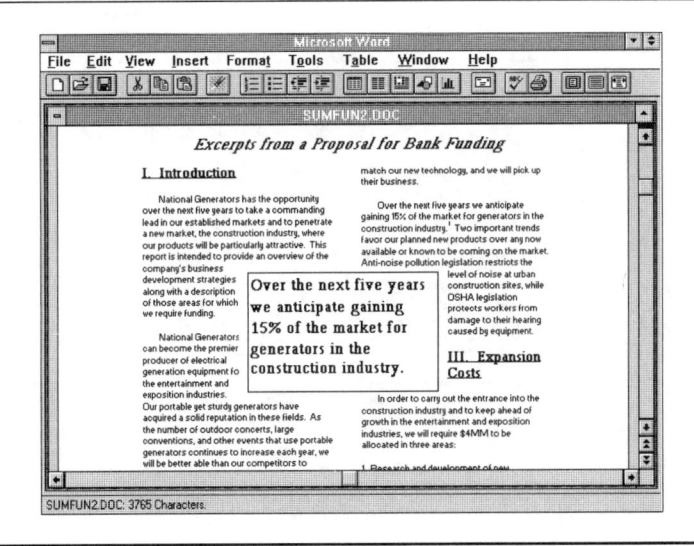

Working with frames is best done in page layout view since that is the view where you can move and resize frames. For this lesson, give the Page Layout command in the View menu if you are not already in page layout view.

As an example, assume that you want to add a frame that will contain a picture to your SAMPLE1 letter. (Of course, it is unlikely that you would actually want to do this since pictures in letters almost always are placed after the text that describes them.) Open the SAMPLE1 letter and click the Insert Frame button in the toolbar. Then click near the middle of the first line of the first paragraph and drag down and to the right. Figure 12-12 shows the result.

To position a frame and describe how the text will move around it, give the Frame command from the Format menu to display the Frame dialog box, shown in Figure 12-13.

When you define a frame's position, you specify both the horizontal and vertical positions. These measurements can be relative to the margin or to the edge of the page; the horizontal position can also be relative to the column. The choices in the Frame dialog box for horizontal position are Left, Center, Right, Inside, and Outside. Inside and Outside refer to even- and odd-numbered pages. If you choose Left, Right, Inside, or Outside and set the Relative

*Figure 12-12.*   *Frame inserted in SAMPLE1 letter*

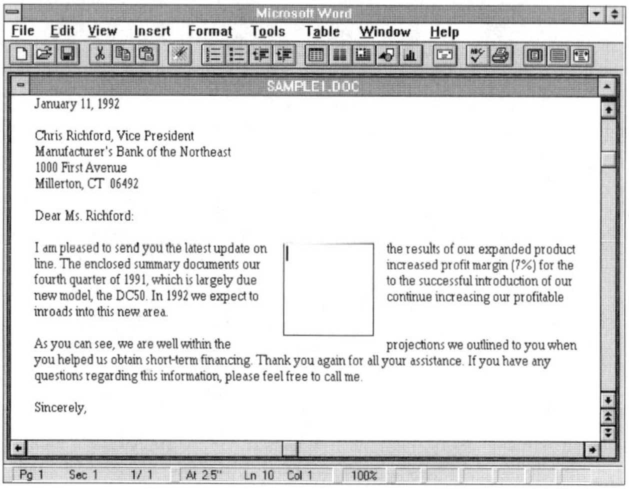

**Chapter 12:** *Formatting Sections* 153

To choice to Page, Word can position the object outside of the margins. The choices for vertical position are Top, Center, and Bottom. For both the vertical and horizontal choices, you can also type a measurement.

For example, to center a picture in the bottom of the text area, you could specify a horizontal position of "centered" relative to the margins and a vertical position of "bottom" relative to the margin. You can also specify a measurement for the position, such as "3.25 inches from the left margin" or "2 inches from the top margin".

You can also specify the Move with Text option for vertical positioning. This tells Word to keep the frame with the paragraph it is next to when you view it in normal mode. This is useful for positioning headings with text.

The Text Wrapping choice tells how the text near the frame will appear. If you want the text to move around the frame, choose Around; otherwise, choose None. You can also set the size of the frame from the Frame dialog box. To change the size of the frame without using the Frame command, simply select the frame and drag one of the handles, as you learned for graphics in Chapter 7.

To experiment with positioning text in frames, add text to the frame in the SAMPLE1 document. Put the insertion point in the frame, and then type the sentence **This is a large sentence in a movable frame.** Select the text and make it larger with the Character command from the Format menu. Your screen should now look somewhat like the one in Figure 12-14.

As you can see, frames are a very powerful feature if you need to position text or graphics exactly in your next instead of having them flow in a normal

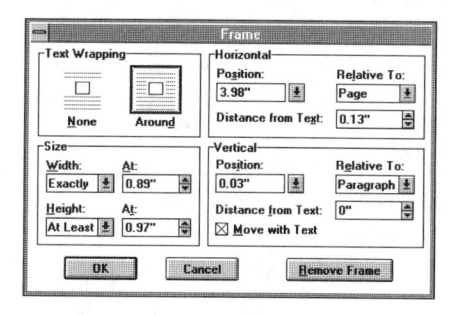

*Figure 12-13.*    *Frame dialog box*

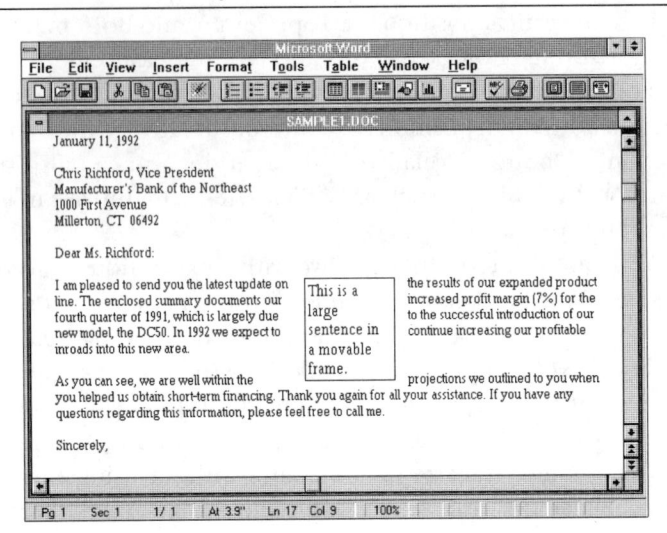

*Figure 12-14.*     *Text added to frame*

fashion. Formatting frames is very much like formatting other items in Word, so you should feel free to experiment with them.

## Lesson 58: Setting Margins and Paper Size

Use the Page Setup command from the Format menu to specify the page margins and other options that affect the look of your sections. Figure 12-15 shows the Page Setup dialog box for margins. Note that there are three choices at the top, and the first dialog box you see is for the Margins choice.

Some users get confused between margins and indents. Page margins are measured from the edge of the paper; paragraph indents are measured from the left and right page margins. Page margins are set in the Document command for the entire document, while paragraph indents are set by the Paragraph command for each paragraph.

If you are going to bind the document, you may want to set a gutter width after selecting Different Odd and Even Pages in the Header/Footer com-

**Chapter 12:** *Formatting Sections* 155

*Figure 12-15.*   Page Setup dialog box for margins

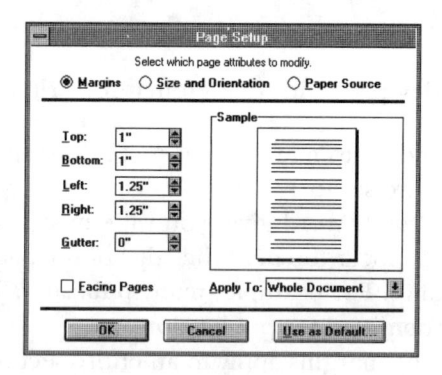

mand. The *gutter* is the center space between two pages of a book that is not used in printing; in this case, it is the amount of space that is used in binding the document. Since binding a document or punching holes takes up a certain amount of space from the left side of odd-numbered pages and the right side of even-numbered pages, Word allows you to stretch the margins, alternating between left and right pages. Set the gutter width to the amount that would be lost in binding. When your pages are printed and bound, the text will not run into the gutter and will thus be easier to read. Note that the margins on this book are wider on the inside of each page, since the binding steals a bit of paper width.

If the difference between inside and outside margins and gutters is confusing, select the Facing Pages button in the Page Setup dialog box. The choices in the Margins area now change to the following:

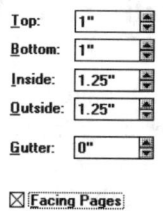

Note that you can now directly specify just the inside and outside margins without worrying about even and odd pages.

Word determines the line length of a page in this way:

line length = page width − (left margin + right margin + gutter)

The top and bottom margins are set by default to 1 inch, and the left and right margins are set to 1.25 inches. These four values are the ones you are most likely to reset. Word gives you wide margins so that your headers and footers do not appear too near the edge of the page. You may, however, need different settings. For example, many publishers insist on a 1.5-inch border around text submitted for publication.

In Word, the margins apply to an entire section. You can use the choices in the Apply To drop-down list in the Page Setup dialog box to specify where you want them applied. If you choose Whole Document, Word changes the margins in all the other sections. The Selected Text option causes Word to add section breaks before and after the text and apply those margins just in the new section.

If you select the Size and Orientation choice at the top of the Page Setup dialog box, the dialog box changes to that in Figure 12-16. This dialog box lets you change the paper size and the orientation of the paper. The Orientation choice specifies how you have loaded the paper into the printer: Portrait (the normal fashion) or Landscape. (These two choices are sometimes known as tall and wide, respectively.) You can remember the difference between these two by thinking of fine art paintings: portraits are tall and narrow and your eyes move from top to bottom, while landscapes are short and wide and your eyes move from left to right.

## Lesson 59: Repaginating and Page Breaks

Word keeps track of each page break in your document in normal mode by default. This makes the program run a little more slowly than if it didn't do this, but it is usually not noticeable. To turn off automatic repagination, use the Options command in the Tools menu, choosing the General choices. In page layout mode, Word always repaginates your document as you edit. If

**Chapter 12:** *Formatting Sections* 157

***Figure 12-16.*** *Page Setup dialog box for size and orientation*

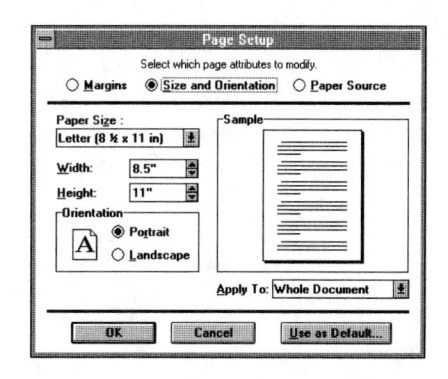

you don't have Word automatically repaginate and you want to cause Word to update all the pagination and show where the page breaks fall, use the Repaginate Now command from the Tools menu.

Word puts a line of widely spaced dots across the page at the places where page breaks occur:

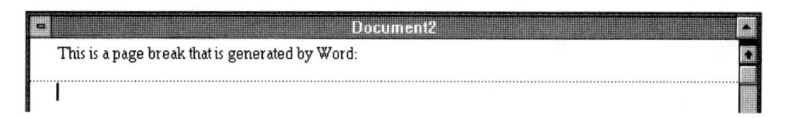

To force Word to start a new page, set the insertion point at the desired location and give the Page Break command from the Insert menu, or press (CTRL)-(ENTER). If you are in normal mode, Word prints a line of tightly spaced dots across the screen to indicate the forced page break:

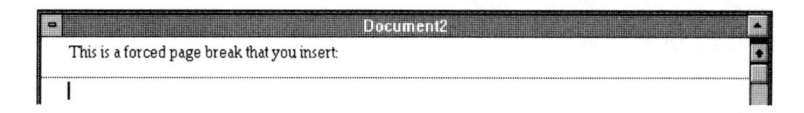

If you want to get rid of a page break, go past it and use the (BACKSPACE) key to delete it.

If you want to be sure that a particular paragraph appears at the top of a page, you can format the paragraph to cause a page break instead of inserting a forced page break. To do this, select the paragraph, give the Paragraph command, and select Page Break Before in the Pagination choices.

If you want to move from page to page, you can use the Go To command from the Edit menu. You can also open the Go To dialog box by double-clicking the page number in the lower-left corner of the document window. The Go To dialog box looks like this:

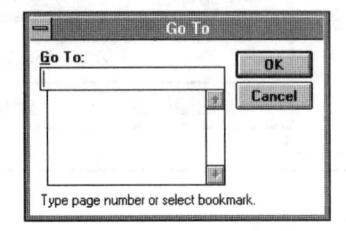

Enter a page number, and Word moves the selection indicator to the beginning of that page. If your document has more than one section, you can also use the Go To command to go to a particular page in a particular section. For example, to go to page 7 of the third section, type **7S3** in the Go To dialog box.

## Review

Add a header and footer to the MAGAZINE file. Put the page number in the right corner of the header and a description of the article in the right corner of the footer.

Make the file two columns and view the results in normal and page layout modes. In print view mode, change the page number in the header to the middle of the page.

Change the margins to be narrower by .5 inch in each direction. Note how that changes the document in normal and page layout mode.

# 13

# Using Styles to Simplify Formatting

Up to this point you have had to specify the formatting characteristics for each paragraph in your text. Microsoft Word also allows you to define a set of *styles* for your documents that is automatically used when you format. When you use styles instead of formatting each paragraph, you specify the style for each type of paragraph (such as a normal paragraph or a section heading), and Word formats the paragraph by finding the corresponding style in the document's set of style characteristics in the document's *style sheet*—the collection of styles.

Word is one of the few word processors offering formatting styles, so even if you are familiar with many other word processing packages, this concept may be unfamiliar to you. In recent years, advanced desktop publishing packages have adopted styles as the preferred method for formatting.

A style sheet can be thought of as a formatting guide that contains a list of types of paragraphs and the formats associated with them. For example, to format a normal paragraph in your text, your instructions might be "justified text, indent the first line 1/2 inch, and skip a line before the paragraph."

Instead of having to format each paragraph this way when you enter or edit the text, you simply tell Word that you are entering a normal paragraph. Word looks up the formatting for your normal paragraph in the style sheet and applies it to the paragraph.

Using styles in Word consists of two steps. First, you must create the style sheet by defining the types of styles you want. To do this, you use the Style command from the Format menu. In addition to defining styles, you can use the many predefined styles that come with Word. After you design the styles, you format your document by labeling its elements with styles. As you will see, there are many ways to specify the styles used in your documents. Word also lets you copy style sheets from document to document easily.

One of the excellent features of formatting with styles is that you can have many different style sheets in different documents that use the same style elements but format them differently. Thus, a normal paragraph in one style sheet might be double spaced and ragged right, but in another it might be single spaced and justified. You might use the first style sheet to print rough drafts so you can correct mistakes easily and then use the second style sheet to print your final document.

Word lets you specify the types of styles you want and allows you to modify and add styles easily; you do not need to stick to predefined styles. You might have styles for normal paragraphs, long quotations, running heads, section headings, and so on.

Using styles does not prevent you from using direct formatting but you will probably find that using styles almost exclusively makes writing and printing easier. You can, however, use some direct formatting when it is faster or when you are sure you will not want to change the format.

A big advantage of styles is that, if you have used only styles and want to change the format of one type of paragraph in all of your different documents, you do not need to change any of them individually with direct formatting—simply change your style sheets. Your new formatting is automatically used.

For example, you may have a style called Chapter Heading that corresponds to boldface, 24-point, centered text. If you later want all the chapter headings to be underlined and left aligned, you only need to change the style; you do not need to search through all of your files for the chapter headings.

If you want to begin using styles but do not yet want to create your own styles, you can use the predefined styles supplied by Microsoft. These appear in the Style command along with your own styles. Of course, you can modify the attributes of these predefined styles if you wish.

If you want to convert a directly formatted document to styles, you should first unformat the entire document. To unformat a document, select the entire document by pressing (CTRL) and clicking in the selection bar at the left of the document, press (CTRL)-(Q) to make all paragraphs normal, and then press (CTRL)-(SPACEBAR) to remove all character formatting.

The next lesson shows you how to create two styles from scratch and how to specify your own style elements. The lessons after that show how to work with styles in your documents.

## Lesson 60: Creating a Style Sheet

Now that you understand the concept behind style sheets, the next step is to add a style to a document's style sheet with which you can experiment. In addition, you will modify some of the predefined styles.

The rest of this chapter uses the report shown in Chapter 12 for its examples. You may want to enter the first section heading and the first few paragraphs of the report so you can try out examples as they are presented. When you enter the text, be sure not to use any direct formatting commands. The top of the text is shown in Figure 13-1.

To start making styles, give the Style command from the Format menu. In this small dialog box, select the Define button to see all the options, which are shown in Figure 13-2.

You will create one style for this sample sheet for the report title. You will also modify two other styles: the Heading 1 style used for the section headings and the Normal style used for all regular text paragraphs.

There are two ways to define a style:

- Give a paragraph the formatting you want, and then give the Style command, enter the name of the style, and select OK.

- Start with an unformatted paragraph, give the Style command, give the formatting commands that define the style by using the buttons in the Change Formatting area, and select Apply.

162  Part II: *Using Word to Format*

*Figure 13-1.*   Top of report with formats removed

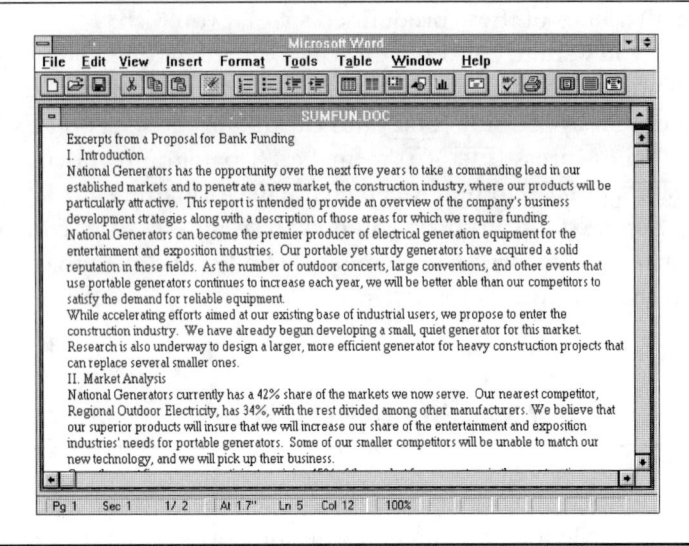

To begin, select the title paragraph. This is currently in Normal style (as is everything in a file before you start giving style commands).

*Figure 13-2.*   Style dialog box

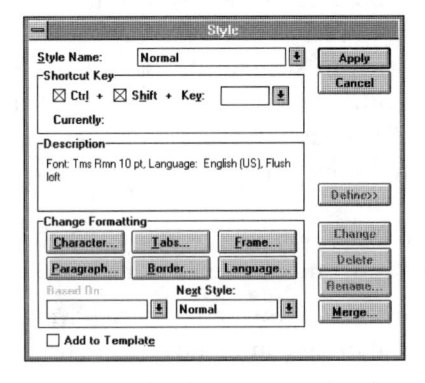

**Chapter 13:**  *Using Styles to Simplify Formatting* 163

The ribbon shows what style is used on any paragraph:

[ribbon: Normal | Tms Rmn | 10 | B I U | align buttons | indent buttons ]

Add some direct formatting to this paragraph so you can see how Word learns formatting from text. Make the characters 18 point, bold, italic, and centered, with one line after. The top of your document now looks like this:

[window: SUMFUN.DOC — *Excerpts from a Proposal for Bank Funding* — I. Introduction]

Now give the Style command. Enter the new style's name in the box labeled Style Name. For this example, type **Title** and select the Define button. Note that the character and paragraph formatting for this paragraph are shown in the Description (by example) box:

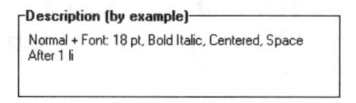

[Description (by example)
Normal + Font: 18 pt, Bold Italic, Centered, Space After 1 li]

Select the Add button, and the new style is defined.

Next, you want to modify the predefined style called heading 1 so you can use it on the headings in the report. Select the heading 1 name in the Style Name drop-down list at the top of the dialog box; the box now looks like the one in Figure 13-3.

In the case of the headings, you want them to be in Tms Rmn font, bold, underlined, 14 point, and kept with the next paragraph. Note that this predefined style already comes with some formatting, such as "Bold Underline", and "Space Before 1 li".

To change the formatting to what you want, you can use the Character and Paragraph buttons in the dialog box, just as if you were using direct formatting. These buttons bring up dialog boxes that look identical to the ones for the commands from the Format menu. When you are finished changing the formats for this style, select the Change button and then the Yes button.

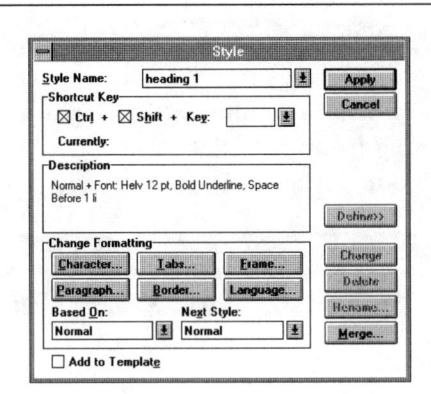

***Figure 13-3.*** *Style dialog box with heading 1 selected*

Next, change the style for normal paragraphs. Select Normal from the list of styles, select the Paragraph button, and specify 12 points before and justified. Again, select the Change button.

You have now added a new style and changed the formatting in two predefined styles. Select Cancel to close the Style dialog box. Don't worry—this is one place where clicking Cancel does not lose the work you have done in the dialog box. Clicking Apply would apply the last style you edited to the current selection, which is *not* what you want to do right now.

## Lesson 61: Using Styles in Your Documents

Now that you have a style sheet, you can start applying styles to your documents. When you use Word, you can either set up a style sheet and enter the styles as you type new text or you can convert a directly formatted document to styles.

You can give text a style by selecting the text and selecting the style from the drop-down list in the ribbon. You can also select the list by pressing CTRL-S. This list is a drop-down list of all the styles created for your document. The list looks like this:

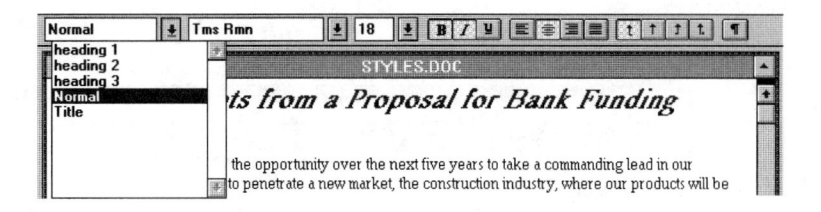

**Chapter 13:** *Using Styles to Simplify Formatting* 165

For example, select any part of the first section heading, "I. Introduction". Select heading 1 from the ribbon to indicate that this is a heading. The result is shown in Figure 13-4. Notice that the paragraph is now formatted properly and that "heading 1" now appears in the style drop-down list. Now select any part of the document title, drop down the style list, and choose the Title style. You can continue adding styles to the rest of the document.

To see the power of style sheets, suppose you decide to have the normal paragraphs justified instead of with left-aligned formatting. Give the Style command, select the Define button, select Normal from the list, select the Paragraph button, change the formatting to justified, select Apply, and select Cancel. As soon as you return to editing, all your normal paragraphs are changed to the new style, as shown in Figure 13-5.

*Figure 13-4.*   Section heading with formatting

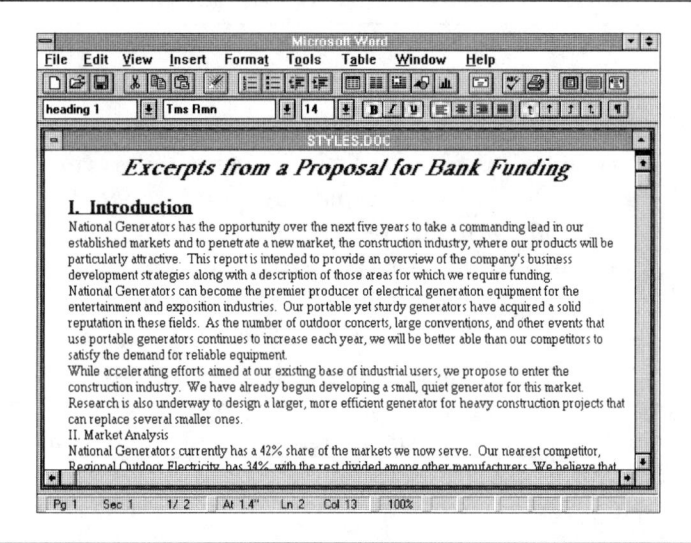

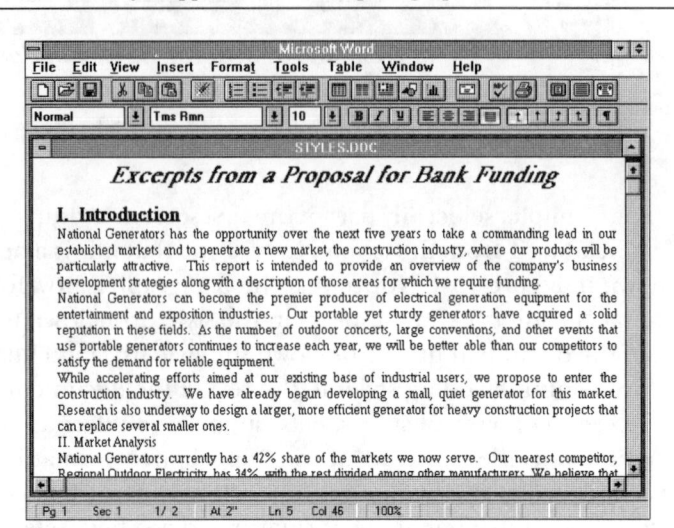

***Figure 13-5.*** *New style applied to normal paragraphs*

## Lesson 62: Working with Style Sheets

### Styles in Templates

A style sheet is saved as part of a template, and you may want to create your own master style sheet in a template. A *master style sheet* would hold all the style definitions you normally use. You can create a file, perhaps called MASTER.DOT, and read the styles from that master into your document when you want to be sure that the definitions in the document match the master.

The process of merging styles is fairly easy. Give the Style command and click Define; then, while the Style dialog box is open, select the Merge button. Select the template that has your master style sheet and select Open, and the styles from the master are merged in your current document. In the merging process, Word takes three actions:

- If the same style name exists in the master and the target document, the document's formatting for that style name is changed to the master's format.
- If the master has a style that does not exist in the document, that style is added.
- Any styles in the document that are not in the master are left as they are.

This method for keeping style sheets opens up new areas for using styles. For example, it is usually most convenient to edit text on the screen when it is single spaced (so that more lines fit on the screen) but more convenient to edit it on paper when it is double spaced (so you can write additions or corrections between the lines). You can keep a master document that has its Normal paragraph formatted for double-spacing. When you merge this master file's style sheet into a single-spaced document, it causes all the Normal paragraphs to be double spaced. You can then print the document and close it without saving the changes (in this case, the double-spacing).

You can use the template feature, described at the end of this chapter, to assure that new documents use the master styles. Put the styles you want new documents to have (such as the styles from your master style sheet) in the template you use to open new documents. New documents will use them automatically.

## Basing Styles on Other Styles

You may have noticed that the description box in the Styles dialog box starts out with "Normal +" for each predefined style. This, plus the Based On choice near the bottom of the dialog box, are part of an advanced style feature that lets one style be affected by another. By default, all predefined styles are based on the Normal style.

To see this, assume that a style called A is based on a style called B. The formatting for A is "B + Bold", and the formatting for B is "Normal + Centered". This means that A is like Normal but bold and centered. If you now change the formatting for B to be "Normal + Justified", A automatically changes to justified alignment as well. This is because A is still "B + Bold", so A changes to whatever B is and adds bold.

The power of this feature is that since everything is based on Normal, you can change one formatting feature of the Normal setting and have that change be reflected in all other formats as well. For instance, assume that you use the Tms Rmn font throughout a document and you decide you want to use Helv instead. You need only change the font for the Normal style, and all styles that are based on Normal also change to Helv.

A formatting characteristic in a style based on another style does not change if the changed style has the same characteristic. For example, if your headings are based on Normal but they use the Courier font and you change the font for the Normal style to Helv, the fonts in the heading styles stay in Courier. This means that you can safely change the formatting of your "base" styles without having to respecify all the formatting for styles based on them.

To specify which style you want to base another style on, first select the style you are changing, and then choose the style it is based on in the Based On drop-down box. The formatting shown changes to reflect the differences between the style and the style it is based on, instead of the differences between it and the Normal style.

## Lesson 63: Getting the Most from Style Sheets

Style sheets can make formatting all your documents, from letters to entire books, a much easier task. Even for large reports it is unlikely that your style sheet will contain more than 15 styles, and only 5 or so will probably be used with any frequency. If you want, you can remove styles in a style sheet by using the Delete button in the Styles dialog box.

You will find that using style sheets has many advantages over direct formatting, and in the few places where styles are not appropriate, you can still format directly. Once you start thinking in terms of style elements ("this is a heading," "this is a normal paragraph," and so on), you will find that your printed documents are much clearer because they are presented in a more organized manner.

Copying styles from one piece of text to another is identical to copying other paragraph formats. You can convert files that use direct formatting to style sheet formatting by applying a style to one paragraph and then copying that style to all other paragraphs to which it applies. You can also search for styles with the Find command.

If you edit with the ribbon showing, you can use the Style box at the left side of the ruler for more than just choosing styles. If you have selected a paragraph that already has formatting on it and select a style from the list, Word lets you redefine the formatting for that style to be the formatting in the paragraph.

To print your style sheet, give the Print command and choose Styles from the Print drop-down list in the dialog box. Word prints each style and its elements.

## Lesson 64: Using Document Templates

Most business letters have the same general format. The letterhead in business stationery is always in approximately the same place. The date is usually in the same place and, although the position of these elements changes from letter to letter, the closing name and address are the same. It would be nice to have a way of placing all that information in every new letter you start and a way to create similar base documents for memos, reports, and so on.

Word's document templates fulfill those needs and more. A document template is a standardized document you can create that contains the following elements:

- Text you want the document to start and end with (such as the date, your name and address, and the closing text for letters)
- A style sheet
- A glossary
- Macros
- Keyboard equivalents
- Menu assignments
- Toolbar customization

When you create a new document, you choose the template you want for that document in the Use Template section of the New command. Up to now, you have been choosing NORMAL.DOT, the default template. However, you can choose any template you want. After you create a standard template for letters, for example, you will choose that template in the New dialog box whenever you begin a new letter.

To create a template, you use the File Save As command. Choose Document Template from the Save File as Type drop-down list. Whatever you have in the document window will be saved as the common text for the template. Your current styles, glossary entries, macros, keyboard equivalents, menu assignments, and toolbar changes are saved as well.

You can also create a template by modifying an existing one. Give the Open command, select Document Templates in the List Files of Type drop-down list. You now see a list of only the templates. Choose one, open it, modify it as you wish, give the File Save As command, and enter a new name for the template.

Templates have many uses. For example, Figure 13-6 shows a template for the minutes of a regular meeting. The template also has a style sheet with formats for items commonly included in the minutes, such as action items and

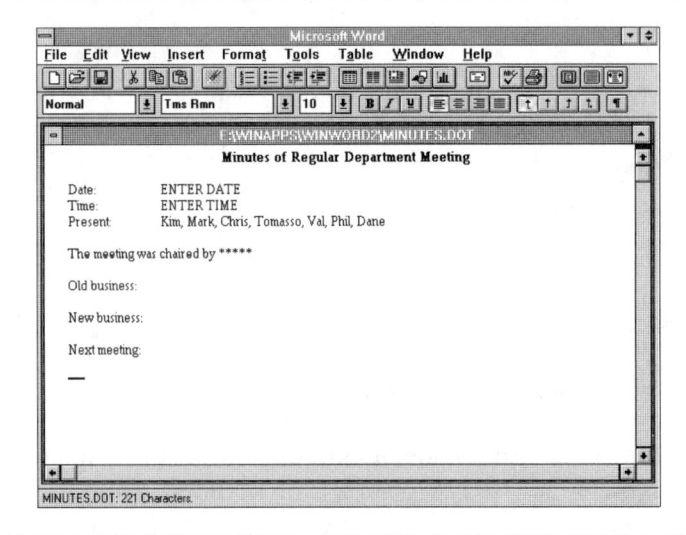

*Figure 13-6.*   Template for meeting minutes

open questions. Since the same people come to the meeting each week, their names are kept in the template's glossary as well.

## Review

Look in books and magazines and think about how they might use styles for the various types of paragraphs such as headings, subheads, and normal paragraphs.

Think about the types of documents you use that could benefit from a template. If you create similar documents, determine which parts of those documents could be stored in the template. Also think about what styles and glossary entries should be stored in the template.

# III

## Other Word Features

# III

# 14

# Creating Form Letters

When Word first appeared, only a few word processing programs included features that let you create form letters from a file of names and addresses. This feature is sometimes referred to as *mail merge*. Today, many programs give you this capability in a limited fashion. The merge feature in Word is more sophisticated than in other word processing programs and produces letters that look much more personalized.

The basic concept behind the merge feature is fairly simple. Your *main document* contains the letter you want to send to many people, with special placeholders (*fields*) for the parts that change from letter to letter (like the recipient's name and address). Your *data file* contains the names of the fields and the information that Word puts into the fields in the main document. All the information for each letter is in one paragraph or one row of cells (called a *record*) of the data file. (You will see more uses for fields in Chapter 22.)

The main document contains the text that is the same in each letter, while the data file contains the text that is different from letter to letter. Both files are regular Word documents that you can edit and format by using the methods you have learned so far.

Instructions in your main document tell Word which file is to be the data file. You create the main document with Word. You can create the data file with Word, a database management system like Paradox or dBase, or a spreadsheet program like Excel. The format of the data file is very straightforward; it is not difficult at all to set up data files to go with your main documents.

When you print your file with the Print Merge command from the File menu, Word reads the first record from the data file, substitutes the field information for the field names in your main document, formats your letter, prints it, then reads the next record from the data file, and so on.

You can include fields in the middle of a paragraph, and Word formats the paragraph with the new information in it. Thus, if you have a field called "Amount" and that field in one record of your data file is equal to 1533, Word properly reformats a paragraph that contains the sentence "You still owe us $1533, which we would like you to send immediately."

You assign a name to each field consisting of up to 253 letters, such as "Amount" or "LastPayment". Note that there is no space in the name "LastPayment"; all field names must be one word. You use the field name in both the main document and the data file, and the names must match. However, the order in which the field names are used in the main document does not need to match the order in which the field names appear in the data file. In fact, you can use the data assigned to a field many times in your main document.

## Lesson 65: Creating the Main Document and Data File

You enter the body of your main document just as you normally enter text with Word. For now, don't enter any field names; Word helps you with that after you create the data file. Instead, type **XX** where the fields would go.

Type the example in Figure 14-1, which is a main document that could be used to inform customers of balances due. Note the "XX" where the field names from the data document will be put later. Save this file as BALANCE1.

You can create the data file manually, but it is much easier to use the Print Merge feature. The Print Merge command, given from the File menu, creates a new file that has a table in the exact format needed for merging. Tables are

**Chapter 14:** *Creating Form Letters* 177

---

*Figure 14-1.* BALANCE1 text

---

August 15, 1992

XX
XX
XX
XX, XX XX

Dear XX:

Our records show that your outstanding balance is $XX, and that we have not received any payment from you since XX. If there is a disagreement about this amount, please feel free to call us about it.

Sincerely,

Sharon Myers
National Manufacturing

---

discussed in Chapter 15, but you can use them here without knowing much about them.

Before giving the Print Merge command, be sure that the BALANCE1 file is open and that the insertion point is at the beginning of the main document. This is important because the Print Merge command has to put information about your data file there.

For this example, you need the following fields to match the BALANCE1 letter:

Company
Name
Address
City
State
Zip
Amount
LastPayment

It doesn't matter whether you use upper- or lowercase letters.

***Figure 14-2.***   *Print Merge dialog box*

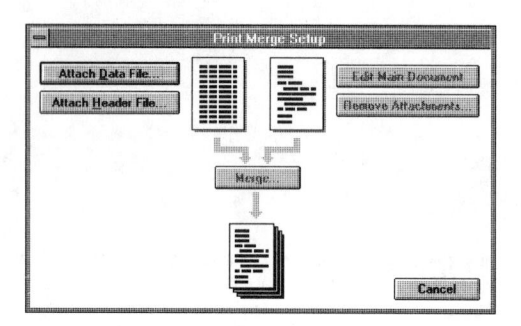

When you give the Print Merge command from the File menu, you see the dialog box shown in Figure 14-2. Select the Attach Data File button to work with the data file. This displays the dialog box shown in Figure 14-3. Select the Create Data File button since you want to create a new data file.

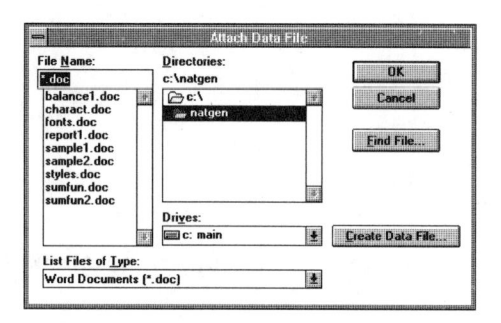

You then see the Create Data File window, shown in Figure 14-4. Enter the name of the first field in the Field Name box and select the Add button (or press (ENTER)). Remember that the order of the fields in the data file does not matter. In this case, type the name **Company** and select Add, type **Name** and select Add; and so on, for all the field names. When you have finished, the window looks like the one in Figure 14-5. Select OK to close the window.

***Figure 14-3.***   *Attach Data File dialog box*

**Chapter 14:** *Creating Form Letters*                                                                179

*Figure 14-4.*     *Create Data File window*

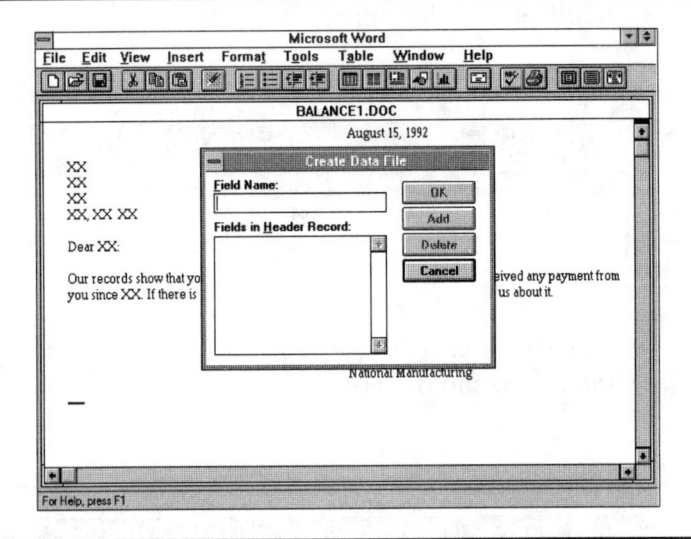

Word now displays a standard Save As dialog box. This allows you to save the data file that you have just specified on disk. Enter **PAYMENT1.DAT** for the filename and select OK. Word now performs two actions:

*Figure 14-5.*     *All field names entered*

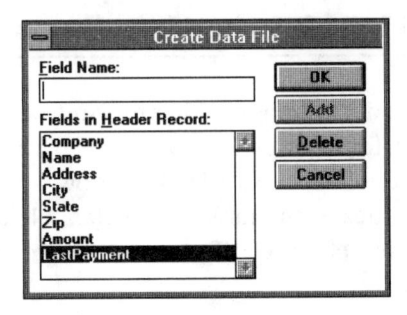

- It starts the data file in a second regular document window, the top of which looks like this:

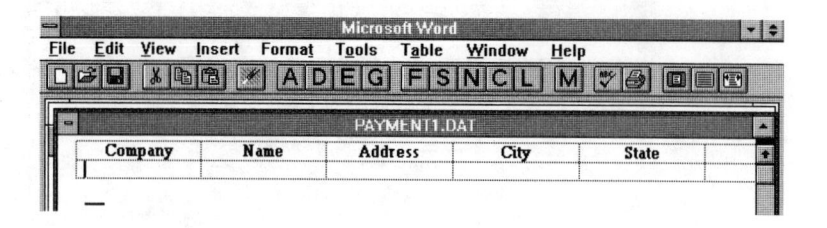

- It opens the print merge helper bar at the top of the main document window, as shown here:

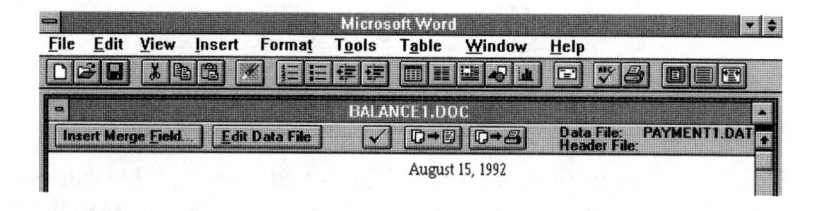

Don't be concerned if this action displaces your first line a bit (the date, in this case) or if the name of the data file is displayed. Also, note that the toolbar changes when the data file is active; the toolbar buttons can be used for manipulating the table, but you won't need them for these examples.

## Lesson 66: Finishing the Main Document and Data File

Switch to the data file by clicking its window, if it is visible, or by using the Window menu if, for example, the BALANCE1 window takes up the full screen and is covering the PAYMENT1.DAT window.

The dotted lines in the table in the data file are the cell borders. Notice that some of the cells are off the window to the right; that is perfectly

**Chapter 14:** *Creating Form Letters* 181

acceptable. As you add text to this table, some of the text may wrap in the cells. The way the data looks in the table does not affect how it looks in your printed form letters. Word wraps text in the cells of a table just like it does in paragraphs.

You now want to start entering the data. To enter data into a table, you simply type what you want and press the (TAB) key to move to the next cell. To start a new row in a table, put the insertion point in the last cell in the last row and press (TAB) again. This is described in more detail in Chapter 15.

For now, start typing the information for the form letters. The first company name is Industrial Mining Co., so type that in the first cell in the blank row:

| Company | Name | Address | City | State |
|---|---|---|---|---|
| Industrial Mining Co. | | | | |

Press (TAB) and type the name, **Michael Townsend**, as shown here:

| Company | Name | Address | City | State |
|---|---|---|---|---|
| Industrial Mining Co. | Michael Townsend | | | |

Enter all the information for the first record in the same way. The first fields look like this:

| Company | Name | Address | City | State |
|---|---|---|---|---|
| Industrial Mining Co. | Michael Townsend | P.O. Box 4110 | Cambridge | MA |

The fields on the right look like the following:

| State | Zip | Amount | LastPayment |
|---|---|---|---|
| MA | 02139 | 127.53 | 7/21/92 |

To start the next record, be sure the insertion point is in the last cell (the one under "LastPayment") and press TAB:

PAYMENT1.DAT

| Company | Name | Address | City | State | |
|---|---|---|---|---|---|
| Industrial Mining Co. | Michael Townsend | P.O. Box 4110 | Cambridge | MA | 02139 |

Fill in the second record as well. The fields on the left look like this:

| Company | Name | Address | City | State | |
|---|---|---|---|---|---|
| Industrial Mining Co. | Michael Townsend | P.O. Box 4110 | Cambridge | MA | 02139 |
| City of Olsenburg | Tamara Fine | 91 Oak Avenue, Suite 320 | Olsenburg | IL | 60606 |

The fields on the right look like this:

| Zip | Amount | LastPayment |
|---|---|---|
| 02139 | 127.53 | 7/21/92 |
| 60606 | 118.18 | 6/31/92 |

If you want, you can add other records to see how they print out.

Give the Save command from the File menu to save this work on disk. When Word displays the Summary Info window, just select OK to disregard it. Switch to the main document (the BALANCE1 letter). You want to replace each "XX" with the name of the appropriate field. You cannot simply type in the field names, however; you need to put in the special merge characters.

**Chapter 14:** *Creating Form Letters* 183

*Figure 14-6.* Insert Merge Field dialog box

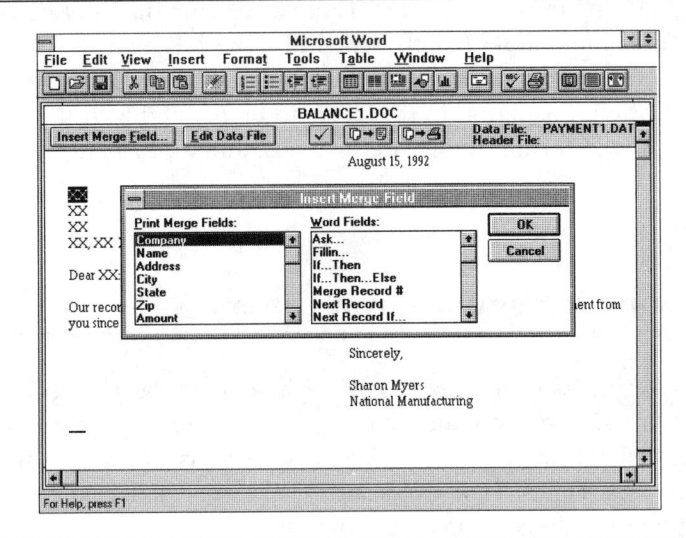

The easy way to do this is to use the print merge helper bar at the top of the window.

Switch to the BALANCE1 file, select the first "XX", which will be the person's name. (Don't select the paragraph mark after the "XX".) You want to replace this with the field called "Name" so click the Insert Merge Field button in the print merge helper bar. This brings up the dialog box shown in Figure 14-6.

Select "Name" from the Print Merge Fields list on the left of the dialog box and select OK. Word then replaces the "XX" with "Name" enclosed in the field markers, as shown here:

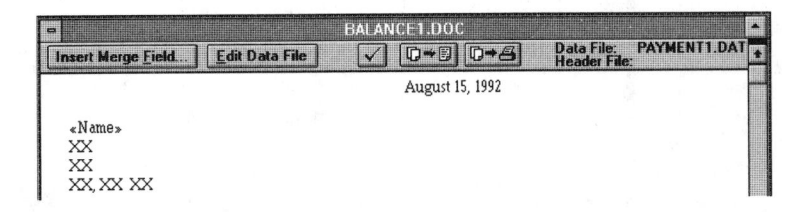

Select the second "XX", which you want to be the company, click the Insert Merge Field button, and select "Company" from the list. Keep doing this until your document looks like the one in Figure 14-7.

You can add formatting, such as italics, to the field names if you wish. This causes the information in the fields to be printed with the formatting. Note that you add formatting to the main document; formatting in the data file is ignored.

## Lesson 67: Printing Form Letters

Printing with the merge feature is very similar to regular printing. Give the Print Merge command from the File menu after setting up your printer with the Page Setup command. Select the Merge button in the middle of the dialog box. Figure 14-8 shows the Print Merge dialog box when the selected document is already a main document.

*Figure 14-7.*   *Completed main document*

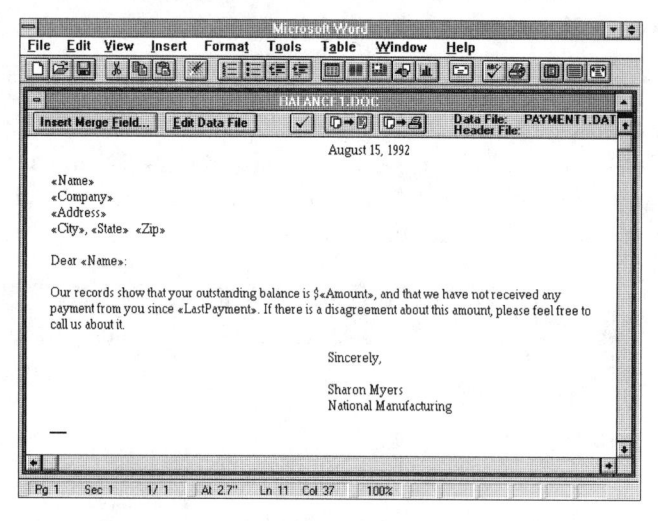

***Figure 14-8.*** *Print Merge dialog box*

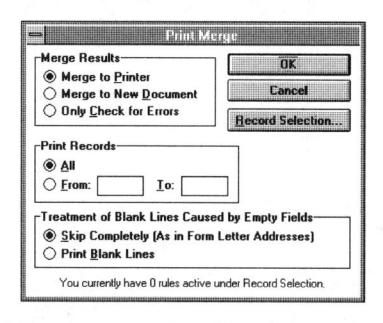

The three choices in the Merge Results section define what happens when you select OK. Merge to Printer causes the results to be sent to the printer, while Merge to New Document causes the results to be saved in a new file. You can use the latter choice if you want to make some changes in the letters before printing them out. Only Check for Errors is used when you have complex main documents.

The Print Records choice lets you specify which records in your data file you want to use. You can enter record numbers in the From and To choices to restrict the records you print. For example, if you want to print from the first three records, enter **1** and **3** for these options.

The last set of options tells Word what to do when you have blank lines caused by fields with no data. For example, if one of the records in your data file has no information for the Company field, you might want to not print the blank line that would result in the main document. However, if you were printing mailing labels, you would want to print that line so that the labels lined up properly.

Figure 14-9 shows the letters Word prints out when you merge the BALANCE1 letter. As you can see, Word filled in the fields in the body of the paragraph and correctly wrapped the text.

If you have a large data file, particularly if you brought the data file over from a database management system, you may not want to print all the records. The From and To options let you restrict the records by record number, but you may want more control. The Record Selection button in the Print Merge

*Figure 14-9.*   *Letters printed by the Print Merge command*

August 15, 1992

Michael Townsend
Industrial Mining Co.
P.O. Box 4110
Cambridge, MA  02139

Dear Michael Townsend:

Our records show that your outstanding balance is $127.53, and that we have not received any payment from you since 7/21/92. If there is a disagreement about this amount, please feel free to call us about it.

                                       Sincerely,

                                       Sharon Myers
                                       National Manufacturing

August 15, 1992

Tamara Fine
City of Olsenburg
91 Oak Avenue, Suite 320
Olsenburg, IL  60606

Dear Tamara Fine:

Our records show that your outstanding balance is $118.18, and that we have not received any payment from you since 6/31/92. If there is a disagreement about this amount, please feel free to call us about it.

                                       Sincerely,

                                       Sharon Myers
                                       National Manufacturing

**Chapter 14:** *Creating Form Letters* 187

dialog box brings up the dialog box shown in Figure 14-10. In that dialog box, you can choose the records you want based on selections such as "Amount greater than 1500" or "City equal to New York".

## Lesson 68: Using Merge Instructions

The previous example showed a simple merge file with many fields. A unique feature of Word that makes letter writing even easier is *conditional insertion*. You can check the value of a field and insert different text depending on the value of the field. For example, if the information in the amount field is over 1000, you can insert a sentence describing the dire consequences of not paying promptly. Your data file can also have a field called "RegularCustomer" that contains a "Y" or "N", and you can use this to decide what type of salutation to use.

The merge feature has many instructions that you can use; some are described in this lesson, but the full use of merge instructions is beyond the scope of this book.

To enter merge instructions, put the insertion point where you want the instruction in the main document and use the Insert Merge Field button in the print merge helper bar. The merge fields are listed on the right side of the

*Figure 14-10.* Record Selection dialog box

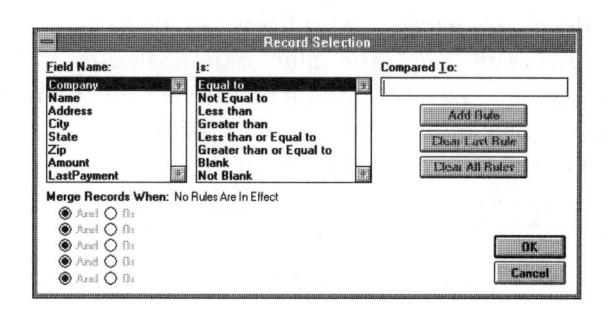

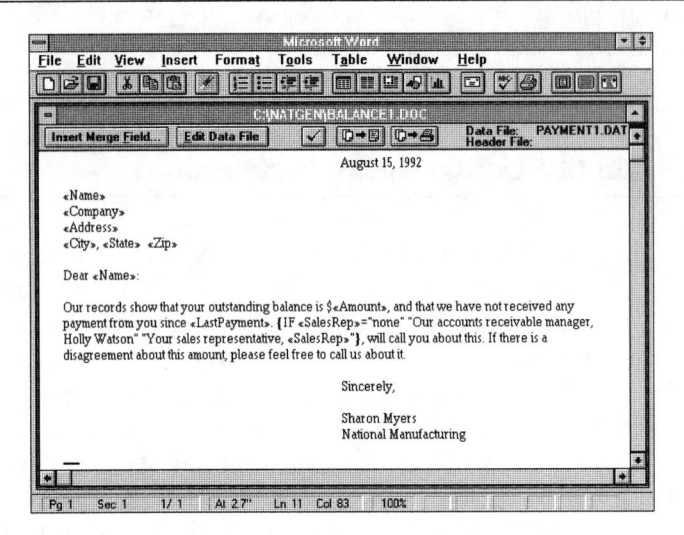

*Figure 14-11.*   *Main document with IF instruction*

Insert Merge Field dialog box (see Figure 14-6). For example, when you choose If...Then...Else from the dialog box, Word inserts the following:

{IF Exp Op Exp "TextIfTrue" "TextIfFalse"}

You need to fill in the correct fields and values in this instruction, as you will see in the next example.

The main document in Figure 14-11, BALANCE2, is similar to the BALANCE1 document except that it has an IF instruction used with a text field. The IF instruction checks the value of the "SalesRep" field and prints one of two possible sentences, depending on whether the information in "SalesRep" is "none" or some other value. The data file is also similar to the previous one but has an extra field added, as shown here:

| State | Zip | Amount | LastPayment | SalesRep |
|-------|-------|--------|-------------|--------------|
| IA    | 02139 | 127.53 | 7/21/92     | Jan Phillips |
| _     | 60606 | 118.18 | 6/31/92     | none         |

**Chapter 14:** *Creating Form Letters* 189

Figure 14-12 shows the new output.

*Figure 14-12.*     *Output from BALANCE2 letter*

August 15, 1992

Michael Townsend
Industrial Mining Co.
P.O. Box 4110
Cambridge, MA  02139

Dear Michael Townsend:

Our records show that your outstanding balance is $127.53, and that we have not received any payment from you since 7/21/92. Your sales representative, Jan Phillips, will call you about this. If there is a disagreement about this amount, please feel free to call us about it.

                        Sincerely,

                        Sharon Myers
                        National Manufacturing

August 15, 1992

Tamara Fine
City of Olsenburg
91 Oak Avenue, Suite 320
Olsenburg, IL  60606

Dear Tamara Fine:

Our records show that your outstanding balance is $118.18, and that we have not received any payment from you since 6/31/92. Our accounts receivable manager, Holly Watson, will call you about this. If there is a disagreement about this amount, please feel free to call us about it.

                        Sincerely,

                        Sharon Myers
                        National Manufacturing

You can also use the IF instruction with integer fields to test whether a number is greater than, less than, or equal to a field value. For instance, if your data file has a field named "CustYears" that is the number of years a customer has been with your firm, you might include the following sentence in a letter:

{IF «CustYears»>5 "We value your longstanding relationship with us."}

The SET and ASK merge instructions allow you to enter information when you print. The SET instruction sets a field once for all letters, whereas the ASK instruction prompts you for a new value for each letter. You can include a string with which Word prompts you.

## Review

Imagine you have an office supply business. Create a client order list including name, title, address, phone, item, and quantity purchased. Next, create a billing letter template and create customized bills for each client.

Think about how to use the information in the order list with the merge instructions. For example, think about how to thank a client for a large order.

# 15

# Working with Tables and Footnotes

## Lesson 69: Introduction to Tables

Although Word's table feature is a bit more complicated than just using tabs, you will find that the tables it produces are better looking and easier to manipulate. With the table feature, the lengths of the lines of text in your tables shrink and grow naturally as you delete and add text to items, and the formatting within a column or row can be controlled more carefully. Since most business writing includes tables of many sorts, you should learn to use the table feature so you can create more attractive and informative tables.

You have already seen an example of tables in Chapter 14. The Print Merge command creates a table for the data file. Most often, however, you will create and format tables yourself by using a small number of Word commands.

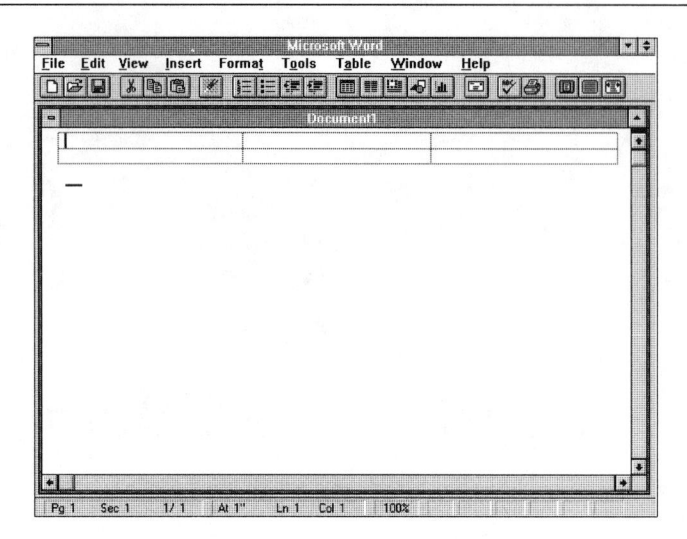

***Figure 15-1.*** *Table with two rows and three columns*

A table is made up of cells. A *cell* is a block in the table. A horizontal line of cells is a *row;* a vertical line of cells is a *column.* For example, the table in Figure 15-1 has six cells: three in the first row and three in the second row.

Usually, the information in a row pertains to a single item. All the cells in a column usually deal with one type of data (such as dates, amounts of money, descriptions, and so on). You can manipulate tables by individual cells, rows, and columns. As you will see, all the rows in a table do not have to be identical or have the same number of columns.

You can specify the format of the information within a cell just like you can in a paragraph. In fact, a cell can contain more than one paragraph. Within a cell, Word automatically wraps words just as it does in the paragraphs in your document, as shown here:

| This text in this cell is automatically wrapped at the cell border. | | |
|---|---|---|

**Chapter 15:** *Working with Tables and Footnotes* 193

*Figure 15-2.* Table menu

```
Table
Insert Rows
Delete Rows
Merge Cells
Convert Table to Text...
Select Row
Select Column
Select Table    Alt+NumPad 5
Row Height...
Column Width...
Split Table
√ Gridlines
```

The table feature uses many Word commands in the Table menu, shown in Figure 15-2. This menu changes when you do not have a cell selected, such as when you are starting a table. To start a table, give the Insert Table command from the Table menu. To change the height and width of cells or of rows and columns of cells, use the Row Height and Column Width commands. As you will see later in this chapter, you use the Insert Cells and Delete Cells commands to add or remove cells. You can also convert text that is in tabular format (text separated by tab characters) to a table by using the Convert Text to Table command.

When you work with tables, it is often useful to see the boundaries on cells. The default is for you to see a grid for all the tables in your text. (Note, however, that the grid will not print.) You can turn this default off with the Gridlines command, but you should have table gridlines visible as you experiment with the tables in these lessons.

## Lesson 70: Creating Tables

In a new document, give the Insert Table command to start a new table. You will see the following dialog box:

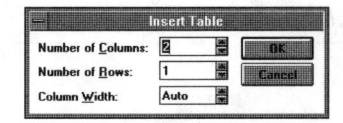

Change the value for Number of Columns to 3 and the Number of Rows to 1, and select the OK button. Word displays the table with one row:

For this example, you want to make two narrow columns and one wide one. You can put the insertion point in a cell by clicking in it or using the direction keys. In this case, the insertion point is already in the first cell, as you want. Give the Column Width command, and you see the dialog box shown here:

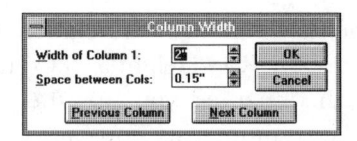

Width of Column 1 lets you change the width of the selected column. Space between Cols indicates the space between columns in the row. It is usually best to leave a little room between the columns so the text of the columns does not run together.

For this example, use the Column Width command to set the width of columns 1 and 2 to 1.5 inches and the width of column 3 to 3 inches. To do this, change the column width for column 1 to 1.5 inches, select Next Column, change it to 1.5 inches, select Next Column, and change it to 3 inches. The table grid looks like this:

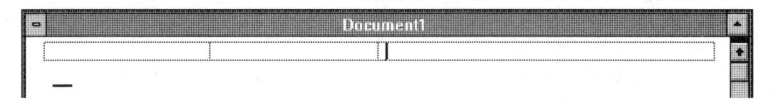

**Chapter 15:** *Working with Tables and Footnotes* 195

The Row Height command from the Table menu displays a dialog box that lets you make settings that apply to the entire row:

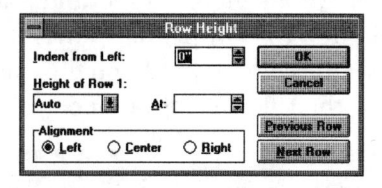

The options are as follows:

- Indent from Left sets the indentation for the first cell in the row from the left margin.
- Height is the height of the row. Usually you leave this set to Auto, indicating that Word should adjust the height based on the contents of the cells. You can also enter an exact amount such as **1 in** if you wish.
- Alignment tells Word how to align the row between the margins (left, right, or center).

Note that the Row Height choices apply to the entire row, not just the cell you selected. All cells in the row change if you change one of these settings.

You can now see how to enter text in a table. Put the insertion point in the first cell and type **Task**. Press the (TAB) key to move to the next cell, type **Who**, press (TAB), and type **Comments**. The table should now look like this:

Be sure the insertion point is at the end of the third column and press (TAB) to create the next row. Note that you do not press (ENTER) in the third column because a cell can have more than one paragraph in it. When you press (TAB) (from the far-right cell), Word creates another row:

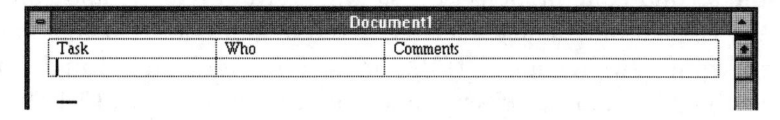

In the first cell in the second row, type **Select new blade supplier**. Note how Word automatically wraps the text within the column. Fill out the rest of the column as shown in Figure 15-3, and then add the next two rows. Remember to add new rows by pressing (TAB) at the ends of the rows.

You can also set the column widths on the ruler without the Column Width command. Display the ruler, as shown here:

| Task | Who | Comments |
| --- | --- | --- |
| Select new blade supplier | Roger | Get newest catalogs first |
| Check fuel lines | Jane | Talk to Robert about current federal and state codes |
| Make new invoice forms | Roger | Enter information from Excel |

You can then drag the column marks—the "T" characters—to change the width. Because cells in a column can have different widths, whenever you want an entire column to have the same width, select the column and use these marks to change the table.

Since each cell has a paragraph in it, you can change the character and paragraph formatting easily. To select a column, move the pointer near the top of the cell in the first row or give the Select Column command. The pointer becomes a downward-pointing arrow. Click this pointer to select the column, as shown here:

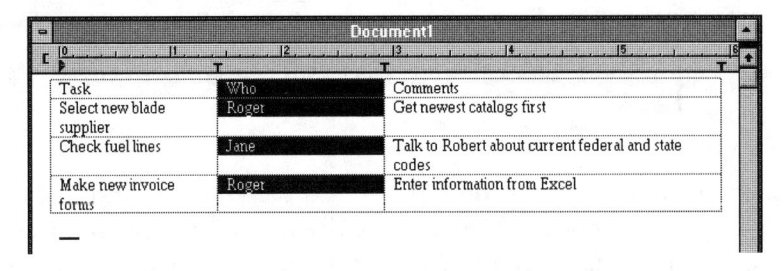

| Task | Who | Comments |
| --- | --- | --- |
| Select new blade supplier | Roger | Get newest catalogs first |
| Check fuel lines | Jane | Talk to Robert about current federal and state codes |
| Make new invoice forms | Roger | Enter information from Excel |

For example, assume that you want to center the text in all of the cells in the second column. Select the column, give the Paragraph command from the Format menu, and select centered alignment. (You could also center a paragraph by pressing (CTRL)-(E) or using the toolbar, as you do in text.) The paragraphs in those cells become centered, as in Figure 15-4.

**Chapter 15:** *Working with Tables and Footnotes* 197

*Figure 15-3.*   *Table filled in*

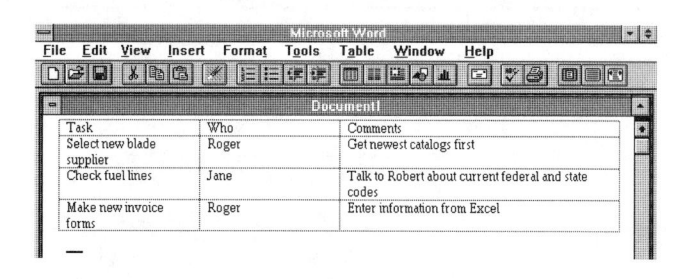

There are many other formatting choices you might want to make for whole rows or columns of cells. For example, you might want to make the whole first row bold. To select the row, double-click in the row's selection bar at the left of the window or give the Select Row command. You might also want to right align or decimal align numbers in some columns.

If you have experimented with selecting and moving in your table, you may have noticed that the actions are somewhat different than in regular paragraphs. To select a cell, you click within the cell's selection bar—the thin area to the left of the text of the cell. To select a row, you double-click in the selection bar of any cell in the row. You saw that to select a column, you select from the top of the column when the pointer turns to a downward-pointing arrow.

*Figure 15-4.*   *Cells with centered text*

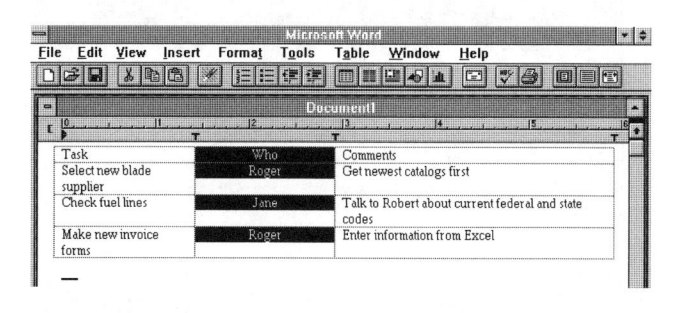

## Lesson 71: Advanced Table Handling

To add rows or columns to your table, use the Insert Cells command. The dialog box is shown here:

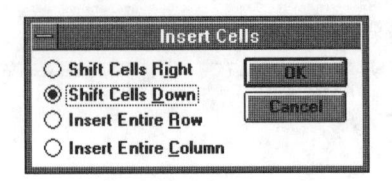

For instance, assume that you want to add a row between the first and second rows in the table. Select the second row (or any part of a cell on the second row), give the Insert Cells command from the Table menu, select Insert Entire Row, and select OK.

The Delete Cells dialog box is similar:

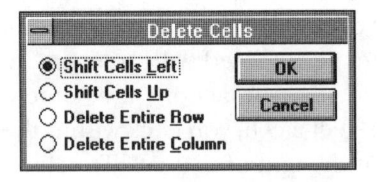

If you have selected a group of cells that are not an entire row or column, you can delete them by specifying which way the rest of the table should be shifted. For example, if you want to delete a single cell from the second row, first select it or put the insertion point in it, as shown here:

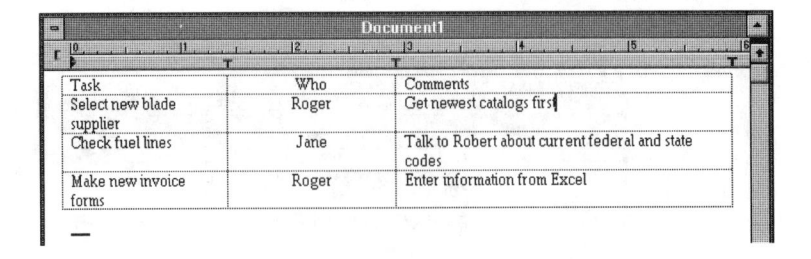

**Chapter 15:** *Working with Tables and Footnotes*

Give the Delete Cells command and indicate that you want to shift the cells to the left (to move the cells that are to the right of the deleted cell to the left when it is deleted), and select OK. Your screen will look like the following:

| Task | Who | Comments |
|---|---|---|
| Select new blade supplier | Roger | |
| Check fuel lines | Jane | Talk to Robert about current federal and state codes |
| Make new invoice forms | Roger | Enter information from Excel |

Notice that the second row now has only two cells instead of three. Word's tables do not require you to have the same number of cells in each row.

If you have selected a group of cells that are not a row or column and you are inserting cells, you can specify whether the added cells should shift the other cells horizontally or vertically. For example, if you want to add a cell to a row, select the cell that will be positioned before the one you want to add, give the Insert Cells command, select Shift Cells Right, and select OK.

The Delete Cells command is necessary because Word does not let you remove cells from a table with the (BACKSPACE) key or the Cut command. If you select some cells and give the Cut command, Word copies the contents of the cells to the Clipboard but does not remove the cells from the table; it leaves the table's cells blank. Thus, to remove cells from the table itself, you must use the Delete Cells command.

If you use the Paste command when there are cells in the Clipboard, Word replaces the cells in the same-shaped area as the cells in the Clipboard. For example, if you select a 2 x 2 section of cells, give the Copy command, and then put the insertion point in a cell and give the Paste command, Word replaces the contents of that cell with the upper-left cell in the Clipboard. Word also replaces the cell to the right of it, as well as the cell below it and the cell diagonally opposite it.

You may already have text with tab characters in it that you want to convert to tables. The Convert Text to Table command makes it easy to convert old-style tables into new tables.

To convert these types of text into a table, select the text to be converted and give the Convert Text to Table command. Word can usually determine how you want to convert, changing tab-delimited columns into table columns.

For instance, you might have formatted a list of names and participants in some seminars as follows:

```
Keller, Stanley, Anderson, Thatcher    Customer service seminar for all C.S.
staff. Receptionists are invited to this seminar.
Nolan, Timmer, Fellston    Group dynamics seminar for engineering staff and
technicians.
```

Note that each paragraph has one TAB character. To turn this list into a table, simply select the paragraphs and give the Convert Text to Table command. Word forms the table:

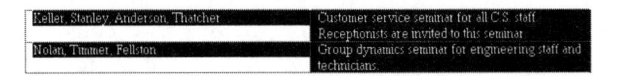

| Keller, Stanley, Anderson, Thatcher | Customer service seminar for all C.S. staff. Receptionists are invited to this seminar. |
| --- | --- |
| Nolan, Timmer, Fellston | Group dynamics seminar for engineering staff and technicians. |

## Lesson 72: Borders for Cells

Remember that the gridlines you see around tables on the screen do not print. You can, however, add borders to tables just as you can to paragraphs (as you saw in Chapter 11). You can add borders to just some cells or to the entire table, depending on what you select. You add borders by giving the Border command from the Format menu. The Border Cells dialog box, shown in Figure 15-5, shows the choices. They are the same here as they were for paragraphs.

You can put borders to the left, right, above, or below a cell. You can also add borders between cells vertically or horizontally. For example, if you select a row of cells, give the Border command, and select the vertical line between the middle guides, as shown in Figure 15-6, Word draws vertical and horizontal lines between the cells in that row.

**Chapter 15:** *Working with Tables and Footnotes* **201**

*Figure 15-5.*   Border Cells dialog box

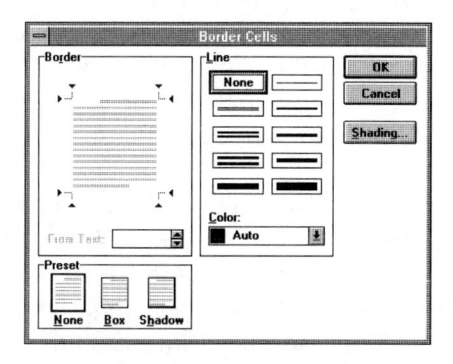

## Lesson 73: Using Footnotes

Many writers find footnotes hard to incorporate correctly in text; however, Word lets you include footnotes easily. In general, footnotes are used for two

*Figure 15-6.*   Specifying a vertical border between cells

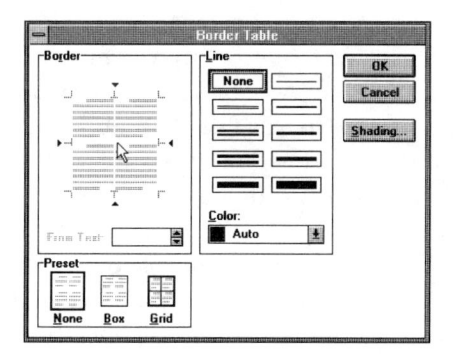

purposes: to give the reference for a quotation or an idea, or to give a supplementary note. They are commonly used in academic and scholarly papers but are becoming more common in financial reports.

Footnotes consist of the *reference mark* (usually an asterisk or a number) and the *footnote text*. To enter these, use the Footnote command from the Insert menu. Most people prefer to use sequentially numbered footnotes. Word keeps track of the current footnote number and even renumbers your footnotes if you take one out. By using the Options button, you can choose whether you want the footnotes printed on the page where they are referenced, at the end of each section, or at the end of the document.

To insert a footnote, put the insertion point at the place where you want the reference mark and give the Footnote command from the Insert menu. The following dialog box appears:

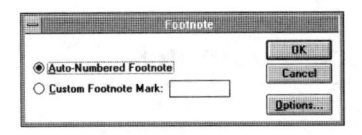

If you enter a character (or up to ten characters) for the footnote reference mark, Word uses that as the reference mark. If you leave the Auto-Numbered Footnote option selected, Word automatically numbers the footnotes in sequence.

When you select OK, Word splits the main text window, creating a footnote pane at the bottom. You can then enter and edit the footnote text in this pane and return to where you were before you entered the footnote by clicking in the top pane or pressing F6. You can also drag the split bar to the bottom of the window if you want to leave the Footnote pane open.

If you want to open the Footnote pane without creating a footnote, press the SHIFT key when you drag down the split bar. If you leave the Footnote pane open as you scroll through your document, Word scrolls the Footnote pane to the first footnote of the page you are on. You can also open the Footnote pane by double-clicking an existing reference mark.

To see how footnoting works, assume that you want to add another footnote to the report you saw earlier in Chapter 12. Remember that report already had some footnotes in it. Move the insertion point to just after the

**Chapter 15:** *Working with Tables and Footnotes* 203

*Figure 15-7.* Adding a footnote

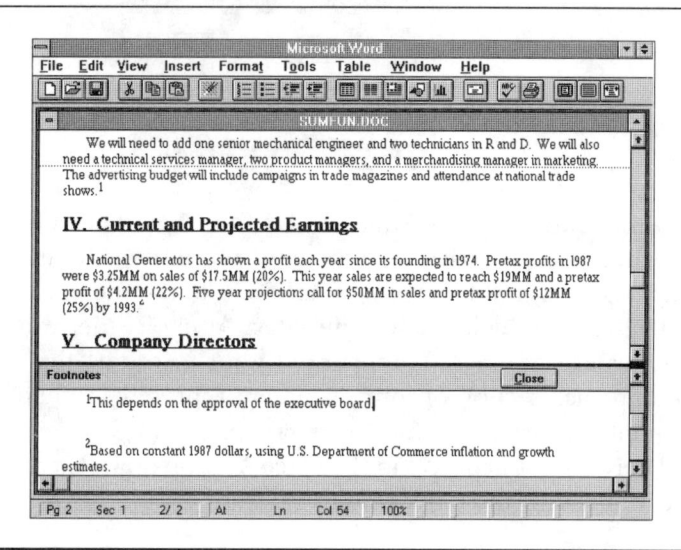

period following the words "trade shows", just before the fourth heading. Give the Footnote command and select the OK button since the automatic numbering choice is already selected by default. Now enter the text for the additional footnote, as shown in Figure 15-7.

Notice that Word automatically renumbers the footnote that follows your new footnote. If you use automatic numbering, Word keeps track of footnotes that you insert or delete and correctly numbers them. To delete a footnote, simply delete its reference mark in the text.

Word lets you change the appearance of the footnotes, the reference marks, and the separators between the text and the footnotes. This gives you flexibility in determining how your documents appear. You can change the formatting of the footnote text and reference marks with direct formatting commands. In addition, you can change their appearance with the Style commands you learned about in Chapter 13.

Selecting the Options button in the Footnote command shows the following dialog box:

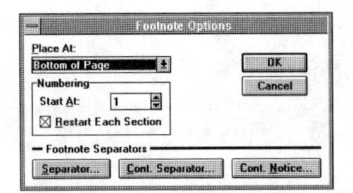

The three buttons in the Footnote Options dialog box allow you to change the characters Word uses to separate the text and the footnotes at the bottom of the page. It is unlikely that you will want to use these.

The Restart Each Section and Start At choices let you choose how the footnotes are numbered. You would want to restart the numbers in each section if each section of your document represents a chapter and you want the numbers to start at 1 for each chapter.

There are four choices in the Place At drop-down list for where footnotes appear in your printed document:

- Bottom of Page puts the footnotes at the bottom of each page, even if there is white space (such as the end of a section or if you have inserted page breaks).
- Beneath Text puts the footnotes directly under the text. If you have white space at the bottom of a page, Word puts the footnotes higher on the page.
- End of Section puts the footnotes on the last page of the section.
- End of Document puts all the footnotes at the end of the document.

These choices allow you to conform to different standards, such as those for academic papers.

## Review

Find a table in a magazine article and add it to your MAGAZINE file. Be sure to use the same character and paragraph formatting that is in the original table.

Add a border with a double line to just the cells in the heading of the table. Then add a border to the other cells with a single line.

Add a footnote to some text near the middle of the document. Go back to the beginning of the file and add another footnote. Note how Word changes the number of the other footnote.

# 16

# Customizing Word

Word has commands that allow you to set various options for the way you use Word. For example, you can adjust the way Word's screen looks and the amount of information that Word gives you.

Most Windows programs let you work only with the menus that come with each program. Word, however, lets you add, move, and remove items on the menus to make using Word easier. You can also change the keyboard combinations used to issue Word's commands.

The settings described in this chapter are remembered when you quit from Word and are automatically used when you start Word again. You can also save different sets of settings and use them at different times—for example, if two people use the same PC and want to use different settings.

## Lesson 74: Setting the Options

The Options command from the Tools menu lets you specify many different types of settings. You have already seen some of these in earlier chapters because the settings affect a wide range of Word's commands. The initial dialog box is shown in Figure 16-1.

There are many icons in the scrolling list on the left of the dialog box. Each icon represents a set of settings. When you click an icon, the settings for that icon appear on the right. For example, when you click the Print icon, the third in the list, the dialog box changes to show choices about printing.

The rest of this lesson explains the contents of the dialog box for each icon.

## View Settings

Figure 16-2 shows the View settings—how things look, what you see, and what you don't. The Window choices tell Word whether or not you want to see special features on the screen. The Show Text with choices tell Word to display guides on the screen so you can determine better what you have entered in a document. The Nonprinting Characters choices cause Word to display special characters in place of ones you normally can't see.

If you want to have more room in your windows, you can choose not to show the horizontal and vertical scroll bars. Turning off the horizontal scroll bar, which is rarely used, gives you an extra line of text on the screen. If you rarely read the messages in the status bar at the bottom of Word's window, you may want to turn off the status bar as well.

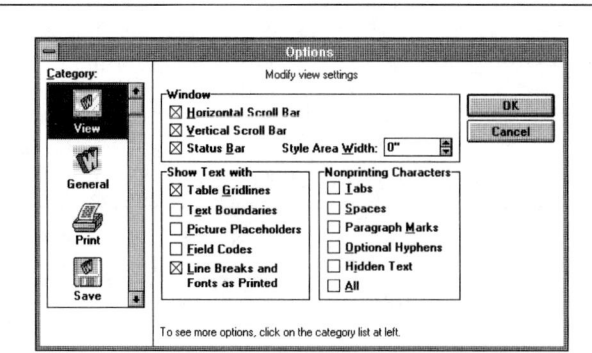

***Figure 16-1.***   *Initial Options dialog box*

**Chapter 16:** *Customizing Word*

*Figure 16-2.*     *View settings*

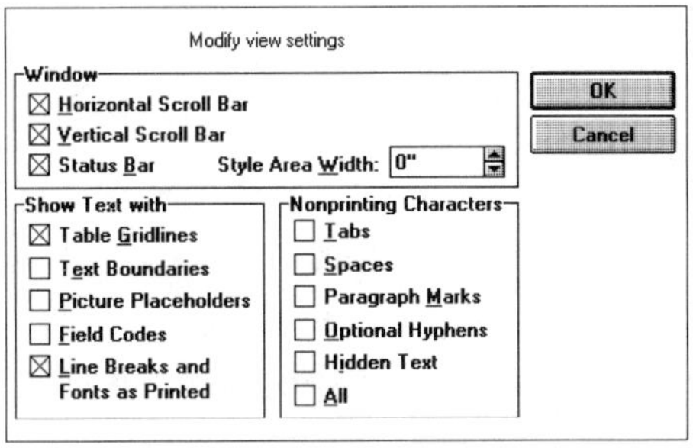

[Dialog box: Modify view settings — Window options: Horizontal Scroll Bar, Vertical Scroll Bar, Status Bar, Style Area Width: 0"; Show Text with: Table Gridlines, Text Boundaries, Picture Placeholders, Field Codes, Line Breaks and Fonts as Printed; Nonprinting Characters: Tabs, Spaces, Paragraph Marks, Optional Hyphens, Hidden Text, All; OK, Cancel buttons]

    The style area is an area to the left of the selection bar. If you have enough horizontal width for your documents and want to see the styles listed next to each paragraph, set the Style Area Width option to a small amount so you can see the listing.

    Table Gridlines displays lines between the cells in a table, as described in Chapter 15. It does not, however, cause these lines to be printed. This option is on by default.

    Text Boundaries is useful when you have positioned paragraphs and tables in a document and you are in page layout mode. This option causes each text box to be surrounded by a dotted border. The Text Boundaries option is off by default.

    Turning on the Picture Placeholders option makes scrolling faster because Word does not show the actual graphic in your documents, only a gray rectangle. This can be especially useful on slower PCs or when you have very complex pictures because of the time Word spends in redrawing each view of the picture.

    Selecting Field Codes tells Word to show the field codes themselves instead of the results of field calculations. Fields are described in Chapter 22.

    Line Breaks and Fonts as Printed causes lines to appear as they will when printed. This is slower than letting Word estimate based on screen fonts, but it assures that the document will print exactly as you see it on the screen.

    The Nonprinting Characters choices display characters that you would not normally see. The characters that appear when you select the choices are shown in the following table:

| Choice | Shows |
|---|---|
| Tabs | Tab characters (→) |
| Spaces | (SPACEBAR) characters (shows as dots) |
| Paragraph Marks | Paragraphs (¶)<br>Newlines (↵)<br>Cell ends (¤) |
| Optional Hyphens | Optional hyphens (¬)<br>Nonbreaking hyphens (—) |
| Hidden text | Hidden character formatting as dotted underline |
| All | All of the above |

## General Settings

The settings described here affect your general use of Word. They are shown in Figure 16-3.

Background Repagination turns on automatic repagination. This is described in Chapter 12.

Typing Replaces Selection causes Word to delete any selected characters when you start typing. This is the standard for most Windows programs but may feel strange to people who have used non-Windows word processors such as Microsoft Word for the PC.

**Figure 16-3.**  *General settings*

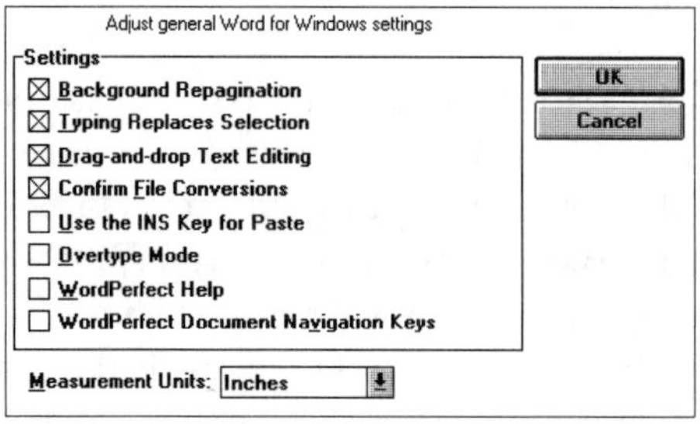

Drag-and-drop Text Editing controls whether that feature is active. Drag-and-drop editing is described in Chapter 4.

Confirm File Conversions tells Word to make its best guess as to what type of file conversion is needed, when you are opening a non-Word file, and then prompt you. If you do not select this setting, Word simply tries its best guess, which is not always correct.

The Use the INS Key for Paste setting allows you to use (INS) as a shortcut for the Paste command from the Edit menu. Many word processors use this, so it is a handy feature.

The Overtype Mode setting is a rarely used feature that causes Word to delete characters to the right as you type, effectively typing over them.

WordPerfect Help lets you use the WordPerfect keyboard command equivalents and, as you use them, tells you the corresponding Word commands. This is very convenient if you are starting to use Word after having used WordPerfect version 5. WordPerfect Document Navigation Keys is similar, but it uses the WordPerfect cursor control key equivalents.

The Measurement option lets you set the units that Word uses when it prompts you for linear measurement, such as in the Paragraph command and on the ruler. You select the choice you want to use when you give measurements. The choices are shown here:

| Choice | Meaning |
| --- | --- |
| Inches | Inches (1 in. = 2.5 cm.) |
| Centimeters | Centimeters (1 cm. = 0.4 in.) |
| Points | 1 point = 1/72 in. (Points are used for measurement by typesetters and are described in Chapter 10.) |
| Picas | 6 picas = 1 in. |

## Print Settings

The Print settings control general options for printing from Word. (Note that printer-specific options are controlled from the Print command.) Figure 16-4 shows the options, which are described in Chapter 8.

***Figure 16-4.***   *Print settings*

## Save Settings

The Save settings change the way the Save and Save As commands work. The options are shown here:

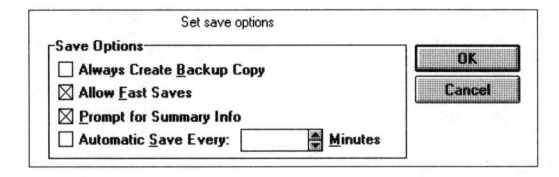

Always Create Backup Copy causes Word to create a backup copy of a file when you give the Save or Save As command. The backup has the document name and an extension of .BAK. You can also change this option in the Save As dialog box.

The Allow Fast Saves option lets Word save files in a faster manner. This is generally good (especially if you are editing long files), but some programs that can read Word files can only read those that have been saved in the slower method. Also, files saved with the fast save method often are larger than files saved with the slower method. After a few fast saves, Word normally reverts to a slow save to reduce the size and complexity of a file.

The Prompt for Summary Info option tells Word whether or not to display the Summary Info dialog box you see the first time you save a file. It is described in detail in Chapter 21. This option is on by default.

Automatic Save Every () Minutes has Word save your work at regular intervals. This is useful if you often forget to save your work and end up working for long stretches without saving.

## Spelling Settings

The Spelling settings are shown in Figure 16-5. You can also get to this dialog box by selecting the Options button in the Spelling command from the Tools menu. The spelling options are covered in Chapter 19.

## Grammar Settings

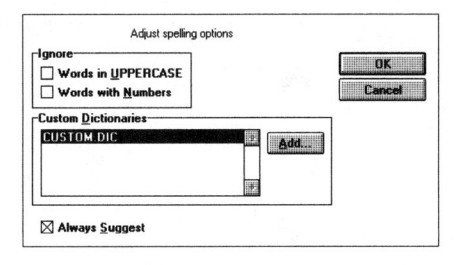

The Grammar settings are shown in Figure 16-6. You can also get to this dialog box by selecting the Options button in the Grammar command from the Tools menu. The grammar options are covered in Chapter 19.

## User Info

The User Info settings let you enter information used by Word. Your name and initials are used by the Summary Info dialog box. These are described in Chapter 21. Your mailing address is used by Word's automatic envelope printing. The choices are shown in Figure 16-7.

*Figure 16-5.*   *Spelling settings*

***Figure 16-6.*** *Grammar settings*

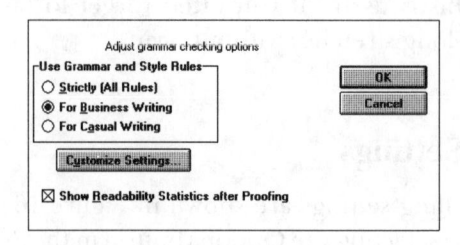

## Win.ini

The Win.ini section lets you modify the Word version 2 settings in your WIN.INI file. It is unlikely that you will ever need to do this, but if you do, it is easier to do it here than by using the methods you use for other Windows programs. Figure 16-8 shows the options.

## Lesson 75: Customizing Menus in Word

Use the Menus settings to add items to menus and remove items from menus. This is a very powerful tool for customizing Word to your needs and

***Figure 16-7.*** *User settings*

**Chapter 16:** *Customizing Word*

*Figure 16-8.*  *Win.ini settings*

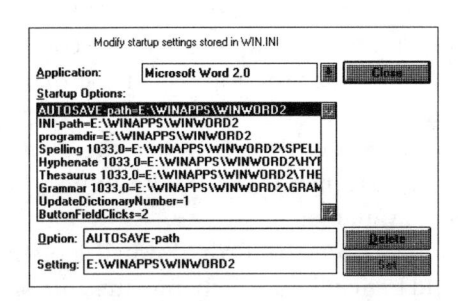

for adding to the menus functions that you use often. The dialog box for the Menus options is shown in Figure 16-9.

The list in the middle of the dialog box contains all the commands that are available to you in Word. These include all the commands normally found on the menus, as well as the names of dialog boxes directly available (such as the Tabs dialog box), all formatting commands (including those from the dialog boxes), and some actions that are usually accessed only through key combinations.

*Figure 16-9.*  *Menus settings*

The Description box at the bottom of the dialog box gives a brief description of what the command you've selected from the list does. The Reset All button resets your menus to the ones that come with Word.

To add a command to a menu, select the command from the list and look in the Menu section near the top left of the dialog box. If the command is already in a menu, the Add button becomes gray and the Delete button becomes available. Select Delete to take the command off the menu. If the command is not in a menu, the Delete button becomes gray and the Add button becomes available.

Word chooses, from the drop-down list of menus, a menu where the command would logically go. To change this, simply choose a new menu from the Menu drop-down list. Enter whatever you want for the name in the Menu Text box and select Add to add the command to the menu. The ampersand (&) character indicates which letter will be underlined and used as the speed selection character for that command. Commands are always added to the bottom of the menu.

## Lesson 76: Changing Keyboard Equivalents

You can add, remove, or change the key combination for a command in a similar way by using the Keyboard settings, shown in Figure 16-10.

After you select the desired command from the list, the Current Keys For section shows the key equivalents already used for the command. To add a new combination, choose the Ctrl and Shift options (if you wish), pick the key from the Key drop-down list, and select the Add button. If that key is already selected for another action, Word tells you that below the Ctrl and Shift options. For example, to make (CTRL)-(B) the Border command from the Format menu, make the following settings:

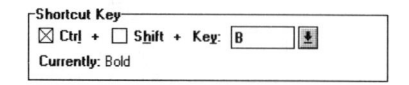

```
┌Shortcut Key─────────────────────┐
│ ☒ Ctrl + ☐ Shift + Key: [B] [▼] │
│ Currently: Bold                 │
└─────────────────────────────────┘
```

To remove a key combination, select it from the list, then select it from the Current Keys For list, and select the Remove button in the dialog box.

**Chapter 16:** *Customizing Word* 217

*Figure 16-10.* Keyboard settings

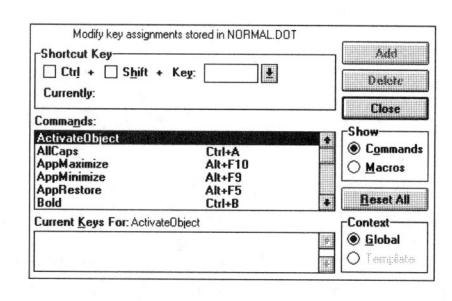

## Lesson 77: Changing the Toolbar

You can change the toolbar in the same way you change the menus and the keyboard equivalents. The Toolbar settings, shown in Figure 16-11, let you add your own tools or remove tools that you do not use.

The Tool to Change drop-down list shows you the tools that are current on the bar. To change one, simply select it in the Tool to Change list, pick a command from the Commands list, choose a new button from the Button list, and select the Change button. Note that the Button list contains a wide variety of buttons, from ones that describe actions to ones that have just letters on them.

*Figure 16-11.* Toolbar settings

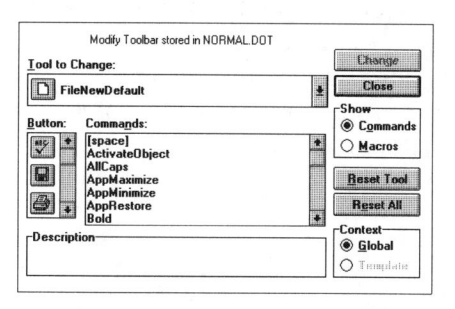

## Lesson 78: Storing Your Settings

The options you specify in this chapter are stored in template files, which are described in Chapter 13. A template file holds many settings. When you open a new file, you associate it with a template and Word then uses the settings for that template.

There is a "super" template called NORMAL.DOT. This template is used to hold *global* settings—that is, ones that you want to use all the time, regardless of the template. If you have made options changes and have not saved a template, when you quit from Word, it will display this prompt:

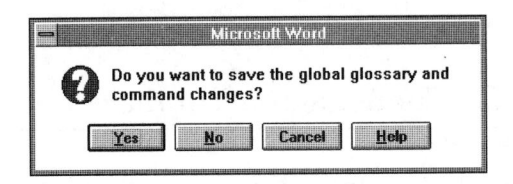

[Dialog box: Microsoft Word — Do you want to save the global glossary and command changes? Yes / No / Cancel / Help]

Select the Yes button to save your changes in the NORMAL.DOT template file.

## Review

If you work in normal mode most of the time, you may want to make a key combination for the Header/Footer command from the Insert menu so you can change the header text without using the mouse. Choose a key combination that makes sense to you for this action (such as CTRL-H) and assign that key combination to that command.

Add the Subscript option (which normally is only available in the Character command) to the Format menu. Look for other actions that you might want on the Format menu.

# 17
# Outlining

There are many circumstances in which outlines help you organize your thinking. Outlines can assist you in determining how important thoughts relate to each other. Writing an outline is also a good way to be sure you have covered all the topics that are relevant to your subject.

If you wish, you can use the features of Word you have already learned to make an outline. If you set the tabs for a document at half-inch increments, you can enter text in a standard outline format. You can use Word's selection features to move groups of items around; you can even use an outline style sheet to specify a different emphasis for each level of your outline. However, Word's new outlining features allow you to do much more.

This chapter shows you how to create and modify outlines by using special outlining features. With these features you can even show existing documents as outlines. If you are familiar with other outlining programs for the PC, you may see similarities between those programs and Word. Once you've learned how to outline with Word, you will find many situations in your daily work in which outlines are very useful.

Every document in Word can also be viewed as an outline. Until now, you have used the normal and page layout modes for editing; since you haven't used any of Word's outlining features, you haven't needed to see your document in outline mode.

It is important to understand that outlines are no different from text documents in Word. Most outline programs create files that can be used only as outlines. Word, however, lets you create an outline and then fill in its parts with text. When you want to see the text, you use normal mode; when you want to see the outline, you use *outline mode*. Outline mode is just a different, more streamlined way to look at your document.

You use outline mode and normal mode for different purposes. You edit and format in normal or page layout mode, as you have seen. You use outline mode to review and change the structure of your text, just as you might decide to switch the position of two major ideas after writing an outline on paper.

In Word's outline mode, when you move a heading, all the text under that heading moves, too. To achieve this result in normal mode, you would have to select a huge amount of text, delete it to the Clipboard, move to the new location, and insert the text there. In outline mode, you just move the heading, and the associated text moves with it.

There is a small price for the convenience of using outline mode: you cannot select text across paragraph boundaries. Because of this limitation, you are restricted to editing a single paragraph. (In outlines, each heading is a separate paragraph.)

If you have a complicated and detailed outline, you may have dozens of subheads under a main heading. When you are working with this kind of outline, you can get lost in the lower level headings and miss the overall picture. Word lets you collapse an outline so that lower level headings are invisible.

Moving between normal mode and outline mode is very easy. You can switch between normal mode and outline mode by using the Outline command from the View menu.

You can tell which view you are in by looking at the top of the window. In outline mode, the outline bar at the top of the window looks like this:

Chapter 17: *Outlining* 221

Outlines can have both *headings* and *body text*. (Body text is like regular text.) Each heading has a level, starting with level 1. Body text does not have a level. As you make an outline, Word remembers the level of headings by saving a paragraph style with each one. These styles are heading 1, heading 2, and so on. Body text is formatted as Normal text. As long as you enter your outline in outline mode, you do not have to add these styles; Word does it for you. (Styles are covered in Chapter 13.)

Because outlines are just like regular documents, Word treats them similarly. You can print an outline with the Print command from the File menu, and you can save it with the Save command from the File menu. In fact, you will find that handling outlines is almost identical to handling regular text files.

## Lesson 79: Creating an Outline

You can enter the text for a new outline in either normal mode or outline mode. It is usually better to enter and edit outlines in outline mode.

When you want to create a new outline, be sure that you use a new document. Switch from normal mode to outline mode by choosing the Outline command from the View menu. If you have the ribbon showing, you can see the level in the Style list. You generally want the ribbon showing when you are in outline mode. However, you lose many possible lines this way, so you might want to hide the toolbar. Your screen looks like the one in Figure 17-1.

Figure 17-2 shows the outline you will work with in this chapter. Begin by entering the first heading, **Contract preparation**, and press (ENTER). Word assumes you want to start at level 1.

Next, type the line **Use standard contract as basis** and press (ENTER). However, you want this entry to be level 2, not level 1. To tell Word that this

***Figure 17-1.***     *Outline mode*

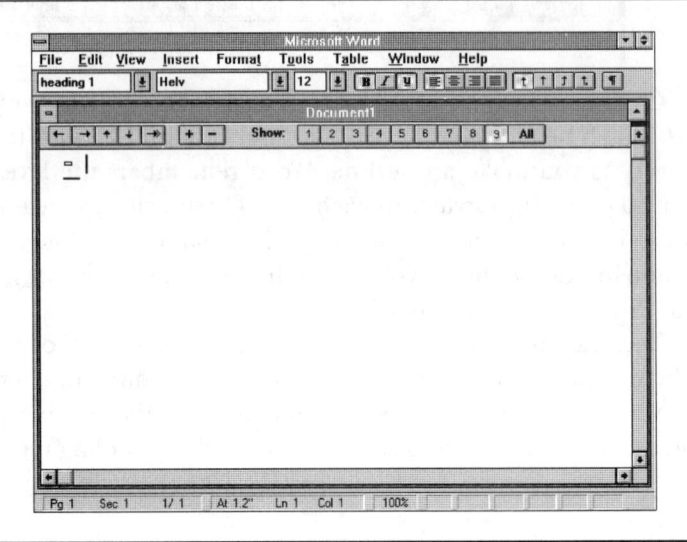

line is level 2, click the right-arrow button in the outline bar, the second button from the left:

Word indents the line, and the style indicator reflects the level you have chosen.

Note that the first line you entered has a hollow plus sign next to it and the second line has a hollow minus sign:

The plus sign indicates that the heading has a subhead beneath it, while the minus sign indicates that the heading does not have any subheads.

Continue by typing the next line, **Add union work clause**, and press (ENTER). Word makes the new heading at the same level as the previous one, so click

***Figure 17-2.*** *Sample outline*

```
Contract preparation
        Use standard contract as basis
        Add union work clause
                Local 112 for installing
                Local 112 and 427 for maintenance
        Add outdoor setting clause
Contract signing
        Phillips at National Generators
        Martinez and Washington at fair
Site preparation
        Verify space requirements
        Erect shelters
        Cable to main sections
        4 500' spans
        Check with Martinez for exact locations
Install generators
        2 30G's for main supply
        2 fuel tanks
        1 33G for backup
        1 extra fuel tank
        Operations shack
```

the right-arrow button again to tell Word that the next line is at level 3. If you prefer to use the keyboard, you can press the (ALT)-(SHIFT)-(→) key combination instead of clicking the arrow in the outline bar.

After you add the two level-3 lines, go back to level 2. To do so, click the left-arrow button or press (ALT)-(SHIFT)-(←). You can see how the left-arrow and right-arrow buttons move the levels up and down. Finish entering all the text and save the file as FAIR1 with the Save command.

So far, you have entered only headings. Many outlines contain body text, such as paragraphs under headings or a title. For this example, use body text to add a title to the outline. To do this, move to the top of the outline, press (ENTER) twice to add some space, and type **Millerton Art Fair** on the first line. To tell Word that this is body text, click the double right-arrow button between the down-arrow and plus buttons:

You can insert topics in the middle of an outline by moving to the beginning of a line, typing new characters, and pressing (ENTER). You can change the level of a heading by selecting any part of the heading and clicking the left- or right-arrow button. You can change a heading into body text by selecting any part of the heading and clicking the double right-arrow button.

It is important to remember to use the left- and right-arrow buttons or `ALT`-`SHIFT`-`→` and `ALT`-`SHIFT`-`←` to shift headings. You should not use the `TAB` key to do this because Word does not recognize it.

## Lesson 80: Collapsing and Expanding

A detailed outline can be very hard to follow, especially if it includes body text. When outlining a complex business report, for example, you can quickly lose track of the outline among all the text.

To avoid this problem, you often want to see only higher level portions of an outline. Word allows you to hide lower level heads and body text by collapsing them. To *collapse* all of the headings below a particular one, simply select that heading (or any part of it) and click the minus button on the outline bar. To restore these headings, click the plus button on the outline bar.

For example, select first the entire level-1 heading, "Contract preparation". Click the minus button in the outline bar twice to hide the two levels of subordinate headings. You can also press the `ALT`-`SHIFT` keys and the `-` key. The result is shown here:

> ✧ Contract preparation
> ✧ Contract signing
>     ▫ Phillips at National Generators
>     ▫ Martinez and Washington at fair

When you collapse a heading, Word puts a gray bar where the collapsed material is, to remind you that there is more under that heading.

You can *expand* a collapsed heading by clicking the plus button in the outline bar or pressing the `ALT`-`SHIFT` keys and the `+` key. Expanding a heading shows only the level immediately below it. For example, if you collapse a level-1 heading and some of the level-2 heads below it have subheads, expanding the level-1 heading does not expand the level-2 heads at the same time. If you have collapsed different levels of headings and want to expand them all at once, press `ALT`-`SHIFT`-`A` or click the All button in the outline bar. This expands all the headings.

Note that the minus and plus buttons on the outline bar collapse and expand the lowest level of heading under the selected paragraph. Thus, if you have a level-3 outline and have selected a top-level heading, clicking the minus on the outline bar hides the level-3 entries only.

It is likely that you will want to view your outline as a whole from various levels. To do this, click the numbers in the outline bar. For example, clicking 2 in the outline bar collapses everything except level-1 and level-2 headings. Collapsing lower level headings in this way is useful when you are analyzing whether points in your outline are properly arranged and have equal weight. The keyboard equivalent for the number buttons is (ALT)-(SHIFT) and the number.

## Lesson 81: Rearranging Your Outline

If you could write an outline correctly the first time you tried, there would not be much use for Word's special outlining commands. Because you use outlines to organize your thoughts, you need to rearrange headings as you decide to change their position or importance. The outline edit mode makes these adjustments especially easy.

If you are moving a heading, it is likely that you also want to move all the ideas associated with it. Word lets you do this. In outline edit mode, when you delete and send a heading to the Clipboard, all subheads and body text under that heading are included, so moving whole ideas is easy.

For example, suppose you want to move "Add union work clause" and its related subheads to follow "Add outdoor setting clause". To quickly select the head and its subheads, click the hollow plus button next to "Add union work clause":

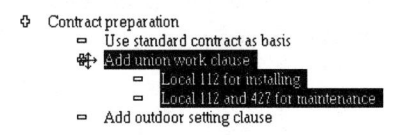

```
     ✧  Contract preparation
           □  Use standard contract as basis
        ⊕▸ Add union work clause
              □  Local 112 for installing
              □  Local 112 and 427 for maintenance
           □  Add outdoor setting clause
```

Click and drag the plus button down to after "Add outdoor setting clause", as shown in Figure 17-3. A dotted line appears, showing you where the selected text will move when you release the mouse button.

The ability to move a head along with the ideas associated with it is especially useful if you have a lot of body text. Instead of scrolling through

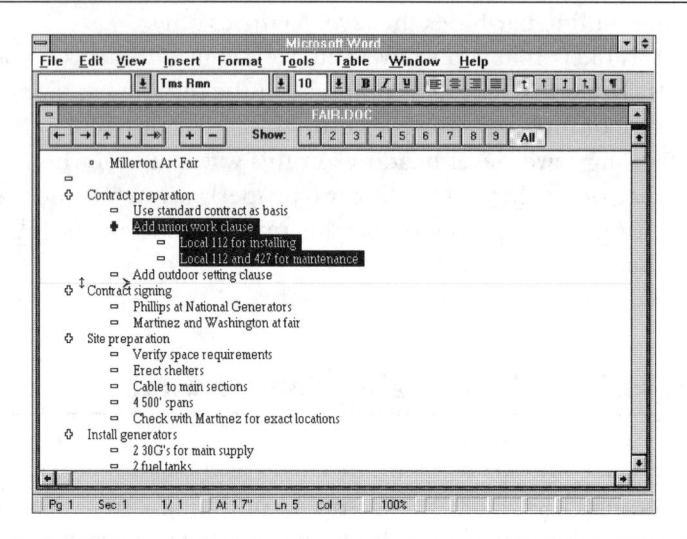

*Figure 17-3.* *Moving the heading down*

many screens of text, you can simply select all the subordinate headings under the heading by clicking the hollow plus button in the selection bar.

## Lesson 82: Numbering Your Outline

Up to this point, all the outlines discussed have been simple outlines without numbers and letters. If you create an outline with numbered headings, you cannot move one of these headings somewhere else in the outline without affecting the numbering. Word gives you a simple way of numbering and renumbering outlines.

This lesson shows you how Word numbers and renumbers outlines. Numbering regular text in normal mode is very similar. Word will, in fact, number anything, not just outlines.

You can add numbering to the selected text with the Bullets and Numbering command from the Tools menu. In that dialog box, choose Outline from the buttons at the top of the dialog box. Figure 17-4 shows the outline numbering options.

**Chapter 17:** *Outlining*

*Figure 17-4.*  Numbering options in the Bullets and Numbering dialog box

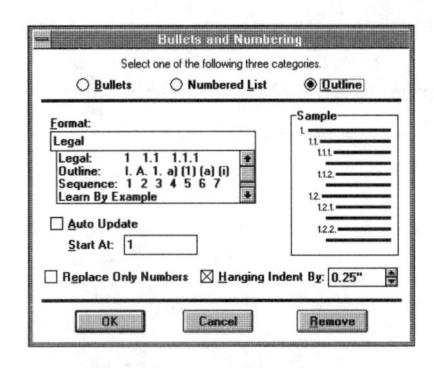

Word can number in cascading numeral format (also called legal format): 1, 1.1, 1.2, 1.2.1, and so on. It can also number in outline format. If you are numbering an outline, Word does not number body text.

For an example of how Word numbers an outline, select the entire outline (not including the title), and give the Bullets and Numbering command from the Tools menu. Select Legal from the Format list and select OK. The outline is now numbered as shown in Figure 17-5.

If you want to use a form of numbering different from the available choices, you have to indicate what form you want. In the Format list, type the format, using the type symbols shown here:

| Type of Numeral | Symbol |
| --- | --- |
| Arabic | 1 |
| Uppercase Roman | I |
| Lowercase Roman | i |
| Uppercase letter | A |
| Lowercase letter | a |

If you want to have different types of numbers for different headings, put a punctuation mark between the types for the different levels. Word puts the punctuation in the outline as well.

Standard outline style is to have uppercase Roman numerals for level-1 heads, uppercase letters for level-2 heads, Arabic numbers for level-3 heads,

***Figure 17-5.***   *Numbered outline*

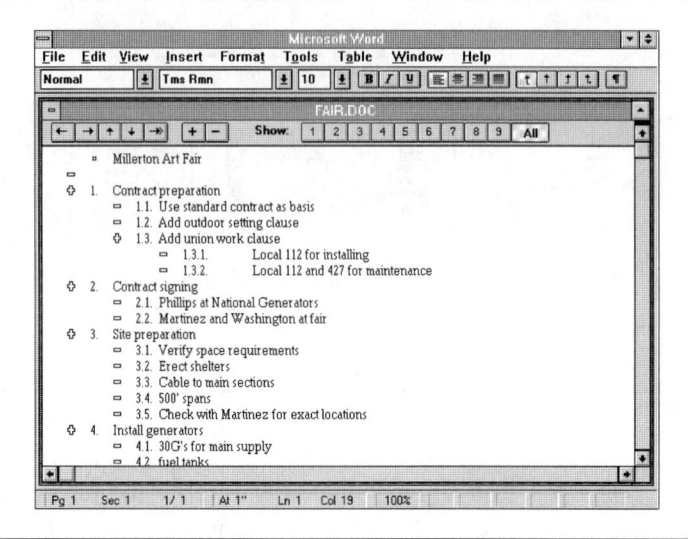

and lowercase letters for level-4 heads. Each of these would have a period (.) after it. To do this enter **I.A.1.a.** in the Format box. You can use any of the following punctuation marks between the levels:

| , | comma |
|---|---|
| - | hyphen |
| / | slash |
| ; | semicolon |
| : | colon |
| ( ) | left and right parentheses |
| { } | left and right braces |
| [ ] | left and right brackets |

Word can also renumber your outlines if you move headings around. For example, if you move the "Add union work clause" heading, select the outline, and give the Bullets and Numbering command, Word correctly renumbers that heading and all the subsequent headings.

When you use the Bullets and Numbering command, Word adds a tab between the number and text. Thus, you should be sure you have set up your document with proper tab settings before you number it. For example, you may want to use hanging indents, which would make the numbers stand out. You can use the Hanging Indent By option in the Bullets and Numbering dialog box to format the paragraphs with the specified format.

## Review

Make an outline that explains the advantages and disadvantages of three possible sites for an annual convention. First list the sites, then add the advantages and disadvantages as subheads, and add more detail under some of the advantages. Rearrange the order of the sites in the outline.

# 18

# Tables of Contents and Indexes

Tables of contents and indexes are not only time-consuming and tedious to prepare manually, but they also must be updated whenever you modify your document. Few word processing packages automatically compile tables of contents or indexes. Those that do usually restrict you to a preset style of printout that may not meet your needs.

With Word, however, you can easily create entries for the table of contents or index, and you have great flexibility in styling your printout. In addition, you can generate a new table of contents or index whenever you choose. These features make Word one of the most popular programs for business and academic use.

The methods used for creating a table of contents and an index are similar. You indicate what you want in your table of contents or index as you edit your document. When you have finished editing and formatting, you give a command that collects the entries and generates a table of contents or index based on the entries and their page numbers. Thus, the table of contents and index are not made automatically, but you can create them or update them at any time with a single command.

## Lesson 83: Planning a Table of Contents

Before you start using Word to generate tables of contents for your documents, you should consider the purpose and structure of a table of contents. A table of contents appears at or near the beginning of a document. It tells the reader what is presented in the document, in what order, and on what page. A document that is only one or two pages long generally does not need a table of contents.

A table of contents can be a simple list of where each section of the document begins, or it can be a detailed road map of the document. For example, the tables of contents of most books contain only the chapter names and beginning page numbers. This keeps the table of contents short (it usually fits on one page) and gives the reader a feel for the general categories and progression of subjects.

Some tables of contents are meant to show almost the entire contents of a document. These are much longer than simple tables of contents and are often hard to browse through. Of course, someone looking for a particular subject will be more likely to find it in a detailed table of contents. However, many authors prefer to create an index for detailed listings and keep the table of contents brief.

The format of a table of contents is also important. If you list two or more levels of headings in a table of contents, using paragraph and character formatting or styles makes the table of contents significantly easier to read. Compare the unformatted and formatted tables of contents shown in Figure 18-1.

## Lesson 84: Indicating Table of Contents Entries

There are two methods for indicating to Word what you want in your table of contents:

- Use the predefined styles heading 1, heading 2, and so on, in your document. You can specify these styles yourself or you can use the outlining feature, which uses these styles automatically. Styles are covered in Chapter 13 and outlining is covered in Chapter 17.

**Chapter 18:** *Tables of Contents and Indexes* 233

- Mark the paragraphs you want to include in the table of contents with fields.

The styles method is much easier than the fields method and is described here. Using styles—particularly if you also use outlining—makes sense since all your chapter titles have the same formatting, all your top-level headings have the same formatting, and so on. The fields method gives you a bit more flexibility, but at the high cost of your having to be very careful to mark every heading.

To indicate the paragraphs you want in the table of contents, use the predefined styles heading 1, heading 2, and so on, in your text. For example, in this book, the chapter names would be heading 1 and the lesson names heading 2.

You can check the organization of your table of contents by viewing your document in outline mode, as described in Chapter 17. When you click one of the numbers in the outline bar, Word hides all of the headings and text at a level below that number.

Note that you have to use styles to mark entries this way. You cannot simply apply direct formatting to the headings. If you do not want to use styles, you must use the fields method for indicating entries. The field method is not described in this book because it uses fairly advanced concepts that do not benefit most users.

*Figure 18-1.* *Tables of contents without and with formatting*

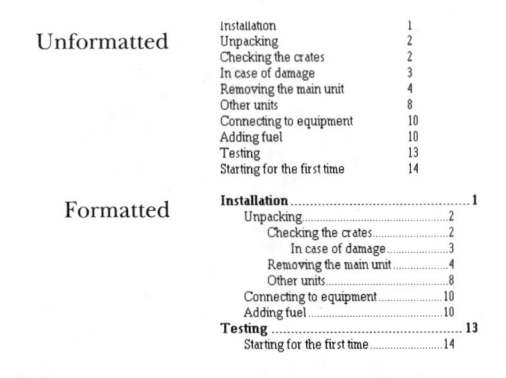

Unformatted
```
Installation                   1
Unpacking                      2
  Checking the crates          2
  In case of damage            3
  Removing the main unit       4
  Other units                  8
  Connecting to equipment     10
  Adding fuel                 10
Testing                       13
  Starting for the first time 14
```

Formatted

**Installation** .................................................. 1
   Unpacking ................................................ 2
      Checking the crates ............................ 2
      In case of damage ............................... 3
      Removing the main unit .................. 4
      Other units ........................................... 8
      Connecting to equipment ............. 10
      Adding fuel ....................................... 10
**Testing** ............................................................ 13
      Starting for the first time ............. 14

## Lesson 85: Creating the Table of Contents

Once you have marked all of the entries, you can create a table of contents with the Table of Contents command from the Insert menu. Briefly, this command performs the following steps:

1. Repaginates your document
2. Searches through your document from the beginning for entries
3. Collects copies of those entries and their associated page numbers
4. Puts the entries at the insertion point

The Table of Contents command has many interesting features that are described in this lesson and later in the chapter. Even if you skip these descriptions, you can quickly generate a simple table of contents just by giving the Table of Contents command. With a bit more planning and work, however, you can create more complex tables of contents and figure lists.

You can give the Table of Contents command at any time after placing the insertion point where you want the table of contents to appear. If you change your document by adding, deleting, or moving text, you should give the command before you print your document so that the table of contents reflects the most current revision. If you have already created a table of contents, Word replaces the old copy with the new one after you verify that you want this done.

When you give the Table of Contents command from the Insert menu, you see the following dialog box:

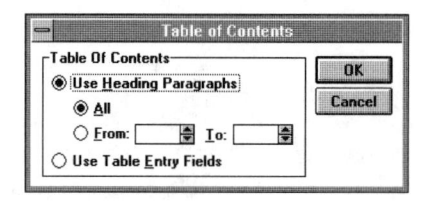

Choose Use Heading Paragraphs and select OK. Word puts the table of contents at the insertion point in your document. You may want to precede the text with a heading such as "Table of Contents" and possibly put it in its own section. Your table of contents will be similar to the one shown here:

```
Installation ................................................. 1
    Unpacking ............................................ 2
        Checking the crates ..................... 2
            In case of damage ................. 3
        Removing the main unit ................ 4
        Other units .................................... 8
    Connecting to equipment ................. 10
    Adding fuel ..................................... 10
Testing .................................................. 13
    Starting for the first time ................ 14
```

Word formats the table of contents with the predefined styles toc 1, toc 2, and so on.

Once you have the table of contents in your document, you can format it any way you want. In general, you use the predefined styles. You can use normal character and paragraph formatting on the text, but it is much better to change the formatting on the styles instead. If you use direct formatting instead of style formatting and remake the table of contents, any direct formatting changes you made are lost.

Word knows where previous tables of contents are in your document, so you do not need to select it when you choose the command again. When it re-creates a table of contents, Word erases only the table of contents entries.

## Lesson 86: Advanced Use of Tables of Contents

Many reports have numerous figures and tables. It is useful to list these elements and let the reader know what pages they appear on. In the same way that you create tables of contents, you can also create other lists.

For example, assume that you want a figure listing like the one in Figure 18-2. To create this list, format your figure titles in the text with the heading 9 style. You use this style because the Table of Contents command looks for all heading styles. Since it is very unlikely that your document uses nine levels of headings, heading 9 will be safe to use for your figure captions.

Because level-9 entries for figure lists would normally appear in your regular table of contents, when you create your regular table of contents, type **1** for From and **8** for To in the Table of Contents dialog box. This creates the main table of contents.

***Figure 18-2.*** *Sample figure listing*

*Figures*

```
Figure 1-1: What's in the crate....................................................1
Figure 1-2: Main unit (front)......................................................4
Figure 1-3: Main unit (back).......................................................4
Figure 1-4: Proper method for removing.............................................6
Figure 1-5: Exhaust unit...........................................................8
Figure 1-6: Electrical unit........................................................8
Figure 1-7: Main connections......................................................10
Figure 1-8: Secondary connections.................................................10
Figure 1-9: Fuel supply setup.....................................................10
Figure 1-10: Fuel safety..........................................................11
Figure 1-11: Starter (front)......................................................14
Figure 1-12: Starter (back).......................................................14
```

To create the figure list, you need to insert a field, a process that is described fully in Chapter 22. For now, simply follow these steps:

1. Put the insertion point where you want the figure list and give the Field command from the Insert menu. You see the dialog box shown here:

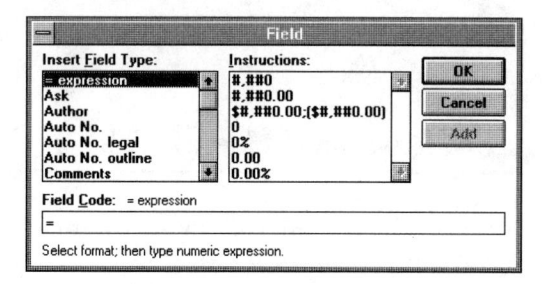

2. Put the insertion point in the Field Code box and remove the "=" that is there.

3. Type **TOC \o "9-9"** in the Field Code box and select OK.

You can use this technique to create lists of figures, tables, charts, and so on. All other aspects of creating tables of contents are identical to those for creating other lists.

## Lesson 87: Marking Index Entries

The steps used to make an index are almost identical to those used for a table of contents, and the results are also similar. However, you cannot mark index entries with styles; they must be marked with fields.

Indexes are very different from tables of contents. In a table of contents, you list the items in your document in the order in which they appear. In an index, you list items that are in your text alphabetically, but sometimes you also list words that do not appear in the text. This is to help your reader search for specific items under different names.

In a table of contents, the text is the same as the text in the headings in your document. The words that appear in an index, however, are not whole lines or phrases and thus must be marked in some other fashion. There are two steps to creating an index: selecting the entries that will make up the index, and then assembling the index itself.

Determining what to include in an index is something of an art. Important words always go into an index, but phrases can be more difficult to categorize. For example, assume a sentence in your text reads, "The 17th century was a period of rapid growth in religious thought." You would certainly index "religious thought," but would you index it under "religion," under "17th century," or both? If you already have many subentries under the word "religion" in your index, you wouldn't want to put the entry "thought" by itself under "religion"; you would want to add "17th century" to clarify it. You might even want to add an entry here for "theology" even though that word doesn't appear in the sentence.

To mark a word or phrase that appears in your text, select it and give the Index Entry command from the Insert menu. Word displays the Index Entry dialog box shown here:

In this case, the phrase "Fire equipment" was selected before the Insert Index Entry command was given.

You will most often want to just select OK here. If you want the page number to appear in bold or italics when the index is created, choose one of those options. The Range option lets you specify a bookmark (described in Chapter 22) to use for the page number instead of the actual page it appears on. You can ignore this option for now.

To mark a word or phrase that is not in your text, place the insertion point at the place you want the index to refer to and give the Insert Index Entry command. The dialog box will look the same except that there will be nothing in the text box. Type the text you want and select OK.

Most indexes are multilevel indexes, meaning that some entries are headings with subentries under them. For example, part of an index with subheadings might look like this:

```
Fans 23
Fire equipment 12
Generators
    Installation 5
    Purchasing 17
Half-height restrictions 21
```

"Fans" and "Fire equipment" are individual entries. "Generators" is a heading, and "Installation" and "Purchasing" are subentries under "Generators". Word allows up to five levels of entries. However, indexes rarely have more than three levels, and most have only two.

Marking multilevel entries is easy. In the text box, you enter the first level, followed by a colon, followed by the second level. For instance, the dialog box for "Installation" under "Generators" looks like this:

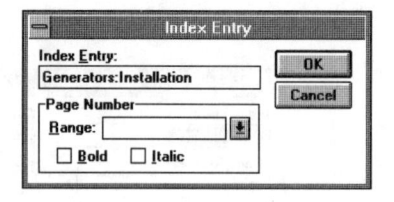

## Lesson 88: Creating an Index

After you have marked all your entries, creating the index is very easy. Simply put the insertion point at the place where you want the index (usually at the very end of the document) and give the Index command from the Insert menu.

When you give the Index command, the following dialog box appears:

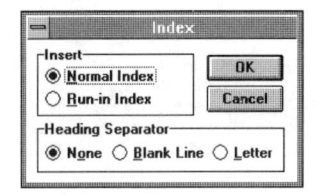

You generally use only the Normal and None options.

You will almost always want a "normal" index. A run-in index is one in which all entries are on the same line with subentries and separated by a semicolon; this is rarely used.

The Heading Separator section tells Word whether you want a break between letters of the alphabet in the index entries. You can have no break, a blank line, or a line with only the letter on it; the letter can be boldfaced, italic, or in a special typeface.

When you execute the command, Word places the alphabetically sorted index entries at the insertion point. You can format the output any way you want, just as with the table of contents. Word uses the styles index 1, index 2, and so on, for the entries, so it is best to change those styles instead of using direct formatting. Note that the entries are identical to the ones that you marked and Word does not capitalize them for you.

It is common practice to have multicolumn indexes. Recall from Chapter 12 that Word can make columns easily. Since most index entries are short, a two-column index usually looks fine. Be careful, however, to check that none of the page numbers in the entries wrap around in a confusing fashion.

## Review

Look in a few books and reports and note how the table of contents is formatted. Pay attention to whether all headings are included or just higher level headings.

In the same books and reports, look at the indexes. How complete are they? Do they use second-level headings?

# 19

# Proofing Your Documents

Much of the time you spend writing is taken up by editing and formatting your document. Good writers know that you also need additional help in making your document look just right. Word includes many tools that let you improve your writing and make it look as good as possible on the page.

Because most people are not perfect spellers, Word has included an easy-to-use spelling checker that works closely with the other parts of Word.

The thesaurus that comes with Word allows you to find synonyms for words and to look at the many meanings a word can have.

Word also has a grammar checker that can find common mistakes in your writing. It looks for things such as overused phrases and incorrect tense.

Word also includes a hyphenation program to help your text look better when printed. Justified text looks significantly better if the long words in the text are hyphenated to reduce the amount of white space between words. Of course, inserting hyphens yourself is tedious. The hyphenation feature frees you from the task of putting hyphens in the words that need them and uses the same dictionary that the spelling checker uses.

Word's proofing tools work in many languages. The default is American English. If you have text that is in other languages and want to check its spelling, you must buy additional dictionaries.

To specify what language you want to proof in, you select the text, give the Language command from the Format menu, and specify the language. The Language dialog box looks like this:

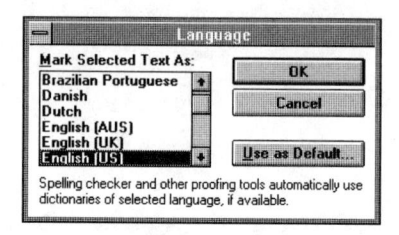

You can also change the default language in this command by selecting the language and selecting the Use as Default button.

## Lesson 89: Introduction to Spelling Checking

The second most useful program for most writers is a spelling checker. (The first, of course, is the word processor.) Even if your spelling is nearly flawless, it is likely that your proofreading is not, and a single spelling mistake in a report or memo can have a very negative effect.

The idea behind spelling checkers is fairly simple. When you run a spelling checker, it reads your document and compares the words in it against a list of all the words it knows. It then tells you the words that it does not recognize. You can correct the words or, if they are proper words that the spelling checker did not know, add the words to the dictionary so the spelling checker recognizes them the next time.

Of course, even a good spelling checker is not perfect; you will probably use words that it does not know, and it will indicate that you have misspelled them. Most dictionaries that come with spelling programs do not include proper names, so a program may think you misspelled something if, for example, it sees the word "Jones" in your text. Also, spelling checkers cannot spot proper words that are used incorrectly in context, as in "I son the race."

The dictionary in Word's spelling checker is quite comprehensive. This makes it unlikely that it will not recognize a correctly spelled word. It is easy to "teach" the spelling checker new words, such as proper names or obscure words.

If Word thinks you have misspelled a word in your document, it can offer help by checking through its dictionary and making a few suggestions for what you intended. For example, if you have the misspelled word "postion" in your document, Word guesses "position" and "positron."

The spelling checker uses two types of dictionaries when it checks a document. It searches these dictionaries invisibly, so you need not keep track of the names.

The *main* dictionary contains all common words. You cannot add words to this dictionary. It comes standard when you install Word.

*User* dictionaries are for words that do not appear in the main dictionary but are still valid. You can tell the speller to check one or more user dictionaries. You create user dictionaries in the Options command from the Tools menu. Most people have just one user dictionary that contains all their additional words.

As it checks your document, Word lists the unrecognized words (those not found in the dictionaries) one at a time. For each word, you have the following choices:

- Add the word to one of the user dictionaries.
- Correct the word in your document by typing the correct spelling or by selecting one of the guesses.
- Ignore the word, indicating that you know it is not recognized but don't care to add it to the user dictionary.

The spelling checker is easy to use. If you are creating a large document, you may want to check the spelling after you enter, but before you edit, all the text, and again just before you print the text.

## Lesson 90: Using the Spelling Checker

Before you give the Spelling command, you need to set up the spelling checker. Give the Options command from the Tools menu, and select the Spelling icon. You see the dialog box shown in Figure 19-1.

The Ignore choices tell Word to ignore certain types of words when it is checking. If you have many acronyms, in all uppercase letters, you may want Word to ignore them (although it is safer to add them to a custom dictionary instead). If you have many words that include numbers, such as in technical literature, you may want to select Words with Numbers for those words to be ignored.

The Custom Dictionaries option lets you choose which custom dictionaries you want to use. To create a new custom dictionary, select the Add button and give a filename. To choose a custom dictionary to be used, select it in the list. You can have more than one custom dictionary selected.

The Always Suggest option tells Word you want it to always make suggestions when Word finds a word that it does not recognize. This is handy, but it also slows down the process of spelling checking. If you find that most of the words that are not recognized are words you are adding to a custom dictionary, you should probably not select this option.

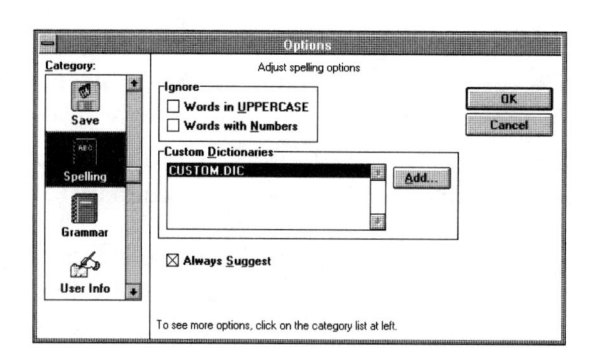

*Figure 19-1.*   Spelling options

**Chapter 19:** *Proofing Your Documents*

When you are ready to check the spelling of a document, open the document, and give the Spelling command from the Tools menu or click the Spelling button in the toolbar:

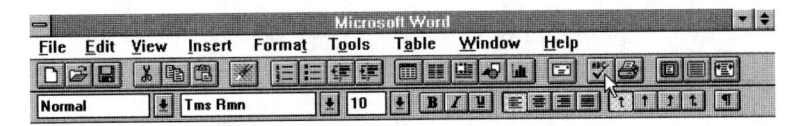

Word displays the dialog box shown in Figure 19-2. Word automatically starts checking your document and shows the first word it does not recognize, in this case "Richford". If the Always Suggest choice in the Options dialog box is on, you also see a list of suggestions.

You now have many choices:

- If you want to change the word in your document to something else, type the new word in the Change To option. Word puts the first suggestion in the list in the Change To option by default, but you

*Figure 19-2.*   Spelling dialog box

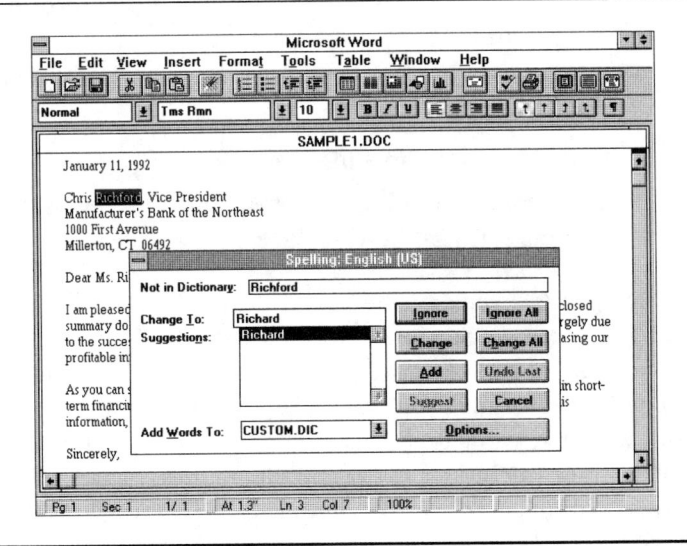

can type over that if you want. You can also select another suggestion from the list, and Word automatically puts that in the Change To option.

- Ignore ignores this word one time. Use this if the word is correct in its context but you do not want to add it to a user dictionary.
- Ignore All causes the Spelling command to ignore this word throughout the document. This differs from the Ignore button in that Word won't stop if it sees the word again.
- The Change choice changes the word in your document to the one in the Change To option one time.
- Change All causes the Spelling command to change the word to the one in the Change To option automatically if it comes to the misspelled word again.
- The Add choice adds the word to the selected user dictionary. You select the user dictionary to add to in the drop-down list at the bottom of the dialog box.
- Undo Last reverses the last change you made. This is useful if you clicked Change instead of Ignore or Add for the last word and realized that the word was valid or that the word that was suggested wasn't right.
- The Suggest button is active only if the Always Suggest choice is turned off.
- Cancel stops the spelling checker.
- The Options button brings up the Options dialog box with the spelling settings showing.

After you take care of the first word that was not in the dictionary, the spelling checker quickly jumps to the next one. This keeps happening until you reach the end of the document or you select the Cancel button.

The first few times you run the spelling checker, you will find yourself adding a slew of words to the user dictionary. You will probably add dozens of proper names (including street and city names) as well as jargon from your industry. Within a week or so, you will add fewer words to the user dictionary and will mostly be finding actual spelling mistakes.

## Lesson 91: Using the Thesaurus

As you are writing, you may get stuck thinking about a word. It is often hard to come up with just the right word for a particular thought. The thesaurus can be helpful in this case.

If you want to find a synonym for a particular word in your document, select the word and give the Thesaurus command from the Tools menu. The dialog box shows the synonyms for that word. If you select the word "pleased", you see this dialog box:

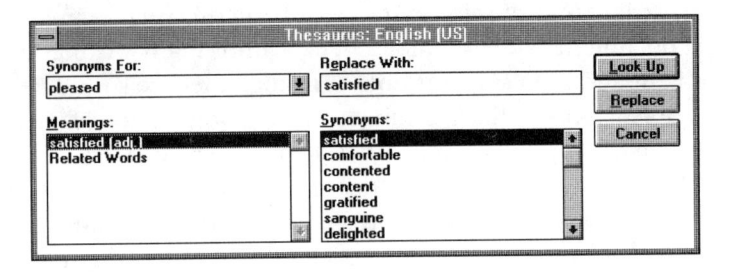

To replace the word in your document with one of the choices in the Synonyms list on the right, select the new word and select the Replace button. For example, select the word "delighted" in the window and select Replace. Word puts that word in your document in place of "pleased".

If you see a word in the list at the right that seems close but not exact, select it and select the Look Up button. This brings up a list of synonyms that may be closer to what you want. For example, select "comfortable" and select the Look Up button; you see the choices shown here:

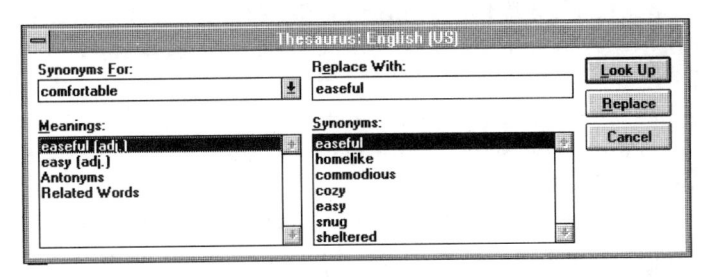

If you select Antonyms, the Synonyms list on the right is replaced by a list of words meaning the opposite of "comfortable". Some words don't have opposites, in which case the Antonyms choice doesn't appear in the list on the left.

## Lesson 92: Grammar Checking

Spelling errors are often the easiest to pick out in writing. However, grammar errors such as the wrong verb tense ("I will ran the race") and poor writing style ("I never want to stay away from there again in my life") can also mar a document. The grammar checker finds many writing mistakes in your document and even suggests how to change them to sound better.

Before running the grammar checker, you should check the grammar settings in the Options command, shown in Figure 19-3.

The Show Readability Statistics after Proofing choice lets you see a summary of your document after you check the grammar. Some people find this information interesting, but it is generally of little value in improving your writing.

You can choose the level Word should check at in the Use Grammar and Style Rules options. These set the rules that are chosen. To further restrict or include grammar rules, select the Customize Settings button. You see the dialog box shown in Figure 19-4.

There are two "rule groups" at the top of the dialog box. The first rule group is for grammatical mistakes. The second rule group is for style—that is, words and phrases that are technically correct but can be improved. You can turn off any of the rules by unchecking them in the list. You would want to turn off a rule only if you find that the grammar checker stops at too many instances of that rule in your document and you generally ignore the checker's advice.

The Catch options specify how far the grammar checker should look to catch split infinitives and multiple prepositional phrases. The default settings are usually fine.

To start checking a document, put the insertion point at the place where you want to start, such as before the first text paragraph of a letter, and give

**Chapter 19:** *Proofing Your Documents* 249

*Figure 19-3.* Grammar options

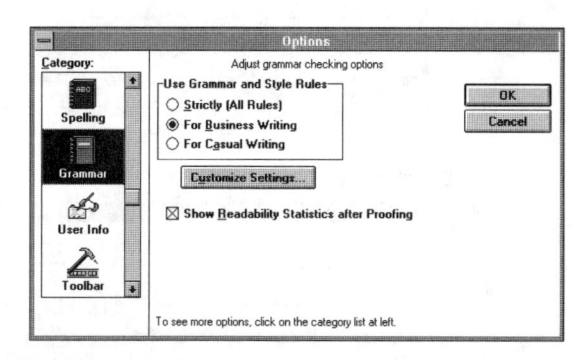

the Grammar command from the Tools menu. Word checks the spelling as it checks the grammar so it can look for usage mistakes. When the checker finds a possible mistake, you see a dialog box like the one shown in Figure 19-5.

In this example, the grammar checker questions whether you want to use the passive voice in "I am pleased". It is often better to use the active voice, as

*Figure 19-4.* Custom settings options

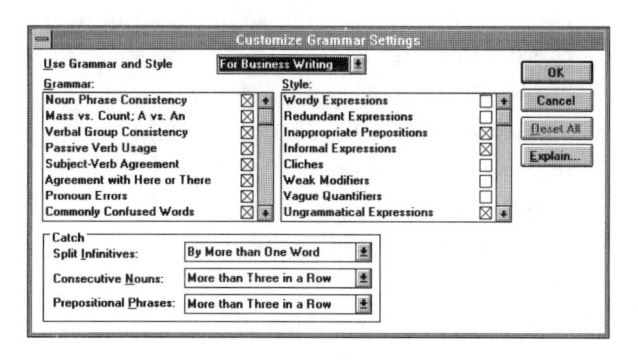

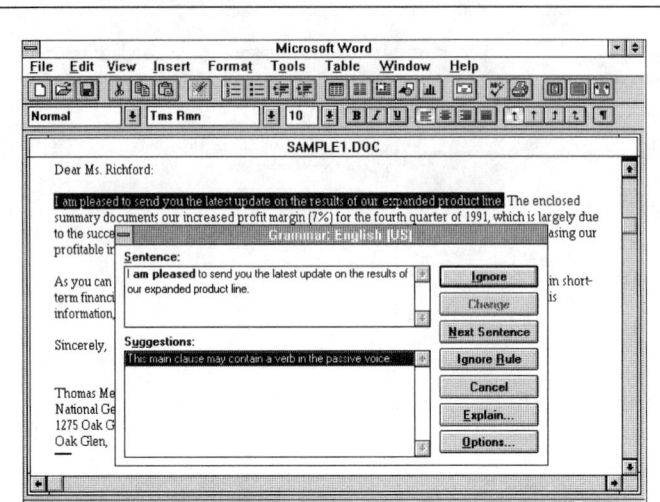

***Figure 19-5.*** *Grammar dialog box*

in "It pleases me", although that sounds too personal in a business letter such as this. The buttons at the right of the dialog box show your choices:

- Ignore causes the checker to skip this problem in this one instance.
- Change corrects the phrase in question to the suggested phrase, if there is one. In this case, there is no suggestion, so the button is not available.
- Next Sentence indicates that you know there are problems with the sentence that you will correct later, so the checker should ignore the entire sentence.
- Ignore Rule cause the checker to skip this type of error throughout the document.
- Cancel stops the grammar checking process.
- The Explain button brings up a dialog box that tells a bit more about the suggestion. In this case, the dialog box shows the following:

**Chapter 19:** *Proofing Your Documents* 251

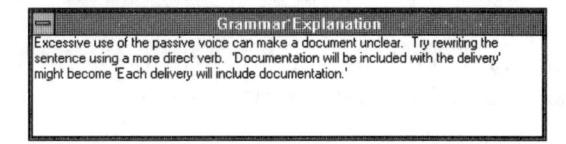

> **Grammar Explanation**
> Excessive use of the passive voice can make a document unclear. Try rewriting the sentence using a more direct verb. 'Documentation will be included with the delivery' might become 'Each delivery will include documentation.'

- The Options button brings up the Options dialog box with the grammar settings showing.

When you have finished checking the document, the grammar checker displays the dialog box shown in Figure 19-6 if you have chosen the Show Readability Statistics after Proofing choice.

Although the grammar checker can help find problems in your writing, you should certainly not rely on it. The rules in it are general and are not a replacement for your spending time editing your writing or finding an editor to help you. For documents where writing is not critical, you will find the grammar checker to be a good quick guide to finding problems.

## Lesson 93: Hyphenation

You may think that there is only one kind of hyphen, but Word has three: normal, nonbreaking, and optional hyphens. Each time you hyphenate a

*Figure 19-6.*     *Grammar statistics dialog box*

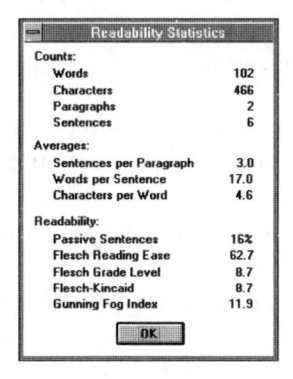

```
            Readability Statistics
Counts:
    Words                          102
    Characters                     466
    Paragraphs                       2
    Sentences                        6
Averages:
    Sentences per Paragraph        3.0
    Words per Sentence            17.0
    Characters per Word            4.6
Readability:
    Passive Sentences              16%
    Flesch Reading Ease           62.7
    Flesch Grade Level             8.7
    Flesch-Kincaid                 8.7
    Gunning Fog Index             11.9
                [ OK ]
```

word, you can indicate the kind of hyphen you want so that wordwrap produces the effect you want.

A *normal* hyphen is one that is always printed. For example, the phrase "self-reliant" contains a normal hyphen since you always want the hyphen to appear in the printed text.

A *nonbreaking* hyphen is like a normal hyphen, except that Word never breaks the hyphenated word if it occurs at the end of a line. For instance, if you use a normal hyphen, you may end up with a paragraph that looks like this:

> There are many different spreadsheets that perform "what-
> if" calculations.

Since there was a normal hyphen between "what" and "if", Word broke the line there. In many cases, this is all right, but in this case it looks a bit clumsy. If you want to prevent Word from breaking a word at its hyphen, use a nonbreaking hyphen, which you enter by pressing (CTRL)-(SHIFT)-(-). The result of using a nonbreaking hyphen is the following:

> There are many different spreadsheets that perform
> "what-if" calculations.

If a paragraph contains many long words, wordwrap causes the paragraph to look very uneven. For instance:

> His telecommunications discussion was
> significantly sidetracked as he started
> expostulating about interplanetary associations of
> antediluvian civilizations.

To make the lines more even, you need to hyphenate some of the words. If you want Word to hyphenate a word, you can enter an *optional* hyphen. You usually do this only when you notice that a particular set of lines is broken unevenly. You can also let Word help you hyphenate your entire document.

An optional hyphen is not used until it is needed. You can include optional hyphens anywhere in a word. To enter an optional hyphen, use (CTRL)-(-). You

**Chapter 19:** *Proofing Your Documents* 253

do not see these hyphens unless they are necessary for proper wordwrap. If you use optional hyphens in the previous example, the result is as follows:

> His telecommunications discussion was significant-
> ly sidetracked as he started expostulating about
> interplanetary associations of antediluvian civili-
> zations.

Deciding which words to hyphenate and adding the optional hyphens can be very tedious and time consuming. Word can help you hyphenate by automatically putting optional hyphens in every word that is at the end of a line and might be split. The Hyphenate command from the Tools menu lets you decide where the hyphen goes in each word at the end of a line or gives you the option of hyphenating without confirmation.

The Hyphenation command from the Tools menu adds hyphens from the location of the insertion point to the end of the document. If you want to hyphenate only part of the document, select that part before giving the command. The Hyphenation dialog box looks like this:

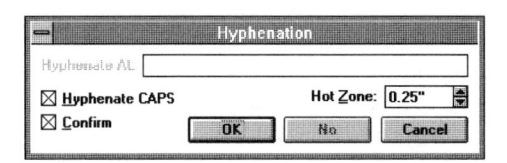

It is unlikely that you will want to have Word confirm hyphenation for each word, especially in a long document. However, if you do choose to have Word confirm each hyphenation, select the Confirm option.

For each word, the program shows you where it thinks the hyphen should go and asks you to enter a response, as shown here:

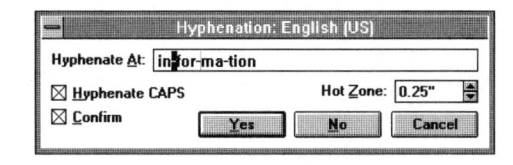

Choose the Yes button to confirm the choice or No to move to the next word.

The Hot Zone option tells Word how close to the right margin the word should be to cause hyphenation. The larger the measurement, the fewer words will be hyphenated.

## Review

Run the spelling checker on letters you have typed in Word. What type of words does it not recognize?

Type the word **running** into a document, select it, and give the Thesaurus command. Investigate the synonyms and note the differences in meaning of each.

Run the grammar checker on a letter you have typed in Word. Consider each suggestion that it makes and see if you can rewrite your letter to incorporate the suggestions.

Type a few paragraphs of your choice and format them to be very narrow. Give the Hyphenation command and note how different the paragraphs look.

# 20

# Sorting

There are often times when you want to sort a list inside one of your documents. If the list is only five or ten lines long, it is fairly easy to sort by hand, but sorting long lists by hand is extremely inconvenient. The Sorting command makes sorting any list easy.

Word can sort both text and numbers. This distinction may seem trivial, but most word processing programs cannot sort numbers the same way they sort words.

Computers think in terms of numbers, not in terms of characters such as letters, punctuation, numerals, and so on. Early computer scientists got around this problem by assigning an internal numeric value to each character. Most computers use a specific system called ASCII to relate characters to internal numbers. The ASCII order, dating back to the 1960s, presents some problems, most of which Word overcomes.

The first problem is that sorting numerals is very different from sorting numbers. Look at the following list:

23
142
5

You would sort this list numerically as "5, 23, 142". However, in ASCII code, the number 1 comes before 2, and 2 comes before 5. Thus, an unintelligent sorter (the kind most word processing programs use) would sort the list as:

142
23
5

Fortunately, Word can sort numerals as numbers rather than as ASCII characters. In fact, Word can also intelligently sort dates, a task that few word processors can do well.

A second problem is that upper- and lowercase letters are separated in the ASCII sorting sequence. Because of this, many word processors sort all words that start with uppercase letters before all words that start with lowercase letters. ("Zebra" would come before "aardvark".) Most of the time you want your lists sorted in alphabetical order, regardless of case. Word sorts upper- and lowercase words together.

A third, minor, problem is that not all punctuation comes before all numerals in the ASCII system. Some characters, such as the equal sign, fall between the numerals and the letters; others, such as the circumflex, fall between the upper- and lowercase letters; and some, such as the vertical bar, follow the lowercase letters.

Word sorts all paragraphs starting with punctuation first, then paragraphs with numbers, and then paragraphs with letters. In general, avoid sorting lists that include punctuation as the first character. The ASCII sorting sequence is shown here:

SPACEBAR
! " # $ % & ' ( ) * + , - . /
0 1 2 3 4 5 6 7 8 9

**Chapter 20:** *Sorting* 

: ; < = > ? @
A B C D E F G H I J K L M N O P Q R S T U V W X Y Z
[ \ ] ^ _ `
a b c d e f g h i j k l m n o p q r s t u v w x y z
{ | } ~

Word sorts international letters in with standard letters so that a word that starts with "ö" is sorted with words that start with "o".

## Lesson 94: Sorting Text

Usually, you want to sort based on entire lines. The most frequent use for the Sorting command is sorting lists in which each item is formatted as an individual paragraph.

Using the Sorting command from the Tools menu is easy. Use the Sorting dialog box:

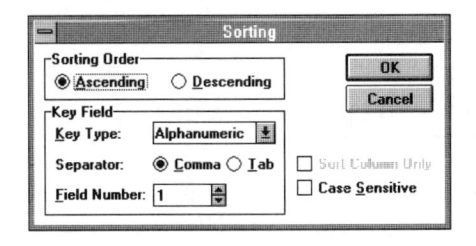

First, select the range of paragraphs you want to sort. (Word sorts only paragraphs, not lines separated by newline characters.) For this example, use the following list:

Chicago
New York
Detroit
Dallas
Houston
New Orleans
Buffalo

Select the paragraphs and give the Sorting command from the Tools menu, and Word sorts the list in the following order:

```
Buffalo
Chicago
Dallas
Detroit
Houston
New Orleans
New York
```

You can tell Word whether you want to sort from "A" to "Z" (*ascending*), which is the default, or from "Z" to "A" (*descending*). Choosing descending produces the following list:

```
New York
New Orleans
Houston
Detroit
Dallas
Chicago
Buffalo
```

In addition to sorting lists in which each item is a separate paragraph, you can sort paragraphs that run many lines. Word simply sorts full paragraphs in this case, based on the first letter of each paragraph.

## Lesson 95: Sorting Numbers

When you give the Sorting command, you can specify how you want Word to sort. In the dialog box, the Key Type drop-down list lets you choose the type of data you are sorting. Your choices are Alphanumeric (text), Numeric (numbers), and Date. If you are sorting based on numbers or dates, be sure to select the appropriate choice.

For example, use the Numeric choice to sort this list:

```
509
22.7
448
100
1000.
17
```

The result would be sorted as follows:

```
17
22.7
100
448
509
1000.
```

You can also sort numbers and dates in either ascending or descending order. Note that Word can handle many date forms.

## Lesson 96: Sorting in Tables

So far you have learned only how to sort based on the first letter in a paragraph. While this is usually what you want, there are some circumstances where you might want to sort a table by a column other than the first one. For instance, you may want to sort the following table on the Amount column:

| Name | Age | Type | Amount |
|---|---|---|---|
| Terrence | 88 | Regular | 88.00 |
| Connors | 150 | Senior | 125.00 |
| Long | 130 | Regular | 130.00 |
| Yee | 50 | New | 67.50 |

Word lets you sort a table by any column if you select just that column. To do this, use the column selection methods discussed in Chapter 11 (if the table was created with (TAB) characters) or in Chapter 15 (if the table was created with the Insert Table command). After selecting the numbers in the column but not the heading, give the Sorting command. For example, if you select the numbers in the Amount column, sorting produces the following table:

| Name | Age | Type | Amount |
|---|---|---|---|
| Yee | 50 | New | 67.50 |
| Terrence | 88 | Regular | 88.00 |
| Connors | 150 | Senior | 125.00 |
| Long | 130 | Regular | 130.00 |

If you select entire rows in a table, the rows are sorted by the first column. If you select a single column, the whole table is still sorted, but the sort is based on the selected column. You can also specify the column to sort on with the Field Number choice in the Sorting dialog box.

## Review

Create a list of names of people with whom you work. Sort it in both ascending and descending order.

Make a two-column table with the names of the same people and their ages. Sort the table by name, and then sort it by age.

# 21

# Retrieving Documents

You have probably noticed that the names of the files used in this book are somewhat descriptive of their contents. The name SUMFUN.DOC, for example, was used for a summary funding proposal. However, MS-DOS file-naming conventions severely limit how much you can indicate in a filename. If you have more than a few dozen files (as you are sure to after using Word for a few weeks), it is hard to remember what each file contains. When you have hundreds of files, opening and closing each one to find a particular file is really time consuming.

Since Word is designed for use in business, where efficiency is a primary concern, Microsoft has devised a method for scanning rapidly through a large number of files. Each Word file has a *summary sheet* where you can list information that is helpful when you search. For example, to search for a letter, you might include in the summary sheet the recipient, the subject, and a few keywords about the contents. Word automatically stores the dates when the letter was created and last updated, so you can also use those in your search.

When you search, Word scans the summary sheets of all the documents on the disks and directories that you specify. You can devise very specific searches (such as one for a file written after July 15, 1992, that lists the keywords "timing" and "starter") or general searches (such as one for all letters to a certain person). This flexibility is very convenient when you are working with dozens or hundreds of files.

You can also have Word search for specific text in the files. For instance, you can locate every letter in which you mentioned "new manufacturing". Note, however, that searching for text in a file is slower than searching for words listed in the summary sheet, especially if you have long documents.

To fill in or search summary sheets, you give the Summary Info command from the File menu. Note that this command works only on Word documents, not on the other files on your system. Also, you can create summary sheets only for files saved with Word's formatting (not for text-only files). The Find File command from the File menu searches through summary sheets as well as through the text in files.

## Lesson 97: Filling In Summary Sheets

Up to now, when Word has prompted you to fill in a summary sheet, you have simply chosen OK and skipped over the sheet (or you may have guessed about how to fill it out). When you save a file for the first time, you fill in the summary information. Here is the procedure for filling in the summary sheets.

Open the SAMPLE1 file and give the Summary Info command from the File menu. The following illustration shows the same dialog box you see when you save a document for the first time:

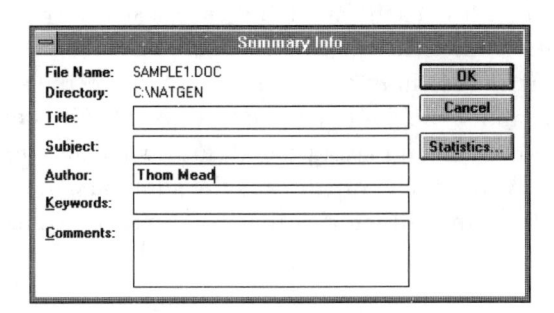

Chapter 21: *Retrieving Documents* 263

The options in the Summary Info dialog box are described in Table 21-1. You might use the field entries shown here for the SAMPLE1 document:

```
                    Summary Info
  File Name:  SAMPLE1.DOC              ┌────────┐
  Directory:  C:\NATGEN                │   OK   │
  Title:     [Letter to Richford 1/11/92]
                                       ┌────────┐
  Subject:   [Update on products and profits]  │ Cancel │
                                       ┌────────┐
  Author:    [Thom Mead]               │Statistics...│
  Keywords:  [DC50 profits financing]
  Comments:  [                    ]
```

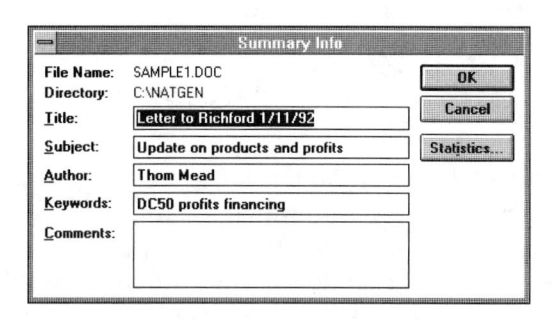

*Table 21-1.*   *Description of Fields in Summary Info Dialog Box*

| Field | Description |
|---|---|
| Title | A title for the document, such as "Request for information on new parts" or "Second notice on overdue accounts" |
| Subject | The document's subject. This is often similar to the title but might have additional information |
| Author | The name of the person who wrote the document. It is good to use both your first and last name since the person searching the summary sheets may not know both. Word automatically uses the name you entered when you installed Word, but you can change the name if you wish |
| Keywords | Words or phrases that are likely to be searched for. Examples are "accounts payable", "urgent", "third notice", and "final" |
| Comments | Remarks about the document. For example, you might use this option for a revision number or a note about what should happen next with the document |

Selecting the Statistics button displays a dialog box like the one in Figure 21-1 that shows fixed information about the file. It also gives you information about the last time the file was edited.

## Lesson 98: Searching for Documents

The Find File command lets you search for documents based on criteria you set, such as the drive on which to look and what to look for. The initial dialog box is shown in Figure 21-2.

When you give the Find File command from the File menu, it searches for the last search criteria you specified and displays the files that match those criteria. When you give the command for the first time, it shows all the Word files in the directory Word runs from. One file is selected in the list at the left, and the contents of the file are shown at the right side of the dialog box.

To find specific files, choose the Search button. You see the dialog box shown in Figure 21-3. You then specify the search criteria in the dialog box:

- File Name is the name (or part of the name) of the file you want to find.
- Type is the type of file you are looking for. You can look for Word files, pictures, and so on. Choose the type from the drop-down list.
- Location is where you want to search. Choose either a drive from the Drive option or a set of paths. In the Drive list, you can also choose

*Figure 21-1.*     *Statistics dialog box*

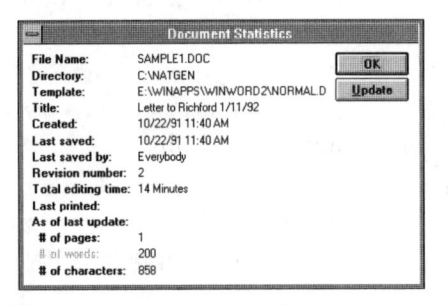

**Chapter 21:** *Retrieving Documents* 265

*Figure 21-2.*   Find File dialog box

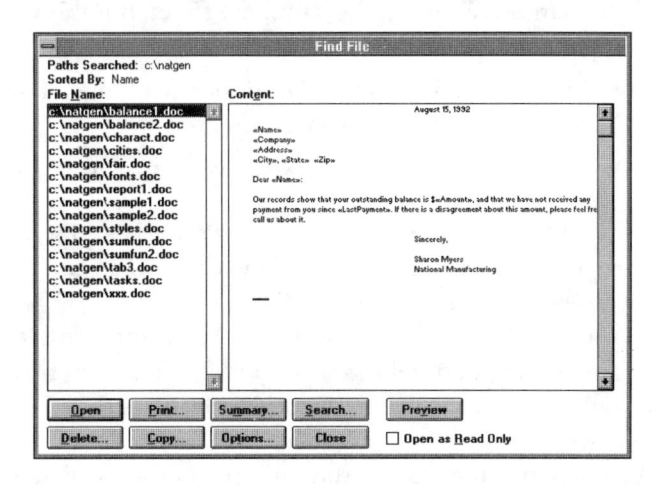

Path Only (the specified path or the current directory), All Local Drives (hard disks that are not on networks), and All Drives (not including floppy drives). The Path option lets you look on more than one path, as described shortly.

- Title, Subject, Keywords, Author, and Saved By are the fields from the summary sheet.

*Figure 21-3.*   Search dialog box

- Any Text is text to be searched for in the documents. This is slower than searching in the summary sheet, but it is very useful if you can remember only some of the content of the file you are looking for.
- Date Created and Date Saved specify a range of dates between which the file was started or saved on disk.
- Options tells what to do with previous searches, described shortly.

To start the search, enter the desired criteria and select Start Search. For instance, to find every file with the keyword "prosecute" in it, type **prosecute** in the Keywords field and select OK.

If you fill in more than one field, Word finds only files that match the entries in all the filled fields. For example, the set of entries shown in Figure 21-4 would find only documents for which the author field contains "Thom" and the Keywords field contains "loan".

You may not want to search an entire disk, particularly if you are on a network. After picking the drive, select the Edit Path button. You see the dialog box shown in Figure 21-5. Choose a path and select Add. When you have specified all the paths you want, Word includes them in the Search dialog box with semicolons, as shown here:

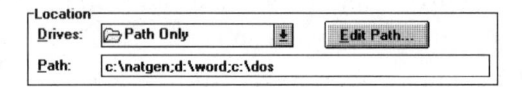

*Figure 21-4.* Finding both "Thom" in the Author field and "loan" in the Keywords field

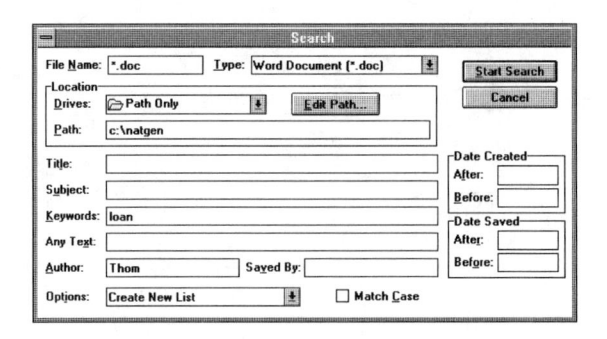

**Chapter 21:** *Retrieving Documents*

***Figure 21-5.*** *Edit Path dialog box*

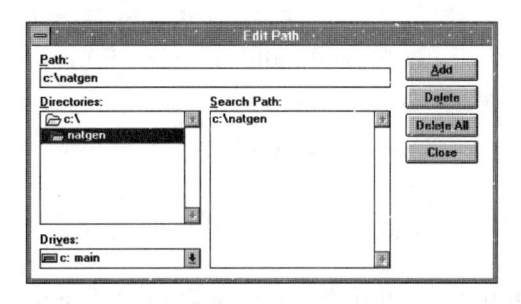

The Options drop-down list gives you many choices about what to do on subsequent searches:

- Create New List ignores the results of the previous search. Use this option when you want to start over.
- Add Matches to List expands the previous search, adding files to the list of files found before.
- Search Only in List narrows the previous search. It looks for the new search criteria only in the files you already found.

For example, assume you searched for all letters from Thom to a particular customer. You discover there are 70 letters. You want to narrow the search by using a keyword. Choose the Search button, enter the keyword in the Keywords field, and select Search Only in List.

After Word looks where you specify, it changes the list in the main dialog box. The buttons at the bottom of the dialog box let you decide what to do next, as described here:

| Button | Action |
|--------|--------|
| Open | Opens the file. Use this after you find the file you want |
| Print | Prints the file |
| Summary | Shows the summary information |
| Search | Lets you search again |

| Button | Action |
| --- | --- |
| Preview | If the file is not a Word file, this button tries to open or convert the file and show it to you |
| Delete | Deletes the file |
| Copy | Makes a copy of the file on your disk |
| Options | Sets the options |
| Close | Closes the Find File dialog box |

The Options button shows the following dialog box:

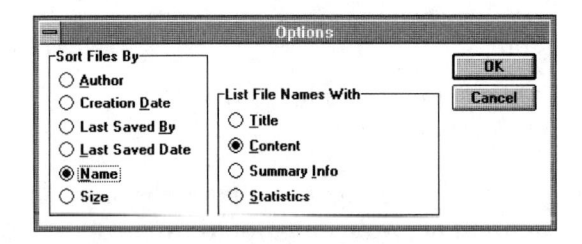

[Options dialog box: Sort Files By — Author, Creation Date, Last Saved By, Last Saved Date, Name (selected), Size; List File Names With — Title, Content (selected), Summary Info, Statistics; OK, Cancel]

The Sort Files By option tells the order in which you want to see the file list. The List File Names With option tells what to show in the area at the right of the main dialog box. The Title option displays one long list, with all the files listed by title. The Content, Summary Info, and Statistics options show the information only for the selected file.

# Review

Go back to the files you have already created and add better summary information to the files. With this new information entered, search for files by using different keywords and other criteria.

# 22
# Fields, Annotations, Bookmarks, and Cross-References

Word for Windows offers many features that make long projects significantly easier to manage.

- Word uses *fields* to mark special items that appear in documents. Although advanced use of fields is quite complicated, you can easily use fields without understanding all of their workings.
- *Annotations* allow you to leave notes for yourself in your document and to later make reference to those notes. You can also use annotations to let other people comment on a document.
- *Bookmarks* make jumping around in your document much faster; you don't have to remember page numbers when you move within the document. Bookmarks are also handy for referring to pages or groups of pages in your document.

- *Cross-references* let you refer to parts of your document by pages or by numbers in a series. For instance, if you have a table you want to refer to, you can put a bookmark at the table and include a special cross-reference. When you print your document, the cross-reference will refer to the table's page.

## Lesson 99: Introduction to Fields

Many parts of documents require a bit more treatment than regular text. Word handles them in special ways. For example, in Chapter 18 you learned how to insert entries for the index. These entries did not appear in your text; they were hidden in your document so when you later generated an index, Word knew what to include. Those entries were fields.

There are dozens of types of fields in Word. Some are fairly easy to understand, like index entries; others are very advanced and well beyond the scope of this book. The most important concept to understand about fields is that Word uses them to insert special text or hidden codes into a document. This lesson shows you how to handle fields so you can use them in the other lessons in this chapter.

Many Word commands enter fields into your documents. You have already seen some of these commands in Chapter 18, such as Insert Table of Contents, Insert Index Entry, and Insert Index. When you used these commands, you saw the results of the fields, not the fields themselves.

To see the actual fields in your document, you use the Field Codes command from the View menu. To see an example of a field, give the New command to start a temporary document. Type the words **This is a field:** followed by a space. Give the Field command from the Insert menu. You see the dialog box shown in Figure 22-1. In that dialog box, scroll to and select "Date" from the field type list on the left, select "MM/dd/yy" (which will appear in the instructions list on the right), and select OK. Then type a period followed by **That was a field.** Your window should look like this (but with the current date):

This is a field: 11/15/91. That was a field.

**Chapter 22:** *Fields, Annotations, Bookmarks, and Cross-References*

*Figure 22-1.* Field dialog box

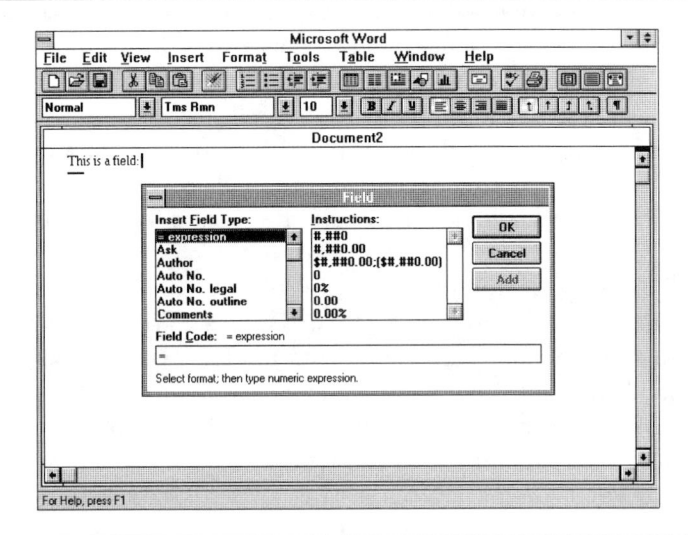

Now give the Field Codes command from the View menu. This causes Word to show fields as their *field codes,* not as the text that is produced by the fields. The window changes to that shown here:

This is a field: {date \@ MM/dd/yy}. That was a field.

A field has three parts: field characters, field type, and field instructions. The field characters look like boldface left and right curly braces. (However, you cannot type a field simply by using these characters from the keyboard; you must use the field commands.) The field type is the first word after the left field character. This tells Word what the field is. In the case of the field you just entered, the field type is "date". Some fields will have *field instructions,* which further define how the field will be displayed, but others won't. In this case, "\@ MM/dd/yy" constitutes the field instructions; they tell Word that this is a date format (\@) and how to display it.

Fields are *dynamic*—that is, they change constantly as you change your document. They have a displayed value when you first enter them in your document, but that value can change when circumstances change. For example, when you worked with tables of contents and indexes in Chapter 18, the page numbers changed when you edited or formatted your document. You did not need to write a new table of contents or index to see the changes; you simply updated the items that were already there. Those items were fields, so you updated the field values to get the new pagination.

To update a field, select it or place the insertion mark in the middle of the field and press (F9). To update all the fields in your document at once, you must select the whole document and then press (F9). This is useful if you have many fields, such as dates, that need to be updated at once. You can find all the fields in your document by pressing (F11) or (ALT)-(F1) to move forward from field to field and (SHIFT)-(F11) or (ALT)-(SHIFT)-(F1) to move backward.

At times you may want to prevent a field from being updated. For instance, you may not want the date to change each day. To lock a field's value (keep its current text value), select the field and press (CTRL)-(F11). To later unlock it, select the field and press (CTRL)-(SHIFT)-(F11).

The Field command from the Insert menu is the easiest way to enter fields other than index entry fields (for which you should use the Index Entry command). For instance, you have seen how to insert the current date in your document. If you open the document at a later date and update the field, the value will change automatically to that of the current date. If you want to know more about fields, see your Word *User's Guide* for a complete list of fields available.

Note that the View Field Codes command does not show certain hidden text, such as annotations (described in the next lesson). If you want to see your index entries or annotations, you must give the Options command and choose to show hidden text.

## Lesson 100: Creating Annotations

You can use annotations to leave yourself easy-to-find notes and markers in your text. Since annotations are stored just as footnotes are, you can add them, move them, and edit them in a similar fashion to the methods you learned in Chapter 15.

When you are writing a long report, frequently you will not have all the information you need. You may want to continue writing the text around the

**Chapter 22:** *Fields, Annotations, Bookmarks, and Cross-References* 273

unknown data instead of waiting until you receive the data to add the sentence or paragraph that goes with it. A convenient method for doing this is to write what you can and then select all the text that is uncertain. Give that text special formatting (such as double underlining) and add an annotation. If you find the missing data before the final draft of the report, simply select the text, unformat it, and add the new information. After you perform the task the annotation reminded you to do, you can easily remove it.

Word treats annotations similarly to footnotes; however, it identifies annotations with your initials and a number instead of with footnote numbers. If many people are marking a document, their annotations have their own initials. This makes it easy to determine who wrote what.

To enter annotations, put the insertion point where you want the annotation to begin and give the Annotation command from the Insert menu. This command adds the mark and opens the annotations pane shown in Figure 22-2. You can add as much annotation text as you want and format it any way you like.

You can edit your annotations by first opening the pane. Give the Annotations command from the View menu. You can also hold down the (CTRL) key while splitting the screen to automatically select the annotations pane. The

*Figure 22-2.*     Annotations pane

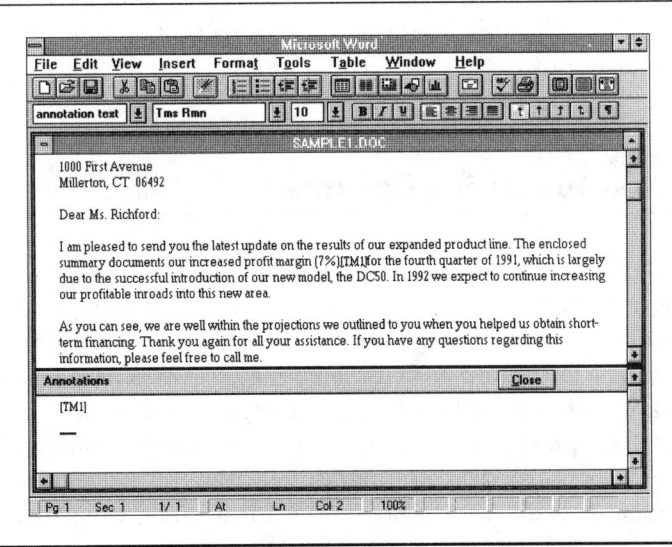

pane shows the annotations closest to your location in the document. To delete an annotation, simply delete its mark in the text. Word will renumber the other annotations so that the order is preserved.

To print just your annotations, give the Print command and select Annotations in the Print drop-down list. To print both your text and annotations in the same output, give the File Print command, select Options, and select Annotations in the Include with Document choices. Annotations appear at the bottom of pages, just like footnotes.

The Go To command from the Edit menu is useful when you are searching for annotations. In the dialog box, enter **A** to move to the next annotation in your document. To find a specific annotation, enter **A** and that annotation's number. To move a certain number of annotations forward or backward, enter **A**, + or –, and the number. For instance, to move five annotations ahead, enter **A+5**.

Many companies use annotations to allow a group of people to comment on a document without allowing them to make changes. This lets the document's author look at all the comments and decide how to make changes based on all of them. Word makes this easy. To start the process, use the File Save As command, choose the File Sharing button, and select Lock for Annotations. Save the file with a new name. From that point on, no one else with a copy of the file can modify it except to add annotations, although they can still view all parts of it. Each person's annotations are added with his or her initials. The only person who can turn off the lock for annotations is the original author.

## Lesson 101: Using Bookmarks

Bookmarks make jumping around a long document very easy. You don't have to remember page numbers (which might change when you edit your document) or search for specific text. Instead, you simply insert a named bookmark and jump to it by name. For instance, if you have a 250-page document that has 20 chapters, you might put a bookmark at the beginning of each chapter; you might also put bookmarks at tables you refer to often.

Word's bookmarks can mark a selection of text, not just a location. For instance, if you create a bookmark for a table, when you give the Go To

**Chapter 22:** *Fields, Annotations, Bookmarks, and Cross-References*         **275**

command from the Edit menu, the entire table will be selected. This is very handy for items that you copy often. When you move the selected text, the bookmark moves with it. A bookmark can be a single character if you wish.

To create a bookmark, select the desired text (or the single character) and give the Bookmark command from the Insert menu. You see the dialog box shown here:

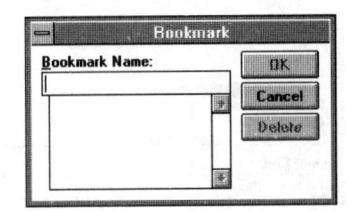

Enter the bookmark's name in the name field (from 1 to 20 characters, with no spaces or colons), and select OK. To jump to a bookmark, give the Go To command from the Edit menu and either type the name of the desired bookmark or select it in the list. To remove a bookmark, give the Bookmark command, select the bookmark you want, and select the Delete button.

## Lesson 102: Using Cross-References

Word can cross-reference any text or page number in a document. You use fields to refer to the chosen items and Word then replaces the fields with the numbers to which they refer. You usually cross-reference to a bookmark.

For example, assume you want to refer to the page number of a specific heading in your document. The heading is "New Operations". You would want its reference to look something like this:

This is described in detail in New Operations on page 32.

To cross-reference to a piece of text, first select the text and make a bookmark for it, as described in the previous lesson. Next, put the insertion point at the place where you want the cross-reference for that section to appear and give the Field command from the Insert menu. Select "Reference" in the field type list and the name of the bookmark in the instructions list.

Thus, to generate the cross-reference just given, you select the "New Operations" heading and make it a bookmark called "newophead" (for instance). Next, type the text that will refer to that heading, put the insertion point where you want the reference, and give the Field command. The selections you would make are shown here:

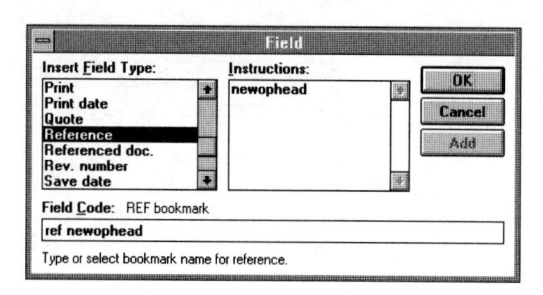

```
┌─────────────────────── Field ───────────────────────┐
│ Insert Field Type:      Instructions:      ┌──────┐ │
│ Print              ▲    newophead      ▲   │  OK  │ │
│ Print date                                 └──────┘ │
│ Quote                                      ┌──────┐ │
│ Reference                                  │Cancel│ │
│ Referenced doc.                            └──────┘ │
│ Rev. number                                ┌──────┐ │
│ Save date          ▼                   ▼   │ Add  │ │
│                                            └──────┘ │
│ Field Code:  REF bookmark                           │
│ ┌─────────────────────────────────────────────────┐ │
│ │ ref newophead                                   │ │
│ └─────────────────────────────────────────────────┘ │
│ Type or select bookmark name for reference.         │
└─────────────────────────────────────────────────────┘
```

Later, when you execute the command, "newophead" will be replaced with the words "New Operations".

To include the page number, add the words **on page** to your text and give the Field command again. This time, select "Page ref." for the field type and the name of the bookmark for the instruction. When you execute the command, Word inserts the page number of that bookmark. Remember that if you repaginate your document after this point, you must select the entire document and press (F9). This updates the "links" between these parts of your document.

## Review

Think about how you would use annotations in your office to have your coworkers comment on work. Consider how they would suggest insertions, deletions, and changes.

In the documents you have created by using Word, think about where cross-references would help refer the reader to another part of the document. Would this add to the readability or make it more confusing?

# 23

# Revision Marks

When you change a document and save the changes, the previous version of the document is replaced by the new one. This is usually what you want when you edit documents. Sometimes, however, you may want to see the changes you are making in your document while you are working on it and have them take effect later. You can use Word's revision marks, called *redlining*, for this purpose.

## Lesson 103: Using Redlining for Revisions

Redlining is commonly used in law offices for making changes to standard forms and contracts. It is also useful for groups of people who work together editing one document. (Compare this to the Annotations feature described in Chapter 22, where each person made only comments, not changes, to a single document.) Redlining shows clearly any text added to or deleted from a document. It also adds a bar to one side of each changed line so you can quickly find where changes have been made.

For example, look at the SAMPLE1 letter. With Word's Revision Marks feature turned on, if you change "pleased" to "happy", the screen might look like the one shown in Figure 23-1. Word's default is to show new or inserted text as underlined and to show deleted text as struck-through. The default also adds a bar to the left side of any line with a change in it.

As you edit, Word continually marks your inserted and deleted text in this fashion. Of course, at some point you will want to remove the underlining and delete the struck-through text so you can print the document and start fresh with no marks. The next lesson shows you how to do this.

To turn the Revision Marks feature on, give the Revision Marks command from the Tools menu. The command's dialog box is shown here:

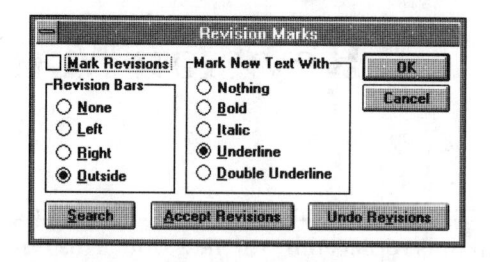

Select the Mark Revisions option and execute the command. When you are editing with Revision Marks on, Word displays "MRK" in the status bar near the right side of the window:

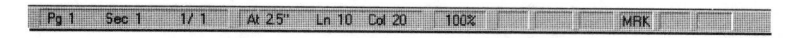

To see how editing with revision marks is different from the editing you have done up to now, start editing the second paragraph of the SAMPLE1 letter. Select "well" and press the (DEL) key. Move the insertion point to after "projections" and type the word **that**. The result is shown here:

| As you can see, we are well within the projections that we outlined to you when you helped us obtain short-term financing. Thank you again for all your assistance. If you have any questions regarding this information, please feel free to call me.

You can also change where Word shows the revision bars in the document window in the Revision Marks command. Some people prefer the revision bars to appear on the right side of the page; in this case, choose Right for the revision bar position. Choosing Outside causes Word to put the revision bars

**Chapter 23:** *Revision Marks* 279

*Figure 23-1.  Revision marks in first paragraph*

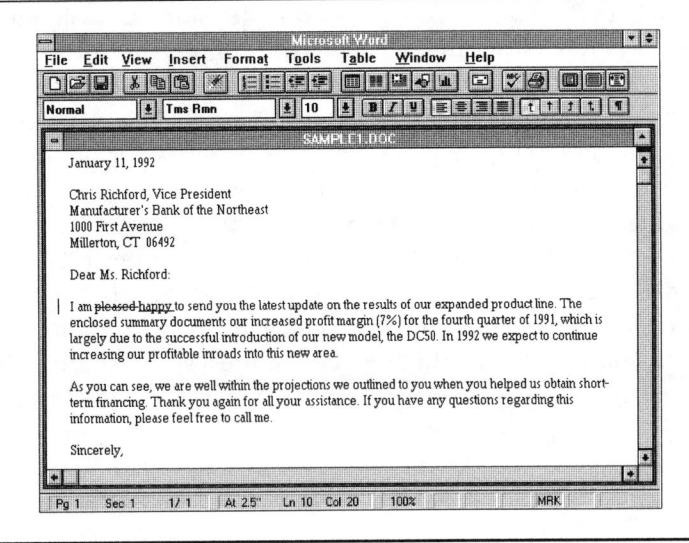

on the outside margins if you are using odd and even pages. If you don't want to see the revision bars, choose None.

## Lesson 104: Saving Revised Documents

When you save a document with redlining turned on, the revisions are saved with the file. Thus, if you leave Word and then come back to edit the file again later, your revisions are still there. This gives you the opportunity to edit your document as much as you want before you decide whether or not to implement the revisions.

When you are ready to accept the revisions, select the revised text, give the Revision Marks command, and select the Accept Revisions button. To accept the revisions on the entire document, select the whole document before giving the command. You can give the command for small portions of the document as well. Word then removes the struck-through text you have marked for deletion and the underlining in the text you have added.

If you decide to undo some of your revisions, select those parts you want to retain in their original form, give the Revision Marks command and choose the Undo Revisions button. Again, you can do this for the entire document or for a selected portion. Word deletes any text you have added since you started revising and retains any text you marked for deletion.

Using the Accept Revisions and Undo Revisions buttons lets you change selected parts of documents. For example, assume that Valerie and Alex are working together on a report. After Valerie writes the report, she puts it on a disk and gives it to Alex. He turns Revision Marks on and edits the text. When he gives the disk back to Valerie, she can easily see what changes he has made. If she disagrees with any of the changes, she selects them, gives the Revision Marks command, and chooses the Undo Revisions button. She then selects the entire document, gives the Revision Marks command again, and chooses the Accept Revisions button.

## Review

Consider the process you use when you revise your own work. Would using revision marks be better than simply making the changes directly? What about in a small work group?

# 24

# Using Word with Other Programs

In Chapter 4, you learned how to use the Clipboard to copy and move text in a file within Word. Often, however, you want to incorporate a copy of an entire file created with another program into a Word file you are editing. For instance, you may keep important charts created with another program in separate files so you can include them in a variety of memos you write using Word.

When the other program you are working with is a Windows program, the simplest way to bring information into Word or to pass information out of Word is to use the Cut, Copy, and Paste commands. You use these commands in other Windows programs just as you do in Word. For example, to copy a picture from a Windows graphics program into Word, you would create the picture, select it, give the Copy command, switch to Word, and give the Paste command.

There are a number of other ways you can interact with non-Word files. You can save Word files in ways that allow other programs to read them. (Most programs cannot read Word files.) You can also read files created by other programs. This chapter describes how to perform these tasks.

## Lesson 105: Opening Non-Word Files

So far, you have used the Open command from the File menu only for Word files. However, the Open command can perform other tasks as well. It can open the following types of word processing documents:

- Microsoft Word for the Macintosh versions 4 and 5
- Microsoft Word for the PC versions 4, 5.0, and 5.5
- Microsoft Word for Windows version 1
- Microsoft Works for the PC version 2
- Microsoft Works for Windows
- Microsoft Excel BIFF versions 2 and 3
- Microsoft Multiplan versions 3 and 4
- WordPerfect for the PC versions 4.1, 4.2, 5.0, and 5.1
- RFT-DCA documents from IBM DisplayWrite
- WordStar versions 3.3, 3.45, 4, 5.0, and 5.5
- Lotus 1-2-3 versions 2 and 3
- Text-only files created by any PC program
- Text files stored with the RTF specification

You can specify which files are visible in the list when you give the Open command. The List Files of Type drop-down lets you specify the types of files that appear in the list. The choices are as follows:

| Choice | Description |
| --- | --- |
| Word Documents | Only documents created in Word |

**Chapter 24:** *Using Word with Other Programs* 283

| Choice | Description |
| --- | --- |
| Document Templates | Only templates (described in Chapter 13) |
| Rich Text Format | Only files created with Microsoft's Rich Text Format (text files that can save formatting characteristics) |
| Text Files | Only text files |
| All Files | All files, regardless of whether Word can open them |

The File command from the Insert menu works like the Open command except that it puts a copy of the contents of the specified file in the current document at the insertion point. You can use this command if you want to read another file into your current file. The File command can read the same file formats as the Open command.

In addition to word processing documents, Word can open many types of graphics documents. Instead of using the Open command, you use the Picture command from the Insert menu. The types of graphics files you can open are listed here with the common file extension used for each file:

- PC Paintbrush (PCX)
- Windows bitmaps (BMP)
- Windows Metafile (WMF)
- Encapsulated PostScript files (EPS)
- TIFF files (TIF)
- AutoCAD (DXF)
- Plotter format (PLT)
- Lotus 1-2-3 graphics (PIC)
- Computer Graphics metafiles (CGM)
- Hewlett-Packard graphic language (HGL)
- DrawPerfect (WPG)
- Micrografx Designer or Draw Plus (DRW)

Many programs can store files in at least one of these formats. For example, almost every graphics program can store documents in either PCX or WMF format.

## Lesson 106: Saving Files in Non-Word Formats

Word lets you save files in different formats. This is useful for transferring formatted information to other word processing programs. The formats you can save in are the same as the ones you can open except that you cannot save in Lotus 1-2-3 or Microsoft Excel BIFF formats.

When you save a Word document in another format, it is likely that some formatting information will be lost. For example, when you save a Word file in the format of another word processor, you lose the styles you may have attached. Word replaces the styles with direct formatting. Word features, such as tables, may also be lost. Remember that many of the formats you can save in do not have all of the capabilities of Word, so you almost always lose formatting information.

## Lesson 107: Linking to Other Programs

Word lets you add information from another Word document, a document from another word processing program, a spreadsheet, or a graphics program to your Word documents. This information is called *dynamic* because it can change outside of Word—for example, if you update it in the original program. When you add information from one of these files, Word keeps track of the file's name and the originating program. You can continue to update the file outside of Word and, with a simple command, have Word check the file to obtain the latest saved version.

Linking is one of the most powerful features of Windows software. Almost every major Windows package uses *dynamic data exchange (DDE)*. DDE allows two programs to send and receive requests for information. For instance, when you copy a part of a spreadsheet to a Word document and later want to update

**Chapter 24:** *Using Word with Other Programs* 285

the figures in the document, Word can transmit that request to the spreadsheet program and get the new figures automatically.

Links to the following type of information are supported:

- Excel data
- Text formatted with the RTF standard
- Plain text
- Pictures
- Bitmaps

To make a link, copy the information from the other program to the Clipboard. Switch to Word and give the Paste Special command from the Edit menu. The following illustration shows the dialog box:

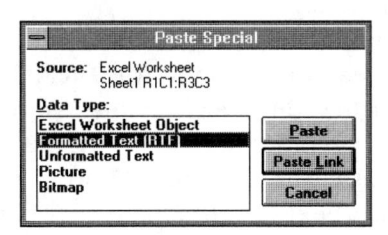

Choose the data type and select Paste Link.

Links are stored in fields, which you learned about in Chapter 22. Use the techniques you learned there to view the contents of the field and to update the field when the data in the other program changes. You can also update links by using the Links command in the Edit menu. The dialog box is shown in Figure 24-1. This gives you control over individually updating the links. However, most links are automatically updated each time you open the Word document so you don't need to worry about the Links command.

## Review

Look at the list of formats Word can open. See if you have a program on your PC that saves in one of those formats and try opening a file in that format.

***Figure 24-1.***   *Links dialog box*

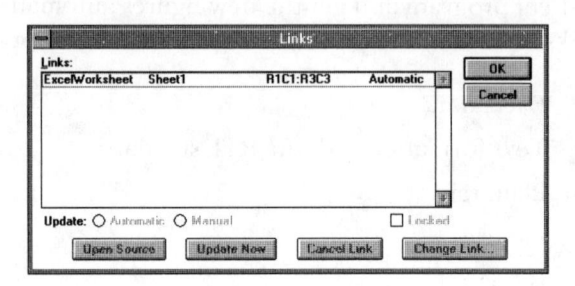

Look carefully at the contents and compare them to the way the file looked in the other program.

Save a file in a format that another program can read and look at the results. Experiment with various Word features such as styles, tables, and graphics and see how they translate when Word saves the file.

If you work in an office that also has Apple Macintosh computers, find out how you can transfer files from your PC to a Macintosh. Save some Word files in formats that can be read by programs on the Macintosh and note the results.

# IV

## Reference

# A

# Keyboard Reference

The following table lists all the Word commands by name.

| Command | Keys |
| --- | --- |
| 1.5 lines | CTRL-5 |
| Activate field | ALT-SHIFT-F9 |
| All caps | CTRL-A |
| Bold | CTRL-B |
| Case change | SHIFT-F3 |
| Center | CTRL-E |
| Close window | CTRL-F4 |
| Copy | CTRL-C |
| Copy selection | SHIFT-F2 |
| Cut | CTRL-X |
| Delete character left | BACKSPACE |
| Delete character right | DEL |

| Command | Keys |
|---|---|
| Delete word left | CTRL-BACKSPACE |
| Delete word right | CTRL-DEL |
| Double-space | CTRL-2 |
| Double underline | CTRL-D |
| Expand glossary entry | F3 |
| Field codes | SHIFT-F9 |
| Find again | SHIFT-F4 |
| Font | CTRL-F |
| Go to | F5 |
| Go to previous position | SHIFT-F5 |
| Hanging indent | CTRL-T |
| Help | F1 or SHIFT-F1 |
| Hidden text | CTRL-H |
| Insert field | CTRL-F9 |
| Italic | CTRL-I |
| Justify | CTRL-J |
| Left align | CTRL-L |
| Lock field | CTRL-F11 |
| Maximize document | CTRL-F10 |
| Maximize Word | ALT-F10 |
| Menu bar | F10 |
| Move to beginning of document | CTRL-HOME |
| Move to beginning of line | HOME |
| Move to bottom of window | CTRL-PAGE DOWN |
| Move down one window | PAGE DOWN |
| Move to end of document | CTRL-END |
| Move to end of line | END |
| Move to next character | → |
| Move to next field | ALT-F1 or F11 |

**Appendix A:** *Keyboard Reference*

| Command | Keys |
|---|---|
| Move to next line | ↓ |
| Move to next pane | F6 |
| Move to next paragraph | CTRL-↓ |
| Move to next window | ALT-F6 or CTRL-F6 |
| Move to next word | CTRL-→ |
| Move to previous character | ← |
| Move to previous field | ALT-SHIFT-F1 or SHIFT-F11 |
| Move to previous line | ↑ |
| Move to previous pane | SHIFT-F6 |
| Move to previous paragraph | CTRL-↑ |
| Move to previous window | ALT-SHIFT-F6 or CTRL-SHIFT-F6 |
| Move to previous word | CTRL-← |
| Move selection | F2 |
| Move to top of window | CTRL-PAGE UP |
| Move up one window | PAGE UP |
| Move window | CTRL-F7 |
| Nest paragraph | CTRL-N |
| One line before | CTRL-O |
| Open | CTRL-F12 |
| Paste | CTRL-V or SHIFT-INS |
| Point size change | CTRL-P |
| Point size decrease | CTRL-SHIFT-F2 |
| Point size increase | CTRL-F2 |
| Print | CTRL-SHIFT-F12 |
| Quit | ALT-F4 |
| Reduce hanging indent | CTRL-G |
| Remove character formatting | CTRL-SPACEBAR |
| Remove paragraph formatting | CTRL-Q |
| Repeat command | F4 |

| Command | Keys |
|---|---|
| Resize window | `CTRL`-`F8` |
| Restore document window | `CTRL`-`F5` |
| Restore program window | `ALT`-`F5` |
| Right align | `CTRL`-`R` |
| Ruler | `CTRL`-`SHIFT`-`F10` |
| Save | `ALT`-`SHIFT`-`F2` or `SHIFT`-`F12` |
| Save As | `ALT`-`F2` or `F12` |
| Select column | `CTRL`-`SHIFT`-`F8` |
| Select entire document | `CTRL`-`5` (keypad) |
| Select text | `F8` |
| Shrink window | `ALT`-`F9` |
| Single-space | `CTRL`-`1` |
| Small capitals | `CTRL`-`K` |
| Spelling | `F7` |
| Style | `CTRL`-`S` |
| Subscript | `CTRL`-`=` |
| Superscript | `CTRL`-`SHIFT`-`=` |
| Thesaurus | `SHIFT`-`F7` |
| Underline | `CTRL`-`U` |
| Undo | `CTRL`-`Z` or `ALT`-`BACKSPACE` |
| Unlink field | `CTRL`-`SHIFT`-`F9` |
| Unlock field | `CTRL`-`SHIFT`-`F11` |
| Unnest paragraph | `CTRL`-`M` |
| Update field | `F9` |
| Update links | `CTRL`-`SHIFT`-`F7` |
| Word underline | `CTRL`-`W` |
| Zero lines before | `CTRL`-`0` |

# B
# Word Commands

Figure B-1 shows Word's menus and their commands.

***Figure B-1.*** *Word's menus*

**File**
New...
Open...  Ctrl+F12
Close
Save  Shift+F12
Save As...  F12
Save All
Find File...
Summary Info...
Template...
Print Preview
Print...  Ctrl+Shift+F12
Print Merge...
Print Setup...
Exit  Alt+F4
1 SUMFUN.DOC
2 BALANCE1.DOC
3 SAMPLE1.DOC
4 FAIR.DOC

**Insert**
Break...
Page Numbers...
Footnote...
Bookmark...  Ctrl+Shift+F5
Annotation
Date and Time...
Field...
Symbol...
Index Entry...
Index...
Table of Contents...
File...
Frame
Picture...
Object...

**Window**
New Window
Arrange All
√ 1 Document2

**Edit**
Undo Copy  Ctrl+Z
Repeat Copy  F4
Cut  Ctrl+X
Copy  Ctrl+C
Paste  Ctrl+V
Paste Special...
Select All  Ctrl+NumPad 5
Find...
Replace...
Go To...  F5
Glossary...
Links...
Object...

**Format**
Character...
Paragraph...
Tabs...
Border...
Language...
Style...  Ctrl+S
Page Setup...
Columns...
Section Layout...
Frame...
Picture...

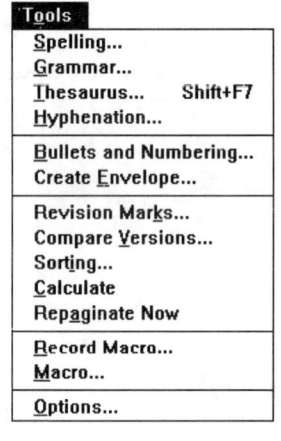

**Table**
Insert Rows
Delete Rows
Merge Cells
Convert Table to Text...
Select Row
Select Column
Select Table  Alt+NumPad 5
Row Height...
Column Width...
Split Table
Gridlines

**View**
• Normal
Outline
Page Layout
Draft
√ Toolbar
√ Ribbon
√ Ruler
Header/Footer...
Footnotes
Annotations
Field Codes
Zoom...

**Tools**
Spelling...
Grammar...
Thesaurus...  Shift+F7
Hyphenation...
Bullets and Numbering...
Create Envelope...
Revision Marks...
Compare Versions...
Sorting...
Calculate
Repaginate Now
Record Macro...
Macro...
Options...

**Help**
Help Index
Getting Started
Learning Word
WordPerfect Help
About...

# Index

1-2-3 graphics, 283
1-2-3 spreadsheets, 282

## A

Adding menus, 214-216
Address for summary info, 213
Aligning paragraphs, 118-120
Alignment
    justified, 119
    left, 118-119
    right, 119
All caps, 100
ALT key, 4, 14
Annotations, 272-274
    command, 273
    printing, 87
Antonyms, 247
Arrow pointer, 9
Art in text, 73-81
Ascending order, 258
ASCII, 255

Author in Summary Info, 263
AutoCAD files, 283
Automatic line spacing, 117
Automatic repagination, 156

## B

Back-to-back printing, 141
Background repagination, 210
Backup copies, 21, 212
BALANCE1 file, 176
Baseline of letters, 102
BMP files, 283
Body text, 221
Bold, 99
Bookmarks, 274-275
    command, 275
Border command, 200
Borders, 128-130
    command, 128-130
    tables, 200
Boundary lines, 135

Break command, 138
Bullets and Numbering command, 226-229

## C

Caret characters, 63-65
Cell widths, 193
Cells, 192
Center alignment, 119
Centimeter, 211
CGM files, 283
Changing fonts, 104
CHARACT file, 97
Character command, 97-104
Characters
    caret, 63-65
    color, 101
    European, 33-34, 257
    formatting, 92, 95
    international, 33-34, 257
    leader, 126
    special, 33-34
    wildcard, 63-65
Check boxes, 30
Checking grammar, 248-251
Checking spelling, 213, 242-246
Clipboard, 47-54, 281
    graphics, 73-74
    replacing with contents of, 65
Close command, 22
Closing a file, 22
Collapsing headings, 220, 224-225
Color characters, 101
Column, 192
Columns, 147-149
    adding and deleting, 198-199
    button in toolbar, 148
    command, 147-149
    newspaper, 147-149
    in sections, 147-149
    selecting, 196
    tabs, 126-128
Commands
    Annotations, 273
    Bookmarks, 275
    Borders, 128-130, 200
    Break, 138
    Bullets and Numbering, 226-229
    Character, 97-104
    Close, 22
    Columns, 147-149

Commands, *continued*
    Convert Text To Table, 199
    Copy, 48-54, 281
    Cut, 48-54, 127, 281
    definition of, 4, 13
    Delete Cells, 198
    Draft, 135
    Exit, 17-18
    Field, 236, 275-276
    Field Codes, 270
    Find, 57-61, 94-95
    Find File, 264-268
    Footnote, 202-204
    formatting, 93-94
    Frame, 151-154
    Glossary, 68-70
    Go To, 158, 274
    Grammar, 248
    Header/Footer, 141
    Help, 16-17
    Hyphenation, 253
    Index, 239
    Index Entry, 238
    Insert Cells, 198
    Insert Table, 193
    Language, 242
    Links, 285
    New, 169
    Open, 22, 81, 170
    Option, 110, 135, 156, 207-217
    Outline, 220
    Page Break, 157-158
    Page Layout, 134-135
    Page Numbers, 146-147
    Page Setup, 154-156
    Paragraph, 110-120, 159
    Paste, 48-54, 74, 199
    Paste Special, 285
    Print, 83-87
    Print Merge, 176, 184
    Print Preview, 135-137
    Replace, 61-65, 94-95, 116
    Revision Marks, 278-280
    Row Height, 195
    Run, 48
    Save, 212
    Save As, 20, 170
    Section Layout, 150
    Select Column, 196
    Select Row, 197
    Spelling, 244

*Index* **297**

Commands, *continued*
    Split, 38-41
    Style, 161-164
    Summary Info, 262-264
    Table of Contents, 234
    Tabs, 125
    Thesaurus, 247
    Undo, 27-29, 49
    Zooming, 137
Condensed characters, 101
Conditional insertion, 187-190
Contents, 231-236
Control Panel program, 84
Convert Text to Table command, 199
Converting text into tables, 199
Copies
    backup, 21
    printing, 85
Copy command, 48-54, 281
Copying formatting, 92, 105-106, 128
Copying styles, 168
Copying text, 47-56
Creating graphics, 75-79
Creating outlines, 221-224
Creating styles, 161-164
Creating tables, 193-197
Creating tables of contents, 234
Cropping graphics, 79-80
Cross-references, 275-276
(CTRL) key, 4, 14
Cursive font, 103
Custom dictionary, 243
Customizing
    keyboard, 216
    menus, 214-216
    Word, 207-217
Cut command, 48-54, 127, 281

## D

Data file, 175
Dates, 266
DDE, 284
Delete Cells command, 198
Deleting text, 8, 24-25
Descending order, 258
Dialog boxes, 29-31
Dictionaries, 243
Direct formatting, 91-93, 160
Disks, 21
Displays, 37

DisplayWrite, 282
Document Control menu, 13, 38, 41
Document formatting, 133
Document templates. *See* Templates
Document window, 5
Documents
    Document1, 5
    main, 175
    retrieving, 261-268
    searching for, 264-268
Double underline, 100
Double-sided printing, 141
Draft command, 135
Draft Output option, 87
Drag-and-drop editing, 54-56, 211
Dragging (mouse), 10
Draw window, 75-79
Drawings. *See* Graphics
DrawPerfect files, 283
Driver for printers, 83
Drop-down lists, 30
DRW files, 283
DXF files, 283
Dynamic data exchange (DDE), 284

## E

Editing, 17-18
    definition of, 3
    drag-and-drop, 54-56, 211
Encapsulated PostScript files, 283
End-of-file marker, 7
(ENTER) key, 15-16, 115, 116
Envelopes, 87
EPS (Encapsulated PostScript files), 283
European characters, 33-34
Even and odd pages, 140-141, 154-156
Excel, 282
Exit command, 17-18
Expanded characters, 101

## F

FAIR1 file, 223
Fast saves, 212
Field codes, 209
Field Codes command, 270
Field command, 236, 275-276
Fields, 175, 270-272
    codes, 270
    dynamic, 271

Fields, *continued*
    printing, 87
    updating, 87
Figure lists, 235
Files
    closing, 22
    converting, 211
    graphics, 81, 283-285
    multiple, 42-44
    non-Word, 282-285
    opening, 22, 282-285
    saving, 20, 279, 284
    text-only, 282-285
Fill, 78
Find command, 57-61, 63-65, 94-95
Find File command, 264-268
Fonts, 101-104
    changing, 104
    characteristics, 102
    monospace, 103
    sans serif, 102
    size, 102
    TrueType, 87
Footers, 140-145
    panes, 141-143
Footnote command, 202-204
Footnotes, 201-204
Form letters, 175-190
    data files for, 180
    definition of, 175
    main documents for, 176
    merge instructions for, 187-190
    printing, 184-187
Formatting
    character, 92, 95
    commands, 92
    copying, 105-106, 128
    definition of, 3
    direct, 91-93, 160
    documents, 154-156
    fonts, 101-104
    introduction to, 91-93
    language, 242
    levels, 92
    paragraphs, 92, 109-130
    searching and replacing, 94-95
    sections, 92-93, 133-158
    styles, 159-171
    tables, 192
    text, 3

Frame command, 151-154
Framing paragraphs, 150-154

## G

General settings, 210-211
Glossaries, 67-72
    creating, 68-70
    definition of, 67
    expanding, 69-70
    opening, 71
    printing, 71
    saving on disk, 71
    special entries, 72
    templates, 169
    uses for, 71
Glossary command, 68-70
Go To command, 158, 274
Grammar, 248-251
    checking, 248
    options, 213, 248
Graphics, 73-81
    creating, 75-79
    cropping, 79-80
    drawing area, 75
    drawing tools, 75
    files, 81, 283-285
    fill, 78
    handles, 77, 79
    pattern, 78
    picture placeholders, 209
    resizing, 79-80
    tools, 76-79
Gridlines, 193, 209
Gutter, 154

## H

Handles, 77, 79
Hanging indent, 114
Header/Footer command, 141
Headers, 140-145
    panes, 141
Headings
    collapsing, 220, 224-225
    expanding, 224-225
    outlines, 220, 224-225
    styles, 232
Help command, 16-17
HGL files, 283

*Index* **299**

Hidden text, 100, 209
    printing, 87
Highlighted text, 10
Hyphenation, 251-254
    optional, 252
Hyphenation command, 253

## I

I-beam, 8
IF instruction, 188
Inch, 211
Indenting, 112-115
Indents, 154-156
    hanging, 114
Index command, 239
Index Entry command, 238
Indexes, 231
    creating, 239
    marking, 237-239
Initials for summary info, 213
(INS) key, 211
Insert Cells command, 198
Insert Frame button, 151
Insert Picture button, 75
Insert Table command, 193
Inserting text, 8-9, 11-13
Insertion point, 8
Installing Word, 5
International characters, 33-34, 257
Italics, 99

## J

Justified alignment, 119

## K

Keeps, 120
Keyboard
    customizing, 216
    dialog box, 31
    equivalents, 13, 289-292
    inserting text with, 12-13
    moving with, 27
    scrolling with, 24
    selecting with, 12-13, 27
    templates, 169
Keywords in Summary Info, 263

## L

Landscape orientation, 156
Language command, 242
Leader characters, 126
Leading, 102
Leaving Word, 17-18
Left alignment, 118-119
Line breaks, 32
Line numbering, 149-150
Line spacing, 116-118
Link to Previous button, 142
Linking to other programs, 284
Links command, 285
Lotus 1-2-3 files, 282-283

## M

Macintosh Word, 282
Macros, 169
Mail merge, 175-190
Mailing address for summary info, 213
Main dictionary, 243
Main document, 175
Margins, 111, 154-156
Match Case option, 59
Match Whole Word Only option, 59
Maximized window, 5
Measurement, 211
Menus, 13, 294-295
    adding to, 214-216
    customizing, 214-216
    templates, 169
Merge instructions, 187-190
Micrografx files, 283
Microsoft Draw window, 75-79
Microsoft Excel, 282
Microsoft Multiplan, 282
Microsoft Word for the Macintosh, 282
Microsoft Word for the PC, 282
Microsoft Works, 282
Modes
    numeric lock, 27
    outline, 220
    page layout, 134-135
    print preview, 135-137, 143
    view, 133-138
Modifying styles, 165
Monospaced font, 103

Mouse
    scrolling with, 23-24
    selecting text, 10-11, 25-27
Mouse pointer, 8
Moving text, 49-56
Moving windows, 41
MRK indicator, 278
Multiplan, 282
Multiple files, 42-44
Multiple windows, 42-44

## N

Name for summary info, 213
Nesting paragraphs, 121
New command, 169
Newline, 32, 115
Newspaper columns, 147-149
Non-Word files, 282-285
Nonbreaking hyphen, 252
Nonbreaking spaces, 32-33
Normal hyphen, 252
Normal mode, 133-134
NORMAL.DOT file, 71, 170
Numbering
    outline, 226-229
    pages, 140-145
    paragraphs, 226-229
    lines, 149-150
Numbers, 258
Numeric lock mode, 27

## O

Odd and even pages, 140-141, 154-156
Open command, 22, 81, 170
Opening
    files, 22, 282-285
    glossaries, 71
Optional hyphen, 252
Options
    command, 207-217
    general, 210-211
    grammar, 213, 248
    Keyboard, 216
    menus, 214-216
    print, 211
    save, 212-213
    spelling, 213, 244
    toolbar, 217
    user information, 213

Options, *continued*
    view, 208-210
    Win.ini file, 214
Options command, 135
    general choices, 156
    view options, 110
Orientation, 156
Orphans, 87, 120
Outdent, 114
Outline command, 220
Outlines, 219-229
    body text, 221
    collapsing headings in, 220, 224-225
    creating, 221-224
    expanding headings in, 224-225
    headings in, 221
    numbering in, 226-229
    outline bar, 220
    outline mode, 220
    printing, 221
    rearranging, 225-226
    styles in, 221
Overtype mode, 211

## P

Page Break command, 157-158
Page breaks, 156-158
Page Layout command, 134-135
Page layout mode, 134-135
Page numbering, 146-147
    odd and even, 140-141, 154-156
Page Numbers command, 146-147
Page orientation, 156
Page range, 85
Page Setup command, 84, 154-156
Paper feed, 85
Paper size, 154
Paragraph command, 110-120, 159
Paragraphs
    alignment, 118-120
    borders, 128-130
    copying formatting, 128
    definition of, 15-16
    formatting, 92, 109-130
    framing, 150-154
    indenting, 112-115
    keeps, 120
    line spacing, 116-118
    nesting, 121
    numbering, 226-229

# Index

Paragraphs, *continued*
    positioned, 150-154
    shading, 130
    tabs, 122-128
    unnesting, 121
Paste command, 48-54, 74, 199, 281
Paste Special command, 285
Pattern, 78
PC Paintbrush, 283
PCX files, 283
Personalizing Word, 5
Pica, 211
Picture placeholders, 209
Pictures. *See* Graphics
Plotters, 283
Point, 211
Points, 102
Portrait orientation, 156
Positioned paragraphs, 150-154
PostScript, 283
Print command, 83-87
Print Merge command, 176, 184-187
Print Preview command, 135-137
Print preview mode, 135-137, 143
Print settings, 211
Printer driver, 83
Printing, 34-35, 83-87
    annotations, 87
    back-to-back, 141
    double-sided, 141
    envelopes, 87
    fields, 87
    form letters, 184-187
    glossaries, 71
    hidden text, 87
    introduction to, 34-35
    line breaks, 209
    non-Word documents, 86
    outlines, 221
    reverse order, 87
    selecting printer, 84
    styles, 169
    summary info, 87
Program Control menu, 13, 48
Program Manager, 5
Program window, 5
Proofing, 241-254
Proportional spacing, 103

## R

Radio buttons, 30
Readability statistics, 248, 251
Rearranging outlines, 225-226
Redlining, 277-280
Reference mark, 202
Repaginate Now command, 157-158
Repaginating, 156-158, 210
Replace command, 61-65, 94-95, 116
Replacing formatting, 94-95
Replacing text, 61-65
REPORT1 file, 43
Resizing graphics, 79-80
Restore box, 5, 41
Retrieving documents, 261-268
Reverse Print Order option, 87
Revision marks, 277-280
    command, 278-280
RFT-DCA files, 282
Ribbon, 99-100, 169
    Show All button, 110
Right alignment, 119
Row Height command, 195
Row heights, 193
Rows, 195
    adding and deleting, 198
    formatting, 192
RTF (Rich Text Format), 282
Rule groups, 248
Ruler, 111-112, 124, 196
Run Clipboard command, 48

## S

SAMPLE1 file, 20
SAMPLE2 file, 70
Sans serif font, 102-103
Save As command, 20, 170
Save command, 212-213
Save options, 212-213
Saving a file, 20, 279, 284
Saving templates, 218
Script, 103
Scroll bar, 21
Scroll box, 23
Scrolling, 4, 22-24
Searching, 57-61
    documents, 264-268
    formatting, 94-95

Section Layout command, 150
Sections, 133-158
    columns in, 147-149
    definition of, 92-93
    headers and footers, 140-145
    starting new, 138-140
Select Column command, 196
Select Row command, 197
Selecting
    columns, 196
    columns of tabs, 127
    keyboard, 12-13
    text, 8-9
Selection bar, 26, 197
Serifs, 102
SETUP program, 4
Shading, 130
SHIFT key, 12, 76
Show All button, 110
Size box, 41
Sizing windows, 41
Small caps, 100
Sorting, 255-260
    ascending and descending order, 258
    numbers, 258
    tables, 259
    text, 257
Spaces, 32-33
Spacing
    character, 101
    line, 116-118
    monospace, 103
    proportional, 103
Special characters, 33-34
    Find and Replace, 63-65
Spelling, 242-246
    checking, 244
    ignoring words, 246
    options, 213, 244
    suggestions, 245
Split bar, 38
Split command, 38-41
Splitting windows, 38-41
Starting Word, 5
Statistics, 248, 251
Strikethrough, 100
Style command, 161-164
Styles, 159-171
    applying, 164-166
    Based On choice, 167-168

Styles, *continued*
    copying, 168
    creating, 161-164
    heading 1, 232
    modifying, 165
    outlining, 221
    printing, 169
    ribbon, 169
    style area, 209
    style sheets, 166-167
    tables of contents, 232
    templates, 169
    toc 1, 235
Subject in Summary Info, 263
Subscripts, 101
Summary info, 212-213
    dialog box, 21
    printing, 87
    summary sheets, 261-268
Summary Info command, 262-264
Superscripts, 101
Symbol command, 33-34
Synonyms, 247

# T

TAB key, 181
Table of Contents command, 234
Tables, 122, 191-200
    adding rows and columns to, 198
    alignment, 195
    borders, 200
    cell widths, 193, 196
    cells, 192
    commands, 193
    converting to and from text, 199
    creating, 193-197
    form letters, 176
    grid, 193
    gridlines, 209
    pasting into, 199
    row heights, 193, 195
    rows, 192
    selection bar, 197
    sorting, 259
Tables of contents, 231-236
    advanced, 235
    creating, 234
    marking, 232-233
    planning, 232

*Index* **303**

Tables of contents, *continued*
    styles, 232
Tabs, 122-128
    columns of, 126-128
    leader characters, 126
    setting, 124
    types of, 123
Tabs command, 125
Templates, 169-171
Templates, saving, 218
Text
    boundaries, 209
    converting to tables, 199
    copying, 47-56
    deleting, 8, 24-25
    editing, 19-29
    entering, 5
    highlighted, 10
    inserting, 4, 8, 11-13
    moving, 49-56
    replacing, 61-65, 210
    retrieving, 261-268
    searching, 57-61
    selecting, 6, 8, 25-27
    sorting, 257
Text-only files, 282
Thesaurus, 247
Thumbing, 23
TIFF files, 283
Title bar, 41
Title in Summary Info, 263
Toggle, 98
Toolbar
    100 Percent button, 137
    changing, 217
    Columns button, 148
    Insert Frame button, 151
    Insert Picture button, 75
    introduction to, 7
    Page Width button, 137
    templates, 169
    Whole Page button, 137
TrueType, 87

## U

Underlining, 99-100
Undo command, 27-29, 49
Unnesting paragraphs, 121
Untitled document, 5

User dictionary, 243
User info settings, 213

## V

View modes, 133-138
View options, 208-210

## W

Widows, 87, 120
Width, 196
Width, cell, 193
Wildcard characters, 63-65
Win.ini file, 214
Windows, 37-45
    maximizing, 5
    Microsoft Draw, 75
    moving, 41
    multiple, 42-44
    restore box, 5
    sizing, 41
    splitting, 38-41
Windows bitmaps, 283
Windows metafiles, 283
WMF files, 283
Word
    customizing, 207-217
    icon, 5
    installing, 4
    Macintosh, 282
    PC, 282
    personalizing, 5
    program window, 5
    quitting, 17-18
    starting, 5
Word underline, 100
WordPerfect files, 282
WordPerfect keyboard settings, 4, 211
WordStar, 282
Works, 282
WPG files, 283

## Z

Zoom command, 137